D0793066

Italy
and the
European Union

Italy
and the
European Union

FEDERIGA BINDI

SCUOLA SUPERIORE DELLA PUBBLICA
AMMINISTRAZIONE (SSPA)
Rome

BROOKINGS INSTITUTION PRESS
Washington, D.C.

Copyright © 2011
THE BROOKINGS INSTITUTION *and*
SCUOLA SUPERIORE DELLA PUBBLICA AMMINISTRAZIONE (SSPA)

Library of Congress Cataloging-in-Publication data
Bindi, Federiga M.
   Italy and the European Union / Federiga Bindi.
      p.   cm.
   Includes bibliographical references and index.
   Summary: "Presents a comprehensive study of Italy's role in the European Union and what that country needs to do as a 'medium-size power' to increase its influence in the EU, chiefly by putting forward well-defined goals and consistent strategies through credible actors"— Provided by publisher.
   ISBN 978-0-8157-0496-6 (alk. paper)
   1. European Union—Italy.   2. Italy—Politics and government—1976–1994.   I. Title.
   HC240.25.I8B56 2011
   341.242'20945—dc22   2010045030

9 8 7 6 5 4 3 2 1

Printed on acid-free paper

Typeset in Minion

Composition by R. Lynn Rivenbark
Macon, Georgia

Printed by R. R. Donnelley
Harrisonburg, Virginia

Contents

Acknowledgments

This book is the result of some fifteen years of work and there are many people to thank. First and foremost, my family for supporting me through all of these years: my parents, Luigi and Donatella; my sisters, Lavi and Nico; my husband, Giulio, and former spouse, Cristiano; and, of course, my beloved son, Giorgio Alessandro.

Thanks to those who are watching over us from the sky: Giorgio and Uaua, who never failed in believing in me, even when nobody else did. I also could not have researched the 1990s without Uaua's meticulous archiving work. I miss you both every day and I know you are rejoicing up there as this book finally comes about! Ana Fraga, unforgotten friend and intellectual stimulus, hosted and supported me in Lisbon (and beyond) in joy and in sorrow, in support but never in judgment—the void left by her premature departure will be impossible to fill.

I would like to also acknowledge Khalid and Alessia, trusted friends and confidantes all these years.

I received plenty of academic advice, but a few people in particular were important at different stages. First and foremost is Giuliano Amato, whose class at the European University Institute (EUI) on the origins of the Italian Constitution changed my approach to the study of Italy and of policymaking; words are not enough to express my gratitude for his invaluable advice and support all these years. Leonardo Morlino and Yves Meny came to my rescue when my PhD thesis at EUI—from which this book in part originates—was stuck in the middle of nowhere. Manuel Braga da Cruz, in Lisbon, and Mario Teló, in Bruxelles, hosted and supported me with generosity for a long time at their institutions. Antonio Zanardi Landi's help proved fundamental in securing interviews with top people when he was secretary general at EUI. Pierre

Gerbet and Martin Saeter nourished my first academic explorations abroad. Antonio Varsori was an enthusiast teacher of Italian foreign policy and offered precious advice. Lapo Pistelli encouraged me to write for the first time on a continuous basis on Italy, the EU, and international politics. Fernando Gentilini took time to teach me how to write in a decent way. Luciano Bardi and Kjell Eliassen bravely got me published academically on Italy and the EU for the first time—I am glad we still work together! Giorgianna Appignani gave me my first teaching job at SUNY-FIT and provided much wise counsel over the years—teaching European and international relations to fashion students has been an incredibly rewarding challenge! Ortensio Zecchino introduced me to the University of Rome Tor Vergata; Alessandro Finazzi Agrò, Luigi Paganetto, Renato Lauro, Alessandro Ferrara, Rino Caputo, Antonio Lombardo, Lorenzo Catucci, Antonietta Pulini, Marina Tesauro, Matilde Nardi, Silvia Quattrociocche, and many others adopted me at Tor Vergata. Giovanni Tria, from Tor Vergata, brought me along to SSPA. Giorgio Freddi introduced me to the fascinating world of public administration and public policy analysis. Among "my" generation, I'm in debt to Francesco Clementi, Serena Giusti, Stefano Grassi, Giovanni Guzzetta, Francesca Longo, Maxiliano Lorenzi, Andrew Moravcsik, Andrea Romano, Francisco and Annette Torres, Amy Verdun, and Luca Verzichelli for advice, support, intellectual stimulus, and cooperation. The parliament chapter owes much to Stefano's and my chapter in *National Parliaments on Their Ways to Europe.*

The Brookings Institution proved to be the perfect venue to wrap up my work. There, Jeremy Shapiro's and Dan Hamilton's sarcastic—but often to the point—comments were an invaluable intellectual stimulus, as was Carlos Pascual's cooperative way of working. Thanks to the Council for the United States and Italy—and in particular to Cesare Merlini, Denis Redmont, and Sergio Marchionne—for financing the fellowship that allowed me to spend more than two incredible years at Brookings! Thanks also to Jean Monnet Action of the European Commission and to Luciano Di Fonzo, in particular, for financing part of the research for this book and for supporting the Tor Vergata Jean Monnet Center of Excellence. If all of the European Union were like you, its popularity would rocket to the sky! The Brookings Institution Press, headed by Bob Faherty, is the best publisher one could dream of, and if the English language sounds right, it is thanks to the wonderful work of Janet Mowery and Janet Walker, and of Gwyneth Sick in Rome, the first to tackle the book with a keen editorial eye.

I am also in debt to the some 150 people I interviewed over the years; I would love to name them all, but this would be impossible, first and foremost for privacy reasons. When studying policies and policymaking, pure academic analysis may not be enough. The periods I spent working in government and politics were therefore essential in finding the data and facts otherwise difficult to retrace and yet fundamental to understanding how foreign and domestic policy works and in gaining access to the right people. I am thus in debt to Enrico Letta for the early years in the European People Party (EEP) family; to Michele Cosentino for the months spent at the Italian Embassy in Lisbon and for his precious advice afterward; Umberto Ranieri for my first period at the Farnesina; to Clemente Mastella for the work we did at the EEP and for the period spent at the Ministry of International Trades—where I benefited from the special guidance of Pietro Celi; to Franco Frattini, for the recent, incredibly stimulating years at the Ministry of Foreign Affairs—very few people would have had the courage and intellectual honesty to hire someone and give her the absolute freedom to write, even when this could mean a risk of exposing himself to eventual criticism! Also, for details on the ministry and the Italian EU and foreign policy, I greatly benefited from the guidance and advice of Marta Dassù, Ferdinando Nelli Feroci, Massimo Gaiani, Andrea Tiriticco, Giandomenico Magliano, Rocco Cangelosi, Sebastiano Cardi, Stefano Tomat, Nicola Verola, Luca Gori, Luca Giansanti, Ettore Sequi, Giampiero Massolo, and Vincenzo Scotti, who was also the first minister for EC policies.

Last but not least is my team, otherwise known as "pulcini." Working with you all these years has been a source of great inspiration and material help. My thanks in particular go to Palma as parts of the history chapter draw on our 2005 book, *The Future of Europe*; to Valeria for help on the 20-20-20 directive, EMU, and the Alba case; to Irina, Ilaria, and Giulia for their work on the notes and the bibliography. Finally, the book would have never come about without the precious input and support of Marco A., Marco "Zinzi," Valentino, Elena, the two Andreas, Daniela, Sophie, and Carlo, and the many others who at one point or another crossed the path of our group.

While many have helped me along the way, any mistakes herein are obviously all mine.

1

Introduction:
Italy's Future Role in the European Union

The purpose of the book is to analyze three aspects of the relations between Italy and the European Union from different points of view: the political actors' historical attitude toward the foundation and development of the European Community/European Union (EC/EU); the institutional and legislative mechanisms regulating the Italy-EU relationship; and Italian negotiating strategies in "high" and "low" EU politics. The aim is to provide an in-depth, comprehensive analysis of how Italy relates to the European Union.

The book endeavors to fill a gap in the existing literature: as yet, there is no exhaustive study on Italy's interaction with the EU. This lack is particularly striking as Italy is considered—and considers itself—one of the most pro-European countries in the Union. Italy has undoubtedly contributed significantly to the process of European integration, yet the country is also widely known for its passive attitude in the day-to-day negotiations that make up the formative phase of EU policymaking.

In explaining this rather contradictory behavior, the book argues that the incomplete "Europeanization" of a country can affect its influence in EU policymaking; it also argues that the variables underlying the negotiating potential of EU member states are of a domestic nature.

The fundamental hypothesis of the book is that a "medium-size power," such as Italy, can be one of the leading countries in shaping EU policies only in the presence of well-defined aims, credible actors, and consistent strategies. Without these factors, the nation's influence will be strongly diminished, if not entirely irrelevant. In analyzing the Italian case the chapters in this book consider the following issues and questions:

—*Actors and procedures (formal and informal): relevant variables in defining Italy's interests and national positions.* How are national interests defined in Italy? Who are the relevant actors? What procedures are followed (formal and informal)? How are national positions defended?

—*Aims and strategies.* What are Italy's aims, interests, and objectives in EU policymaking? How much have these changed over the years? Is there continuity or discontinuity from one government to another? Are Italy's EU policies coherent with one another, or do they tend to diverge, and even contradict each other?

—*Impact.* What is the outcome of all this? How has Italy's action affected "high" and "low" politics in the EU? Is Italy a proactive or passive actor? Does it succeed in shaping EU policy?

The book is organized as follows. In chapter 2, I describe the intellectual path that led to the research underlying the results presented here. I first review early studies of European integration (federalism and functionalism) and how they later evolved in two opposite directions: multilevel governance and liberal intergovermentalism. I discuss how these two approaches diverged in the context of the roles played by member states in the European decisionmaking process. I then analyze how the literature has dealt with the issue of relations between the member states and the EU. As the study of member states in the EU decisionmaking process is, with few exceptions, a young field within the larger area of European Studies, the broad goal of this book is—by focusing on the Italian case—to add knowledge about the role of member states in shaping the EU decisionmaking process and, in turn, to properly weigh the influence of decisions made at the European level on those member states.

Chapter 3 explores Italy's relations with the European Communities and Union in historical terms. Italy owed much to its early membership in the Communities to Prime Minister Alcide De Gasperi and Foreign Minister Carlo Sforza. In the 1950s membership in the European Coal and Steel Community (ECSC) represented a means of securing the newborn Italian democracy, though their decision was opposed by a number of influential actors at the time. Since the early 1980s, all major parties have become supporters of the European integration process. There was discontinuity in the strength of support for the EU in the years from 1994 (the first Berlusconi-led government: Berlusconi I) to 2008 (Berlusconi IV). With the 2008 elections, European affairs lost their salience in the electoral debate and again became a shared bipartisan issue. Did the domestic perception of European affairs influence the way Italy projected itself abroad and acted within the EU? How? With what results? Chapter 3 focuses on how the different governments and political actors have dealt with European policies and on the role Italy has played in shaping the process of European integration.

Chapter 4 is devoted to the study of the Italian political system and the attitude of both political parties and public opinion toward the process of European integration. I first describe the changes that have taken place in the Italian political system since the 1990s, discussing the main features of the old and new political system both domestically and with respect to Italy-EU relations. I describe how membership in the Community—initially a unilateral decision of the then-leading Christian Democratic Party—gradually became a shared value of all the parties of the political framework and then again a divisive issue, alongside transatlantic relations, in the mid-1990s. I then discuss how, while governmental stability improved, Italian foreign policy became, on the contrary, increasingly less predictable; European and transatlantic policies were transformed into divisive issues both within and between the two coalitions. And with a plethora of parties in each coalition, some of the minor political parties acquired a veto power that far exceeded their effective political force. Indeed, they have often used this power in foreign policy issues, and EU affairs represents one of the major areas of contention. Chapter 4 also discusses the Italian public's opinion of the EU, unquestionably one of the most favorable in Europe toward the integration process.

Chapter 5 describes how the Italian parliament deals with European affairs and what effects the EU has on it. I focus first on the years before the early 1990s, when the influence of the Italian parliament on EU affairs was near zero. If, until roughly 1995, the Italian parliament demonstrated "low-level Europeanization" (its structural adaptation was weak, minimal time and energy were devoted to the scrutiny of EC law, and there was a general lack of interest in playing a greater role), since the mid-1990s the Italian parliament has successfully addressed many issues that had remained unresolved for years, thus greatly reducing the gap between itself and the national parliaments that were best organized in the scrutiny of EU affairs. While maintaining its traditional model of "paper-based scrutiny," the parliament now has in place a full-fledged system organized around permanent committees specialized in EU affairs. It has expanded the scope of its scrutiny of EU policies, is regularly informed of developments in EU affairs, has developed clear procedures for scrutiny and fact-finding, and is even protected in its prerogatives by the introduction of a "scrutiny reserve system." Chapter 5 also distinguishes between the formative phase of EU law and the implementation of EU law—the field of European affairs where the Italian parliament exerts the most control.

Last but not least, the chapter briefly addresses the question of the Italian constitutional framework and how its peculiarities have affected the way the parliament has approached European issues. It also discusses the evolution of the normative discourse about the relation between national and EC law; and it explains how the Italian Supreme Court moved slowly from denying the supremacy of EC law to acknowledging its effects, transforming the latter into national law. This development, naturally, has affected the way Italy deals with European affairs.

Chapter 6 is devoted to the executive and to the way the Italian government deals with European affairs. First, I address the question of Italy's form of government, as established by the Constitution and as it evolved after the reforms of the late 1990s and early 2000s. Then I look specifically at how the different actors in the government deal with European affairs. The analysis begins with the Ministry of Foreign Affairs, because in Italy, traditionally, it has played the main role in European affairs. Within the ministry, the two main actors handling European affairs are the minister himself and the secretary of state for European affairs, both assisted by the Directorate General for European Integration. Since 2000, however, a number of reforms have delegated partial responsibility for EU policies to the Presidency of the Council (that is, the Prime Minister's Office). Since 1999, in fact, the Presidency of the Council has been responsible for the "participation of the Italian State in the EU" and for the "actuation of EU policies." Acting in coordination, the Presidency of the Council and the Foreign Ministry are to ensure the promotion of Italy's positions within the European institutions. At the Presidency of the Council, the relatively new Department for EU Affairs is entrusted with following EU policies. It also gives logistical and technical support to the new Interdepartmental Committee for Community and European Affairs (Comitato Interministeriale per gli Affari Comunitari Europei, or CIACE), which coordinates EU policies among the ministries. Chapter 6 looks at how coordination takes place, both within and across departments and ministries. Last but not least, the chapter examines the role the Permanent Representative in Brussels has played in the past and is playing now.

Chapter 7 investigates the role played in Italy's EU affairs by regional and local authorities and by organized interests. The chapter seeks to answer questions such as: Can the regions oppose "scrutiny reserve" to proposed EU legislation? Do they do follow-up analysis?

The regional case is particularly interesting as in October 2001 the Italian Constitution was modified to provide Italy with a federal framework. Before the 2001 constitutional reform, the Italian institutional framework was based on the hierarchical supremacy of the central government over regional authorities. In drafting law, regions had to respect the principles fixed by the central legislative power, while the central government's decentralized authorities checked the administrative acts of the regions. This constitutional reform served to create a new philosophy—namely that the Italian Constitution should no longer enumerate regional competencies, just state ones. Regions can now act in every area that the Constitution does not specifically attribute to the state and enjoy, at least on paper, ample powers in EU policies. Chapter 7 therefore discusses whether these powers are effective in dealing with European affairs and how the different regions address them.

The second part of the chapter focuses on organized interests with regard to the European Union. How are Italian interests presented and defended at the EU level? What strategies do they follow and how effective are they?

After looking at the actors dealing with EU policies, the closing chapters focus on Italy's negotiating strategies and behavior within EU negotiations. In 1966 Stanley Hofmann introduced the distinction between *high politics* and *low politics* in the EC policy process. The terms are now commonly used by scholars in the field: *low politics* refers to "technical" negotiations—that is, day-to-day negotiations about EC law; *high politics* refers to negotiations about EU constitutive and "grand" policies, such as treaties, foreign policy, and security. Chapter 8 studies the role played by Italy's EU high politics. I first examine the drafting of the Single European Act (in 1985), followed by the preparation of the Treaty of Maastricht in 1990. In both instances, Italian action was pivotal for the success of the negotiations. The story is different, however, for developments during the 2003 Intergovernmental Conference (IGC), also led by the Italian presidency. Here, the lack of support by both France and Germany ultimately led to the negotiations' failure. The next cases examined in the chapter relate to Justice and Home Affairs—in particular, the controversial case of the European arrest warrant—and to the aborted cases of a Common Foreign and Security Policy, and the so-called "Alba" mission to Albania. The latter two cases present elements of both success and failure for Italy and are therefore of particular interest.

Finally, chapter 9 deals with two relevant cases of low politics. One regards the strategy used by Italy in its negotiations over the Economic and Monetary Union. How was that strategy implemented and to what effect? Did the outcome respond to the Italian national interest? How did the government act to preserve it? The second case study is related to the negotiations over the EU's so-called 20-20-20 directive on renewable energy. This is a very interesting case for Italy. The time span covers two different governments, whose actions and behaviors were quite different. The case therefore provides a broad overview of Italy's negotiating style. While in the first phase coordination was almost impossible because of deep differences among departments and ministries, with the change of government, approaches to negotiations changed completely and Italy was able to successfully define and defend its national interests. How effective it was, however, remains open to debate.

The conclusion looks at the crux of the matter from two perspectives: one, the degree of Europeanization of the Italian system; and two, Italy's influence on both high and low politics in the EU. Regarding Italy's degree of Europeanization, I review whether and how Italy's governance and state structure, constitutional practice, political discourse, policy output, and other matters have been affected by the process of European integration. Regarding Italy's influence, I make some observations about the impact Italy has had on EU policymaking, both in drafting laws and in creating intergovernmental policy.

In the end, the conclusions test my fundamental hypothesis—that a "medium-size power" such as Italy can only be a leading country in EU policymaking in the presence of certain variables. I conclude that there are political and institutional mechanisms that facilitate the ability of member states to elaborate adequate national positions, and lacking such mechanisms, the member states will lose negotiating efficacy. In particular, relevant intervening variables appear to be:

—a *consociative political culture,* at least as far as participation in the EU is concerned (that is, agreement among elites about the importance of promoting national interests in EU decisionmaking procedures);

—mechanisms of *interministerial and intraministerial coordination,* which make it possible to define positions that take into account all the nation's different interests;

—*adaptable national institutions,* which allow a country to adjust quickly, as the EU structure and its decisionmaking procedures are subject to frequent changes.

Finally, well-defined *aims,* credible *actors,* and consistent *strategies* strengthen a nation's influence, keeping a medium-size power like Italy from becoming irrelevant in Brussels.

2 | *The Theoretical Framework*

When the field of European Studies was young (roughly from the late 1950s to the early 1980s), the main scholarly challenge was to describe the new institutional setting, to explain how it came into being, and to foresee possible future developments. From the mid- to late 1980s, the focus moved to explaining the changes introduced by the Single European Act (which took effect in 1987) and what these meant in institutional terms and for the future. Since the early 1990s, European Studies has proliferated and branched in so many directions that one book alone could never cover it thoroughly.

What happened during the early stages of European Studies, however, still affects us today; it has certainly influenced the way the research presented here was examined and interpreted. In those early years, scholars were often driven by *their own* expectations about European integration—that is to say, by whether they were in favor of the process or skeptical about it. Their attitudes influenced scholars' selection of topics to be analyzed, as well as their choice of methodology. According to William Wallace, "The widespread use of politically charged concepts in the European political debate—federalism, sovereignty, supranationality, integration itself—both [makes] the task of dispassionate definition more difficult and makes the desirability of rediscovering conceptual common ground more pressing."[1] Scholars differed over long-term political goals (whether there should be a United States of Europe or a Union of States), over working methods (supranationalism vs. intergovernmentalism), and over leading actors (EU institutions vs. nation-states).

Apart from a few isolated voices, it is fair to say that the majority of specialized scholars in the early days of European Studies shared a pro-European (that is, a pro-federal) view of the integration process. After all, enthusiasm was needed to approach such a new and (at the time) almost uncontemplated subject. Over the years, a split occurred. On the one side, pro-integration scholars devoted themselves to the study of European institutions. On the other, international relations (IR) specialists—generally more skeptical about the European integration process—emphasized the role of nation-states as the main EEC/EU gatekeepers. Indeed, the split between these two groups has not been limited to scholarly approaches; at times, it has led to personal petty disputes, seemingly more ideological than scientific. One such instance was the conflict between *federalists* and *neofunctionalists* in the 1950s. At a later date, disputes were rampant between *neofunctionalists* (and their evolutionary equivalents, such as "scholars of multilevel governance") and the supporters of *liberal intergovernmentalism*. Whenever relevant, the following pages will recall the most significant of such debates.

One of the results of the division among scholars was that non-IR types, when looking at the member states, focused primarily on the top-down effect—that is, on the *consequences* of integration for the member states, a phenomenon usually defined as Europeanization. Only to a far lesser extent did they consider the bottom-up approach—that is, the role played by the member states in *shaping* EU policies. Until recent times, therefore, few studies were dedicated to the influence that member states (or other national actors) exert on EU policymaking. Few scholars have asked who influences what, how, and to what extent? These questions lie at the heart of this book.

Whatever the research focus—top-down or bottom-up—four common types of studies, with different strategies, have emerged for researching relations between the member states and the EU:

—*Comparative "horizontal" studies.* These works compare the overall policymaking process in (almost) all of the member states, an exercise that is becoming more difficult as the number of member states grows. Interesting examples include an early work edited by Dietrich Rometsch and Wolfgang Wessels, which argued that EU and national decisionmaking were merging into a single cycle,[2] and a more recent volume edited by Simon Bulmer and Christian Lequesne, which concludes that more research is needed: "Research has to learn more about the impact of the member states (and especially of the new member states) on the EU level ("inside-out" studies). . . . More studies have to be undertaken on the role of the 25 national executives in the EU Council of Ministers, on the different negotiating *modi operandi* which necessarily change with ten more member states, and more generally on the influence of the member states inside the Commission and the European Parliament. Enlargement is increasing the activities of member states at the EU level but is also making them more diffuse and heterogeneous. The domestic organization of the new member states and the institutional linkages between their capitals and Brussels have to be investigated on a comparative basis."[3]

According to another study, by Klaus Goetz and Simon Hix, EU decisionmaking simultaneously imposes constraints and opportunities ("exits") for domestic policymakers. "The delegation of policy competencies to the European level and the resulting political outcomes constrain domestic choices, reinforce certain policy and institutional developments and provide a catalyst for change. The establishment of a higher level of governance provides new opportunities to exit from domestic constraints, to promote certain policies, to veto others, or to secure informational advantages."[4]

—*Comparative studies of one institution.* These works pick one national institution—the executive, the legislature, the regions, for instance—and compare it to its counterpart in other member states. One of the most important contributions in this field is the work of the late Vincent Wright, who maintained that the EU's main negotiating roles were in the hands of members' foreign and finance ministers.[5] With Hussein Kassim and Guy Peters,[6] Wright also stressed that interaction between domestic and EU policymaking has implied, for member states, the need for both inter- and intraministerial coordination. National parliaments have had to adapt to the constraints of EU decisionmaking, too, as first Philip Norton and then Wolfgang Wessels and Andreas Maurer have shown.[7]

—*Comparative studies of one policy area/decision.* The focus in such studies is on how the different member states were affected by, or how they influenced, a single policy area (and/or one specific piece of legislation). One example is the work of Yves Meny, Pierre Muller, and Jean-Louis Quermonne on national policies in the field of social policy, industrial policy, and competition law:[8] they draw the conclusion that three types of convergence can be identified: (a) the existence of a European political agenda, since the drafting of public policy is no longer a monopoly of the national actors; (b) the transformation in the system of interests, with a progressive Europeanization of interest groups; (c) the adaptation of national decisionmaking processes to characteristics of those of the Union. This latter factor has led, in particular, to uncertainty created by the lack of a clear and stable leadership, and to both openness and opacity in the decisionmaking processes themselves.

—*Member state case studies.* Finally, there is the strategy of focusing on a single member state, seen in its relations with the EU. The most comprehensive effort in such a sense has been the *X and EC Membership Evaluated* series. Completed in the 1990s, this series includes eleven of the then twelve member states. The more recent Palgrave Macmillan series *X in the European Union* so far only includes France, Spain, and Ireland.[9]

All told, the study of member states in the EU decisionmaking process is, with few exceptions, a young field of study within the larger area of European Studies. The general goal of this book is to add knowledge about the role of member states in shaping the EU decisionmaking process, and in turn, to properly weigh the influence of decisions made at the European level on those member states. I focus specifically on the Italian case. The paragraphs that follow explain the intellectual path that led to the research underlying the results presented in this book.

The Early Studies: Federalists and Neofunctionalists

The Schuman Declaration set as an explicit goal the creation of a European Federation: the United States of Europe.[10] Ernst Haas, in 1958, drafted an early study of the subject: *The Uniting of Europe.* Haas was a German-born American political scientist and a pupil of David Mittrany, one of the first scholars to examine the early international organizations. Fascinated by the creation of the ECSC and the EEC, and by Jean Monnet's role in them, Haas decided to spend one year in Luxembourg to study developments in the field.

From his study of the ECSC in *The Uniting of Europe*, Haas elaborated on the concepts of political integration, supranationality, and spillover, thus giving birth to the so-called *neofunctionalism* movement. *Political integration* is the process through which political actors from different nations are persuaded to shift their loyalties, expectations, and political activities toward a new center whose institutions hold jurisdiction over the preexisting national states. Supranationality was referred to as the "archetype of a federation," a definition drawn by the ECSC High Authority.[11] The concept of *spillover* was borrowed from the principle of "central function" in the classical theory of functionalism. Part of the "expansive logic of sector integration," spillover stood for the spread of integration, to include new, as yet unintegrated, sectors.

Haas also analyzed the decisionmaking processes of the new institutions and their relations with economic and social groups. He identified two main factors at the core of the supranational process: (a) the capability of central institutions to generate strong expectations—be they positive or negative; (b) the tendency of economic and social forces to unite beyond national borders and to create common policies. The system outlined by Haas is thus *dynamic, concrete, and actor-oriented*. The actors are the governments and voluntary associations. The *environment* in which they operate consists of *beliefs, institutions, objectives,* and *competencies*. There are also *inputs* and *out-*

puts, which may transform the environment through specific consequences of either an integrative or disintegrative nature.

Besides Haas, in the late 1950s, the European federalists were among the few to discuss the ongoing European integration process. Analysis conducted by federalists intersected with their activism in the process of European integration. And while Monnet and the federalists may have agreed on the final outcome (a European federation), their views on how to achieve it were significantly different. A pragmatic man, Jean Monnet believed that a political European union was needed to secure enduring peace and prosperity for the continent, but that such a union would only be reached gradually: "I have always felt that the political union of Europe must be built step by step, like its economic integration. One day this process will then lead us to a European Federation," he wrote in the *Journal of Common Market Studies* in 1963.[12] Against Monnet's pragmatic approach, the federalists thought that citizens should stand for a United Europe and that a European Parliament should draft a European Constitution. As Altiero Spinelli and Ernesto Rossi wrote in the *Ventotene Manifesto* (as explained in detail in chapter 3): "The easiest solution [is] a European Federation . . . if there will be in the main European countries a sufficient number of people who will understand that victory will be briefly in their hands."[13] The federalists thus denied any role for the national governments, believing that they were destined to disappear.

Other scholars, in the 1960s and 1970s, were more skeptical about the process of integration: Robert Keohane and Joseph Nye doubted the overall validity of the theory of integration, while Stanley Hoffman believed that nation-states maintained firm control over the decisionmaking processes.[14] The control of the nation-states was particularly pronounced with regard to what Hoffman defined as *high politics* (state security and vital resources, for example) as opposed to *low politics* (technical and administrative issues). When dealing with low politics, national governments appeared to be more eager to cooperate. Eventually, with the crises of the 1970s severely affecting the construction of a unified Europe, European Studies was largely ignored by scholars and political scientists.

The 1980s: Multilevel Governance and Liberal Intergovernmentalism

With the arrival of Jacques Delors and the relaunching of the Internal Market in the mid-1980s, new studies of the EEC soon emerged. In 1989 Wayne Sandholtz and John Zysman affirmed that Haas's spillover concept was still valid and claimed that the relaunching of the European integration process was linked to a number of factors,[15] including:

(a) The structural changes in the international community. The economic growth of Japan left Europe with only two alternatives: to become a satellite of Japan or to react.

(b) The rotation of the governing parties in the member states, with the return of Christian Democratic coalitions and governments. In several countries, the Christian Democrats were in power at the time of the creation of the first Community institutions; they remain the most supportive of the principle of European union. After the defeat of the Socialists in the elections in Great Britain and Germany, the major Communist parties were weakened (in France and Italy); after that, those Socialists still or newly in power (Mitterrand in France, Gonzales in Spain) opted for clear free-market policies.

(c) The role of the European Commission. Guided by Jacques Delors since 1985, the Commission had found in the above-mentioned changes sufficient margin for maneuver to take the lead. Examples include the implementation of research and technical cooperation between European countries (through ESPRIT and RACE—the European Strategic Program for Research and Development in Information Technologies, and Research and Development in Advanced Telecommunications Technologies in Europe); Lord Cockfield's White Paper for the completion of the Internal Market and the subsequent Single European Act (through which new Community competencies were added); an increased reference to qualified majority voting; and the European Parliament's enhanced involvement in the legislative process.

(d) The role of the economic elites. The Commission was strongly supported in its actions, and in some cases its actions were anticipated by the economic elites. The European Round Table (ERT) played a preeminent role, offering a source of inspiration for the abovementioned White Paper.

(e) The receptiveness of the new national governments. Member states began supporting the Commission's proposals, thereby relaunching the Community integration process.

If, in 1983, William Wallace claimed that national governments had been "successful at retaining control of the process of Community policy-making in most areas,"[16] just a few years later, together with Helen Wallace, he claimed that the centrality of the European states had been eroded, in favor of the European level. "It's possible for national governments to hold the gate between domestic and international politics only for a shrinking number of policy areas. More and more, public servants and private actors have developed their own paths across national boundaries; goods, services, money and people flow across such boundaries less and less affected by side action or control. . . . The centrality of the European state has been progressively reduced."[17] Essentially, scholars began to concentrate on the actors involved in the day-to-day functioning of the Union, and to assess, for instance, the roles of lobbies, the European Commission, and the European Parliament.

Calling the EEC a *network form of organization*, in which Commission technocrats, members of national bureaucracies, transnational lobby groups, and multinational companies were all involved, Robert Keohane and Stanley Hoffmann concluded that the old theories were no longer valid.[18] They could not explain the new and complex EEC decisionmaking process, during which informal and formal structures interacted at different levels. A new literature trend was thus launched around the concept of *multilevel governance*. Alongside the works of Helen and William Wallace, studies by Gary Marks, Fritz Scharpf, Simon Bulmer, John Peterson, and Beate Kohler-Koch merit mention.[19] Among the common themes they wrote about were:

—preferences and results as shaped by institutions;

—the complexity of policymaking and how it has spread over several levels;

—member states' efforts to use the EEC to achieve national goals. Governments essentially sought to maintain control over inputs and outcomes, but success rates varied according to the policy areas involved.[20]

Not all scholars used this approach, of course. For instance, according to the Alan Milward school, "Neofunctionalism failed the test of history because it did not ask the crucial question about where the locus of power lay in the postwar period and, in its enthusiasm for a theory, practically did away with the nation-state as the central unit of political organization."[21] Milward's analysis of the origins of the Community is characterized by a reading of rational choices by nation-states. The starting point for Milward's analysis is the realist conception according to which "the modern nation-state is still the ultimate arbiter of its own destiny." According to this theory, a state would choose to move from interdependence to integration only when the first proves insufficient: "Nation-states have a certain portfolio of policy objectives which they'll try to realize in the face of economic and political internationalization. These policy objectives are almost entirely shaped by domestic pressures and economic resources and will therefore vary from country to country and over time. In order to advance these objectives, nation-states will attempt to use what international framework is at hand. Many of these objectives can and will be pursued by expanding what we have called here the inherited framework of interdependence, traditional intergovernmental co-operation among states. However . . . some fundamental objectives after 1945 could not be achieved through such a framework and were therefore advanced through integration."[22] And again: "The common policies of the European Community came into being in the attempt to uphold and stabilize the post-war consensus on which the European nation-state was rebuilt. They were a part of the rescue of the nation-state."[23]

Andrew Moravcsik's analysis starts from the same assumption, that states are rational actors. According to his *liberal intergovernmentalism,* European integration is explained as a series of rational choices made by political leaders. Those choices are determined by the constraints and opportunities created by domestic economic interests, by the relative weight of each state in the international system, and by the role of the international institutions in supporting the credibility of interstate commitments. Accordingly, the assumption is that states act rationally or instrumentally in the quest for stable and defined interests and that Community negotiations can be divided into three phases: the emergence of national preferences, interstate negotiations, and choices in the international institutions. As Moravcsik explains in *The Choice for Europe*: "European integration is the result of a series of rational choices made by national leaders who consistently pursued economic interests. . . . When such interests converged, integration advanced. [p. 3] Interstate bargains are decisively shaped by the relative power of nation states. [p. 7] Choices to pool and delegate sovereignty to international institutions are best explained as efforts by governments to constrain and control one another. [p. 9] Liberal intergovernmentalism holds that European integration was a series of rational adaptation by national leaders to constraints and opportunities. [p. 473] National governments can be analyzed by assuming that each first formulates national preferences, then engages in inter-state bargaining, and finally decides whether to delegate or pool sovereignty in international institutions. [p. 473]"[24] States are thus seen as unitary actors maintaining a rational single voice in international negotiations.

Both Milward and Moravcsik choose the state as their unit of analysis. For the former, this is the *national* state; for the latter, it is the (big) member state, seen in its relationships with other (big) member states. According to Moravcsik, European high politics are determined by "the convergence of domestic policy preferences in the largest member states," from which, however, Italy is excluded.[25] Unfortunately, given that from a formal point of view Italy *is* a big EU member state, Moravcsik never explains why he excludes the country.

For Milward, on the other hand, the key element is the decision of a member state to opt for integration with regard to those policies that can no longer be properly managed at the domestic level. Therefore Milward concentrates on the internal dynamics of the various national states because he is interested in understanding *how* the choice to integrate was reached, within the states themselves. It is irrelevant, for the purposes of Milward's analysis, whether a state is big or small.[26]

Moravcsik also addresses the question of domestic dynamics within the member states, in order to demonstrate the convergence of interests between the "big" states, considered the engines of European integration: France, Germany, the United Kingdom. "From its inception, the EC has been based on inter-state bargains among its leading member states. Heads of government, backed by small groups of ministers and advisors, initiate and negotiate major initiatives in the Council of Ministers or the European Council. Each government views the EC through the lens of its own policy preferences; EC politics is the continuation of domestic policies by other means. . . . Small states can be bought off with side-payments, but larger states exercise a *de facto* veto over fundamental changes in the scope or rules of the core element of the EC, which remains economic liberalization. Thus bargaining tends to converge toward the minimum common denominator of large state interests."[27] The Single European Act, for instance, is explained, on one hand, by the negotiations between France, Germany, and the United Kingdom and, on the other hand, by the "negotiating leverage that France and Germany gained by exploiting the threat to create a 'two-track' Europe and excluding Britain from it."[28] "The importance of inter-state bargains in the SEA [Single European Act] negotiations is consistent with the broader experience of the EC since the mid-1960s. European integration did not proceed steadily and incrementally; it proceeded in fits and starts. Moreover, since the Luxembourg Compromise of 1966, the EC has moved toward intergovernmental ('state-to-state') decisionmaking centred in the Council and summit meetings, rather than toward increasing authority for international bodies such as the Commission and Parliament. . . . Heads of Government and their direct representatives carried out the negotiations. The result represents the convergence of domestic policy preferences in the largest member states."[29]

The problem with such intergovernmental models is that, notwithstanding the analysis of the states' internal dynamics, they still consider those states unitary actors in the European decisionmaking process. In Carol Webb's words: "Intergovernmentalism represents one means of getting to grips with conceptualising the national dimension in Community politics and Community policymaking. But, so long as it is associated with the 'billiard-ball' image in which monolithic governments are seen as preserving their hard shells against external penetration by international negotiating forums like the EC, it cannot be a complete answer. From a national bureaucratic perspective, two aspects are inadequately accommodated within the intergovernmentalist approach. . . . The first is the extent of intergovernmental negotiation and co-ordination which is made necessary by the context of Community issues and the second is the political context in which they are mediated. Intergovernmental negotiations imply the possibility—frequently the reality—of multiple *transgovernmental* contacts. Bureaucracies will attempt to manoeuvre themselves into strong positions and . . . become acquainted . . . with their opposite numbers working on similar problems for other governments."[30]

On the other hand, the supranational models explained above tend to neglect the study of the member states, assuming their decline. Again in Carol Webb's words: "Neofunctionalism's view of the domestic politics of regional integration was forever distorted by its preoccupation with the 'new style' of politics at the Community level. An oversimplified view of interest group politics at the national level led neofunctionalists to underestimate (and underresearch) the political relationships between governments and their domestic constituencies, which can enhance and complicate national participation in the European Community. In fact, the variables which appear to shape governments' responsiveness to functional integration and policy bargaining in an international setting turn out to be more intimately connected with strands in domestic politics than was initially imagined."[31]

Member States Matter

Still, throughout this period, a number of scholars insisted that analysis should continue to focus on the national level. In the field of international relations, Robert Putnam linked the negotiation skills of the national leader to his or her domestic politics. As recalled by Andrew Moravcsik in the introduction to Putnam's book: "The two-level-games approach begins by assuming that statesmen are typically trying to do two things at once; that is, they seek to manipulate domestic and international politics simultaneously. Diplomatic strategies and tactics are constrained both by what other states will accept and by what domestic constituencies will ratify. . . . statesmen are strategically positioned between two 'tables,' one representing domestic politics and the other international negotiation. . . . To conclude negotiations successfully, the statesman must bargain on these two tables, both reaching an international agreement and securing its domestic ratification [p. 4]. Statesmen must make trade-offs between domestic and international goals [p. 10]. The two-level-games approach [differs from previous theories because] complex patterns of interdependence do not simply constrain statesmen, but also create new possibilities for creative statecraft [p. 16]. The two-level-games approach recognizes that domestic policies can be used to affect the outcomes of international bargaining, and that international moves may be solely aimed at achieving domestic goals [p. 17]. Each state is assumed to have a 'win-set,' defined as the set of potential agreements that would be ratified by domestic constituencies in a straight up-or-down vote against the status quo of 'no agreement' [p. 23]. Putnam's article is based on the proposition that the outcome of international negotiations reflects the size of the domestic win-sets . . . larger win-sets increase the number of potential agreements and decrease the probability that nations will defect from those they make [pp. 27–28]." [32]

Putnam's analysis is important because it draws attention to the *domestic constituency*. However, in his approach, the domestic arena is somewhat "hidden" behind the national leader, who stands in as the main actor. Furthermore, while the two-level game undoubtedly explains the behavior of certain actors within the framework of certain Community negotiations, it would be limiting to apply the paradigm to *all* European negotiations. Other IR scholars have therefore stressed the importance of analyzing the domestic constituency.

Thomas Risse, for instance, has claimed that neither the supranational nor the intergovernmental approaches capture the true essence of the European decisionmaking processes. He considers it necessary to "reconceptualize" the EU, starting from an approach defined as *transnational relations*. Recalling authors such as Keohane and Nye, Risse states that such an approach is contrary both to the idea that the state is the only significant player in international relations and to the fact that national governments must be considered as unitary actors. "Policy-making in the EU does not take place in an institutional void. The domestic structures of the member states and the institutional structure of the EU exert independent effects on the ability of actors to shape the European policy agenda, to create 'winning coalitions,' to influence decisions, and to implement them. As for *domestic structures*, we need to differentiate between the structure of the political institutions, societal interests' formation and aggregation, state-society relations, and the norms embedded in the political culture. Domestic structures vary not only among the member states, but also with regard to the issue areas involved." [33]

Scholars of comparative politics, however, are the main advocates of the study of domestic policies. In 1983 Helen Wallace, William Wallace, and Carol Webb wrote that "the intergovernmental and transgovernmental approaches need to be accompanied by a more thorough analysis of domestic political structures and relationships if they are to be usefully applied to Community politics. The phrase 'domestic politics' or the 'domestic context' is a convenient shorthand way of referring to the range of commitments, electoral debts and policy responsibilities which all the EC member state governments must consider in the formulation of their positions on Community issues. Studies of the 'two-track' network linking the Community with domestic politics in the member States have revealed an interesting combination of factors, both positive and negative, which are relevant for an understanding of government roles. In political terms, national governments clearly have to evaluate the costs and benefits of their Community membership if not continuously, then at least in part by ensuring that they remain in tune with the prevailing tide of domestic opinion. This is not fixed or immutable. . . . Governments may not be entirely prisoners of their domestic constituencies, but they can be especially sensitive . . . to the political clout of some groups. . . . Internal political relationships between governments and various sector and general interests are fundamental to the positions taken up by officials and ministers in Brussels. . . . The European Community could be, and indeed has been, used as a 'resource' in domestic politics by hard-pressed governments. . . . Back home, by contrast, a government may be able to avoid too close and too uncomfortable an association with an unpopular or contentious policy by making use of the EC as a political or economic alibi. . . . If national governments sometimes use the EC as a 'prop,' the EC itself frequently has to rely on governments to provide the basic administrative infrastructure which is lacking at the Community level. Thus the national administrative infrastructure becomes an indispensable element in Community policy management and implementation. . . . Commission officials have not worked in a vacuum in their attempts to formulate a Community-wide industrial or regional policy. They have, more often than not, had to sit back and watch representatives of national governments determine the pace (or lack of it) [pp. 28–31]."[34]

William Wallace stressed this idea again in 1990: "The games in Brussels are linked to the outcomes of games played in national capitals and in turn influence the games played in national capitals. But it would be a mistake to see each member state as simply a vertical segment of a multilateral system."[35] This position was also shared by Stephen George, who concluded that the neofunctionalist model is a useful guide to empirical investigation, but no more than that. *Domestic politics*—to be subdivided into political party positioning, electoral reasons, roles of stakeholders and *bureaucratic politics*— need to be assessed as well.[36]

Already in 1983 Simon Bulmer had sought to draw attention to the fact that a vast majority of studies concentrated on the Community institutions. According to Bulmer, this approach neglected the national positions and the differences among them. Bulmer put forward five assumptions grounding the *domestic politics approach*:

(1) the basic unit for the Community is the *national polity*;

(2) each *national polity* is characterized by social and economic conditions that determine its interests and policies;

(3) European *policymaking* represents only a part of the activity of *national polity*;

(4) in formal terms, national governments occupy a crucial position, linking national politics and Community policies;

(5) the *policy style* concept best assesses the relationships between the governments and other political forces in relation to Europe.

The domestic politics approach, according to Bulmer, determines the necessity to analyze the Community policymaking process and national policies in the same way.

Little by little, despite an increasingly complex and supranational EU, it came to be accepted that member states still mattered in negotiating EU policy—an idea that would be reinforced later by the multiple halts in the process of writing the Constitutional Treaty and the Lisbon Treaty.

According to Bulmer and Lequesne there are at least six reasons that "member states matter":[37]

(1) The European Union reflects a balance of unifying and territorial forces/institutions.

(2) Identity, democracy, and legitimacy tend to be located predominantly at the member state level.

(3) Changes within member states have a profound effect on the Union and are closely interlinked with the development of the EU.

(4) Member states, and not just governments, are key players in the politics of the European Union.

(5) The EU is an important factor in the member states' politics.

(6) The dynamics of interaction among member states and the EU are significant in a number of ways:

—national governments and other actors must devise ways of having effective input into the political process at the supranational level (projection);

—national governments and other actors must devise ways of incorporating EU business into their deliberations at the national level (reception);

—the EU creates a changing opportunity structure for all actors at the national level;

—all these types of actors are also subject to new constraints such as policy commitments and legal obligations;

—it is not clear whether the "logic" of political action in Brussels or that of political action in the member states should prevail;

—national governments (ministers and officials), public agencies, national parliaments, subnational parliaments, political parties, interest groups, national courts, and public opinion all interact with the EU.

This book fits into this field of research, conjugating such an analysis with the results of Milward's work. The goal is to understand the web of interaction and variables existing in relations between Italian *domestic politics* and the *European policy cycle*. Domestic politics, in this sense, refers to all political actors and institutions within a member state.[38]

The next few pages are thus devoted to an analysis of the literature that focuses on relations between the member states and the EU, about which we can essentially distinguish three areas of research:

—horizontal comparative studies (that is, the EU and the member states);

—comparative studies focusing on a given national institution (national parliaments and the EU);

—case studies devoted to the analysis of the whole process in a member state.

Horizontal Comparative Studies of EU Member States

To undertake a comparative study covering the entire policy process in the twenty-seven member states demands significant means and comparative skills. Not surprisingly, therefore, the few texts that attempt to do so are often based on secondary data.

In his seminal study of the then twelve member states, Keith Middlemas analyzed the internal organization of the member states in handling and coordinating European issues.[39] He takes France as the reference case (centralized), and classifies the other member states as follows: *Other centralized states* (United Kingdom, Spain, Portugal, Greece); *federal or decentralized states* (Germany, the Netherlands, Belgium, Denmark, Luxembourg); *intermediate states* (Italy, Ireland).

A volume edited by Eleanor Zeff and Ellen Pirro, on the other hand, seeks to study the interconnection between national and European policymaking, focusing on the way in which each member state implements European policies at national and subnational levels.[40] The studies collected in the volume, although significant when considered individually, can hardly be compared: the policies selected are all different.

One of the most relevant analyses in horizontal comparative European studies—for its analytical dimension and methodological rigor—was undertaken in the period 1990–93 by the Institut für Europäische Politik (IEP) under the guidance of Dietrich Rometsch and Wolfgang Wessels.[41] The working group tested three hypotheses and found confirmation for two of them:

(a) *There is a process of Europeanization of the national institutions:* This hypothesis—that there is a "constant effort toward European activity and participation in EC decisionmaking, in order to cope with the requirements of the EC/EU political system"—was confirmed.[42]

(b) *The national and the European institutions are increasingly part of a single decisionmaking cycle:* This hypothesis—that national institutions (governments, ministerial bureaucracies, parliaments, regions, and courts) and European institutions do not act independently from each other—was also confirmed.

(c) *National institutions are converging toward similar organizational models:* This last hypothesis did not find any empirical confirmation. Research showed that governments continue to play a dominant role; there is no substantial passivity on the part of national parliaments (a certain tendency toward a "laissez-faire attitude"); and no common trend could be found in the organizational patterns across member states.

In fact, each national institution and each public administration sector revealed specific and peculiar models of interaction with the Union. The crossing of horizontal and vertical cleavages is such that "the basic trend towards the Europeanization of national institutions differs in scope and intensity according to the member states [so that] there is not one single pattern of institutional behavior and participation but rather a great variety of possible combinations and options within the general trend of Europeanization."[43]

To put it another way, it is possible to identify two types of cleavages in the interaction between national and European institutions: Europeanization and convergence vs. nationalization and divergence. Convergence indicates a "gradual process of constitutional, procedural, organizational and behavioral innovation and adaptation to the EC/EU decisionmaking process by national political institutions, which, in the long-term, could lead to one common politico-constitutional system in the member states, characterized, above all, by the disappearance of pre-existing differences." Divergence points to "the lack of innovation and adaptations of national institutional systems and the maintenance of the politico-constitutional differences in the member states."[44] Both the process of Europeanization and institutional adaptation are influenced by variables like national elections, the particular history or political culture of member states, and their traditional relations in foreign affairs.[45] The authors found that it is possible to "classify" national institutions according to their degree of Europeanization (low, medium, and high).

Though the field of European Studies has grown significantly in recent years, an exact definition of *Europeanization* has yet to be agreed upon. In Hussein Kassim's words: "This concept has been used in such a variety of ways and to describe such different things that it no longer has a precise or clear meaning, . . . it construes the relationship between the Union and the member states in terms of a one-way, top-down relationship."[46]

One of the very first studies on the process of what was then called *Europeification* was conducted by Svein Andersen and Kjell Eliassen.[47] The two

Norwegian authors started from the assumption that until then there had been a tendency to consider the national political systems as relatively closed, while the Community—a new form of transnational system, in which member states and their actors interacted—had become open and complex. Europeification, they explained, has three practical aspects: policy context, policymaking processes, and policy outcomes. The questions the authors sought to address—by analyzing the Community institutions and a number of European policies—were the following: What factors stimulate or block Europeification? How institutionalized are policies (not only at the national but also at the European level)? What characterizes the distribution of interests? At what levels of the decisionmaking process can the driving forces be found? Their research led the authors to conclude that, in reality, there is no single and univocal answer: there are, instead, various degrees of Europeification. Andersen and Eliassen pointed out the importance of the national level in the EU decisionmaking processes and the interlacing between these and the Community. Other studies then followed.

Yves Meny, Pierre Muller, and Jean-Louis Quermonne, for instance, investigated ways in which the drafting and the content of national policies are influenced by the Union.[48] They pondered whether a *European sphere of public policy* truly exists, and whether there is a convergence of the styles, the action strategies, and the content of the public policies in the member states. The three scholars analyzed patterns in how member states defend their interests at the European level; they undertook case studies of how national bureaucracies (Great Britain, Germany, and France) adapted; and they studied the impact of European integration on national social policies, industrial policies, and competition law. They eventually identified three types of *convergence*: (a) a distinct *European political agenda* (the drafting of public policy is no longer a monopoly of the national actors); (b) a transformation of the system of defending national interests (a progressive *Europeanization* of interest groups); (c) new decisionmaking processes due to the particular characteristics of decisionmaking within the Union.

Klaus Goetz and Simon Hix see in European integration a factor of both continuity and change at the domestic level.[49] According to the authors, the process of European integration can have two kinds of impact—which are reciprocally intertwined—on national political systems (actors and institutions):

—Policy competencies can be delegated to the European level and the resulting political outcomes can constrain domestic choices, thereby reinforcing certain policies and institutional developments and providing a catalyst for change.

—A higher level of governance can be established, providing new opportunities to shed domestic constraints, to promote certain policies, to veto others, or to secure informational advantages.

The impact of integration at the domestic level can be direct or indirect. There is *direct impact* when changes are due to specific Community legislative measures, and *indirect impact* in all other cases. Integration can influence the *institutional processes* (new regulatory policy styles, relationships between the legislative and the executive, decentralization) or the *input processes* (the emergence of new political forces or new divisions in existing parties, new coalitions).

Moreover, the decisionmaking processes of the Union provide domestic actors with new opportunities, making it possible for them to operate outside the domestic arena, veto domestic actions, and gain an informational advantage over the national arena. According to Tapio Raunio and Simon Hix, the process of integration seems to have had a negligible effect on the relationship between the executive and the legislative, although it has enhanced the executive's role somewhat and the position of the prime minister within it.[50] Also, administrative variables have gained power over the political ones in decisionmaking by national executives. Influence has been felt most with regard to administrative duties, while national politics now seem to play a lesser role in the drafting phase of decisions.[51] As far as the national parliaments are concerned, Raunio and Hix found that first there was a decline in the importance of the legislature vis-à-vis the executive, but then, beginning in the 1990s, a strengthening of the former over the latter.[52] Still, Klaus H. Goetz failed to find sufficient evidence of "European integration as a major force driving domestic executive change."[53]

Finally, Maria Green Cowles, James Caporaso, and Thomas Risse compared a number of case studies relating to different policies and came to three conclusions about the effects of Europeanization on the domestic structures of the member states: first, in the majority of cases, there is indeed convergence; second, this convergence is at the policy level rather than at the structural level; third, in the majority of cases, convergence is mixed (alongside innovations there are also specific institutional arrangements).[54] Convergence, therefore, does not imply homogenization. The most relevant and original finding by these three authors, however, is the assessment of the factors that prevent Europeanization. They can be summed up in five variables, which are related to the assets and the internal procedures of each member state: *multiple veto points, mediating formal institutions, differential empowerment of actors, organizational and political cultures,* and, to a lesser degree, *elite learning.*

Comparative Studies Focusing on National Institutions and Their Relation to the European Policy Cycle

Studies of a given national institution are more common because they are easier to undertake than those of an entire state. In 1973 Helen Wallace showed the relevance of interdepartmental coordination on European policies, writing: "at the national level each government developed its own procedures and mechanisms to handle Community questions, and to ensure liaisons between national and Community institutions. . . . Each member government and its administration have tackled the demands of Community membership in a manner consistent with their own traditions. There are considerable differences in governmental organization, in administrative style, and in policy goals among the Six. . . . The approach of the single party is significantly different from that of coalition government . . . there are further differences between the recent two-party coalition of West Germany and the rather more fragmented coalitions of the Netherlands or Italy. . . . In the case of Belgium and Italy . . . Cabinets and such have not been closely involved in the formulation of national policy towards the Communities, either because this would have been almost superfluous or because it would have risked breaking apart the governing coalitions."[55]

Almost four decades have passed since Helen Wallace wrote those words, and the Community has become a Union, now with twenty-seven members. It is therefore interesting to compare results from successive studies. There are two recurring sets of questions in studies of the relationship between national executives and the European Union. They are related, on the one hand, to the adaptation process of the governments (Is there a process of adaptation by the national executives? Does this adaptation occur in a uniform way? Can we identify the convergence of the various national models toward a single or at least a similar one?) and, on the other hand, to the identification of those elements that are crucial to ensuring efficient interdepartmental coordination. This last variable is often considered the most meaningful one in relations between member states and the EU.

Still, measuring effectiveness and making it operational are difficult things to do in political science. European Studies is no exception. The late Vincent Wright believed that it is possible to evaluate the effectiveness of member states in relation to European policymaking by looking at their capacity to: (a) anticipate new EU legislation and its impact at the national level; (b) shape the EU policy agenda and tap the resources available in Brussels; (c) smoothly and quickly translate European legislation into national law; (d) implement and monitor European legislation at the street level.[56] Yet even these indicators—or others, such as the ability to contain the costs (or enhance the benefits) of European legislation for the national system—are difficult to measure. Only for the issue of turning Community legislation into national law is there a reliable level of analysis today, by, among others, Finn Laursen and Sypros A. Pappas; Jurgen Schwartze, Inge Govaere, Frederique Helin, and Peter Van den Bossche; Heinrich Siedentopf and Jacques Ziller; Christoph Knill; and Andrea Lenschow.[57]

Anne-Marie Slaughter, Alec Stone Sweet, and Joseph Weiler argued that the relationship between national courts and the constitutionalization process at the EU level depends on the following variables: *judicial self-understanding, national identity,* and *national political culture*—that is, the perception tribunals have of the national political culture and their attitude toward the European integration process (inasmuch as constitutional courts tend to see themselves as both guarantors and an integral part of national identity); *judicial empowerment,* since some courts tend to be more reluctant to accept discipline imposed by EU law; *judicial dialogue and cross fertilization in the national and European political context*—that is, there is not only a "vertical" dialogue between national courts and the European Court of Justice but also a "horizontal" one between national courts; *national and European political context*—that is, the public opinion's perception of the European integration process and how it evolves (are these feelings influenced by national judges?); *the deployment of individual litigants and national courts, the role of the different branches of government and the relative balance of power between them*—that is, how Community policymaking has strengthened the executive, inasmuch as it can now adopt legislation together with EU policymaking bodies, bypassing the national parliament; *the impact of the legal culture*—that is, the role and importance of doctrine; *judicial composition and role of individuals*—that is, the biography of the judges involved.[58]

National Executives and the EU Policy Cycle

Leaving aside, for a moment, the issue of implementation and considering the formative phase of European law—specifically, the role played by national executives—it seems that interministerial coordination is the key element in rendering a government more or less capable of effectively defending its interests in EU negotiations. David Spence affirms that if "negotiations [in the Council] are ultimately about how governments put their point across and defend the 'national' interest in the search of an acceptable compromise, clearly the way in which governments arrive at a definition of national interests is an important part of the process. The ability of public administration to coordinate effectively . . . is crucial."[59] Spence thus puts special emphasis on the role played by Ministries of Foreign Affairs and Departments for EU Policy, as well as on that of the Permanent Representatives. Fiona Hayes-Renshaw and Helen Wallace highlight the existence of different priorities within the national ministries and, accordingly, the varying levels of importance given to intraministerial coordination at home and to coordination with the Permanent Representative in Brussels.[60]

Vincent Wright compared these levels of coordination and demonstrated the consequences of different approaches: (a) a dominant role for prime ministers, together with the ministers of foreign affairs and the ministers of finance, with regard to the most relevant political issues and to constitutional issues; (b) a leading role for ministers of foreign affairs (or finance/economy) in ensuring the link between the national capital and Brussels; (c) adaptive trends at the level of national ministries; (d) different ways of coordinating across countries, notwithstanding a certain degree of emulation and convergence.[61]

Wright was one of the first leading scholars to study how national governments elaborate those positions to be defended in Brussels. Together with Hussein Kassim and Guy Peters, Wright started with the issue of coordination at the national level on European policies, and eventually covered the entire governmental organization in relation to the EU.[62] According to these authors, the process of European integration calls for coordination by the governments involved. For the executives of the member states, it is necessary because of the increasing competencies of the Union, because of the growing responsibilities connected with the term of presidency, and because of the need to protect national interests.

The very nature of the decisionmaking processes, together with the many domestic variables, makes it quite difficult to effectively implement coordination. Domestic variables include the relevance of European issues in the national debate; the party system; the position of the prime ministers and of the other relevant ministers; the capacity of the administrative bodies to produce a coherent set of policy proposals; the level of integration and centrality of the public administration; the level of internal division within the bureaucracies. The way coordination is organized has important consequences both for the different domestic policies and for the whole EU. At the domestic level, the need for coordination has modified the existing institutional balance. On the other hand, at the EU level, if all member states were to adopt systems of coordination as rigid as the Danish one, the European decisionmaking process would soon be stuck. Kassim, Peters, and Wright considered "institutional convergence" and found a number of similarities across EU member states:[63]

—The prime ministers' roles and resources in EU affairs have increased significantly since the mid-1980s.

—The foreign ministers still play a central role, but their monopoly has eroded. In most cases, they act as coordinators of EU affairs, not least because the Permanent Representatives in Brussels respond to them.

—Virtually every national minister is now affected by EU policymaking, and they all have some sort of support unit to deal with it.

—Almost all member states have created ministers of EU affairs, but they are often junior figures.

—Relations between the legislative and executive branches have been affected by EU affairs, generally resulting in a weakening of the legislature.

—Subnational levels (regions, Länder, etc.) are progressively succeeding in participating in the national coordination of EU policies.

They also found a number of dissimilarities:

—The role and powers of each minister (not just of the foreign affairs minister) differ significantly from country to country.

—The member states' coordinating mechanisms vary significantly in shape and goals (some states, such as France, the United Kingdom, Portugal, and Denmark, use them to define their national positions, while others have more modest aims).

—The interconnection between formal and informal coordination, administrative procedures, and political decisionmaking varies too, from well integrated (France, Denmark, Germany) to disconnected (Italy).

—The role of the national parliaments varies, from peripheral (France) to determinate (Denmark).

—The involvement of the subnational level in the coordination process varies, from absent (in centralized countries such as Greece and Portugal), to involved (Italy and Spain), to key (Germany).

—The articulation of the official and political levels fluctuates from well-interconnected countries (France, Denmark, Germany) to fragmented ones, so that the possible construction of a coherent position, in truth, can only take place at the COREPER (Committee of Permanent Representatives) level.

"Institutional convergence" takes place thanks to the pressure applied by the Union's institutional structure as well as learning processes, while persistent national differences seem to be due to six characteristics inherent in domestic politics. The first three of these characteristics are related to the values of the member states, the remaining ones to their institutions.

Policy style: whether decisions tend to be handed down from above, or whether they tend to be consensual; whether the government's approach to policies tends to be active or reactive.

Policy ambitions: the objectives of the government in relation to the Union; whether it favors the process of integration, is neutral, or is even opposed to it; whether the government is prepared to defend particular policies or polities.

Coordination conception: whether coordination is seen solely as an exchange of information or as a way to elaborate the national positions to be defended in Brussels.

Nature of the party system: whether there is a majoritarian system—which ensures better coordination thanks to the more significant hierarchy of the executive and the party code of conduct, or a coalition government—which is less effective because different ministries are controlled by different parties.

Structure of the executive: when there is a weak prime minister (Italy) or ministers have significant autonomy (Austria, Germany), the individual ministers enjoy greater independence of action in the European arena.

Domestic administrative opportunity structure: the existence of vertical rather than horizontal divisions in the public administration; the frontier between the political appointment or career diplomats at the highest administrative levels; the existence of a cabinet system; the nature of the administrative culture.

In other words, the pressures of the Union on the national political systems are mediated through "the existing institutional structures and values that characterize each national political-administrative system . . . the responses of member states reflect the pre-existing balance of domestic institutional structures, as well as the broader matrices of values which define the nature of appropriate political forms in the case of each national polity and the outcome is a pattern of national differentiation."[64] Likewise, the "national systems for the coordination of European policy are strongly influenced by features of the wider national polity, and institutions may seek to replicate their domestic standing in the EU policymaking structure. . . . The national arrangements for managing EU policy are the outcome of interactions among national actors, institutions, and values, as well as between the latter and pressure form Brussels."[65]

Yet the findings of Kassim, Peters, and Wright are only partially confirmed by Goetz and Hix. Indeed, they often conflict. This is not surprising as "research on the Europeanization of national polities has not yet reached a stage where it is possible to set out a widely accepted 'standard version' of executive Europeanization."[66] Goetz thus suggests developing a research strategy capable of defining "more robust casual hypotheses about European integration and executive developments."[67] According to the author, this would entail a thorough and systematic analysis of the following:

—each national executive;

—the modes and procedural features characterizing the executives;

—the impact of the "European integration" variable with other types of variables, which could help explain the changes taking place at the domestic level;

—the changes taking place, in a temporal perspective;

—the ways in which changes have taken place, in an effort, in particular, to understand whether those changes are due to vertical pressure (determined by the Union) or horizontal pressure (cross-frontier).

The Role of National Parliaments in the EU Policy Cycle

With regard to the role of national parliaments in Europe's decisionmaking processes, a pioneering study was conducted by Valentine Herman and Rinus Van Schendelen under the auspices of the European Consortium for Political Research (ECPR).[68]

In the late 1970s, parliaments did not have any direct role in the decisionmaking processes of the EEC. They had minimal influence and control over the legislative production of the Communities themselves. Indeed, "at least for some decades . . . EC policy was considered part of 'external' affairs and, as such, an indisputable prerogative of the 'executive'—outside the legitimate claim for parliamentary participation."[69] Therefore, "national parliaments have increasingly lost in overall importance due to the evolution of [the EU] political system,"[70] leaving space for dominance by the executives—the real decisionmakers when it comes to EU policy.[71]

As the Community turned into a Union, and as the Union has continued to evolve, the framework has changed significantly. We can now identify three phases in the relationship between national parliaments and European issues: limited or no involvement (from the origins to the mid-1980s); first adaptations to the renewed decisionmaking framework of the EEC (following the Single European Act in 1987); and increased specialization and workload (with the creation of specific Committees for European Affairs and attempts to involve members of the European Parliament in their activities). Finally, after the Maastricht Treaty, or Treaty on the European Union (TEU), in 1991, a third phase began, in which the involvement of the national parliaments has been perceived as an answer to the democratic deficit of the Union.[72] The enlargement of the areas covered by Community legislation, the increasing importance of Community law, and the new powers and functions of the Union have all raised the need for improved scrutiny of the Union's legislative acts. Such a necessity has been recognized in successive treaties. With the Maastricht Treaty, indeed, "a more parliamentary climate prevailed."[73] Declaration No. 13 attached to the TEU responds to the concerns of the national parliaments in the European Union. The Amsterdam Treaty featured a protocol on the role of the national parliaments, demanding that governments forward to their respective national parliaments not only all the consultative documents of the Commission (green papers and white papers), but also the legislative proposals of the Commission.

Access to information has been the real turning point for national parliaments.[74] The parliaments' changes in attitude are attributed, on the one hand, to the changed mood of public opinion (which has gone from permissive consensus to reluctant acceptance), and on the other, to the fact that the executives—on issues falling under their competence—started to make use of the European level precisely to bypass the control of their own parliaments.[75]

National parliaments most recently have sought to react to the modified context by providing a more significant parliamentary scrutiny on European issues.[76] This has meant that they have had to determine which kind of scrutiny best served their purposes. And this, in turn, has forced them to ask themselves: *What needs to be scrutinized?* Only legislative acts or also documents such as "white books" and recommendations, or documents related to the second and third pillars?; *Who needs to be scrutinized?* Only the action of the respective governments or also that of the European institutions?; *When should scrutiny take place?* Only when the Commission makes legislative proposals or also when documents are approved in the various readings by the European institutions?; *What degree of scrutiny is appropriate?* Should the legal value of the parliamentary scrutiny be binding, as it is in the case of ratification to amendments or approval of new treaties?; *How should scrutiny be done?* Mainly by specialized committees? What should their relations be with other standing committees? Who should have which powers?[77]

Over the years, all the national parliaments have created specialized Committees for European Affairs.[78] However, this development has given birth to a number of difficult new questions, such as: what relationship should such committees have with other committees (that is, should the latter be consulted in their respective spheres of competence)?

A number of things impede the ability of parliaments to offer a positive contribution to the drafting of EU legislation. One problem concerns the effective capacity of the national parliaments to scrutinize. Indeed, there are several limitations in this respect. First, there are institutional limits: only in a few cases (in Denmark, for example) is the opinion of the parliament binding. Second, the tendency of parliaments to leave international affairs to the executive was originally extended to include European issues. Indeed, until the mid-1990s, European policies were perceived by national parliaments to be a matter of foreign rather than domestic affairs. Third, legislative bodies have often delegated a part of their European competencies to the executive (for instance, with regard to the implementation of Community law). Indeed, if, on the one hand, regulations are self-executing, on the other, directives are so technical and detailed that any parliamentary intervention is usually super-fluous. Finally, the European policy process itself limits the possibility of influ-ence by national parliaments. For instance, qualified majority voting makes it possible for other member states to *outvote* a government that is supporting the positions of its own parliament but not vice versa; also, the transmission of EU documents from the executive to the legislature is often slow and lim-ited to the first proposal of an act, as presented by the Commission.[79]

Another problem national parliaments face is that of their capacity to adapt to the process of European integration. Norton coordinated a comparative study of this issue in ten member states, focusing in particular on the reaction of national parliaments to the SEA and the TEU.[80] His research identified a general trend, but still uncovered significant differences across member states. Such differences appear to be connected to five variables: the national consti-tutions (specifically provisions concerning the Union); the norms and par-liamentary procedures (in particular, the organization, functioning, and powers of the specialized European Affairs Committees); the workload of the parliaments (which can make it difficult in certain countries to manage Euro-pean affairs); the ideological divisions on the process of European integration (leading certain parliaments to consider the supranational level the most appropriate for drafting, discussing, and enacting Community law); the polit-ical culture, as European integration is a source of strife between (or even within) parties in some countries, whereas elsewhere it serves as a shared value and thus becomes a "nonissue."

Another issue that has not been sufficiently addressed by national parlia-ments is how their specialized committees should operate. Should EU com-mittees have the power to assess acts by themselves? Or should competencies be "horizontal," meaning that they should then distribute material to other committees? According to Torjörn Bergman, the influence of national parlia-ments in European affairs depends on at least five variables: public opinion; national political culture; the member state's constitution; relations between the executive and legislative branches; and evidence of an overriding strategy.[81]

Last but not least, each specialized committee's perception of its own task counts: while some committees feel they should provide their own govern-ments with clear instructions and feel responsible for their governments' actions in the EU, others limit themselves to providing expert advice. The dif-ference in attitude and approach depends to a great extent on whether the par-liament in question can bind its own government to adopted positions (as in

Denmark) or whether it can only express a precise opinion, leaving the government then to decide whether to support it (as in France, Spain, or the United Kingdom).

One recent study, notable for its rigorous methodology and the number of case studies presented (the parliaments of all of the then fifteen member states) was coordinated by Wolfgang Wessels and Andreas Maurer.[82] Their objective was to understand "how national parliaments (re)act in and adapt to a dynamic institutional and procedural set-up" [page 17]. Even if the differences across nations are taken into account, the final results show a slow but significant institutional adaptation and *legal constitutionalization.* As far as real participation patterns are concerned, however, the parliaments' impact appears modest: "The role of the national parliaments in the decisionmaking process lies in 'one-level' scrutiny and advice within the model framework of the government-legislature relationship. National parliaments exercise these roles according to the constitutional and political context of the country" [page 19].

To put it another way, Hix and Raunio's hypothesis of a progressive reaffirmation of parliamentary action was confirmed, but only with regard to the formal aspect of parliamentary scrutiny and not with regard to effective influence over the EU decisionmaking processes.[83] According to Maurer and Wessels, adaptation has mainly concerned the creation and/or transformation of specialized European Affairs Committees in three areas: improved specialization within parliaments; more significant activity by specialized committees; greater segmentation and fragmentation of the bodies and parliamentary groups.[84]

Member States as Case Studies

Another way to approach the issue of relations between the member states and the European Union is to select one of them as a case study. Two collections of such case studies have been brought together in publications, yet neither has been followed up with a conclusive comparative volume.

A series of volumes evaluating individual countries' membership in the EC was published in the early 1990s, following the adoption of the Internal Market. It analyzed eleven of the twelve member states at the time and tried to evaluate the costs and benefits of accession to the Community.[85] Certain policies were examined in all of the member states: economic policies (the Internal Market, competition, industry, technology, transportation and communication, energy, agriculture, environment, taxation, regional policies, foreign trade); international relations (foreign policy cooperation, security, development aid); social, cultural, and educational policies (employment, work mobility, industrial relations, social security and health, equal treatment of men and women, consumer protection, education, European identity and cultural policies, media). In each volume, one section is devoted to the political and legal systems (the relationship between the legislative and the executive branches, the electoral system, political parties, local and regional governments, decision-making processes, the legal national system, judiciary procedures, the preservation of public order, the protection of fundamental rights, the organization of the state). The series undoubtedly offers interesting analytical research, but today it is outdated and there has been no follow-up comparative analysis.

Another series, evaluating individual countries' membership in the European Union, has yet to be completed. Among the volumes that have been produced, *France in the European Union* deals with the French contribution to the European integration process, the adaptation of its national institutions, the role and political orientation of parties, French public opinion, and a number of sectorial policies (European Security and Defense Policy [ESDP], the Common Agricultural Policy [CAP], economic and social policies, territorial policies, freedom of movement).[86] The aim of the volume is threefold: to identify the contribution of French policymakers to the European integration process; describe the methods that were adopted; and assess the impact of the European integration process on politics, policies, and policymaking in France. The authors concluded that the European integration process not only made the French policymaking process more complex but also led to a new balance of political power. The executive—in particular, the Finance Ministry and the Bank of France—gained more power, to the detriment of the parliament and the political parties. New actors also acquired new roles and influence (such as regional prefects, judicial courts, and certain environmental lobby groups). The national institutional adaptation occurred both at the top tier of government—where the integration process strengthened the president's role—and at the level of ministries and courts. The parliament, however, proved to be particularly slow in adapting to the integration process.

As for coordination, France seems to be one of the most efficient countries, though it has become increasingly difficult for the SGCI (Secretariat General of the Interministerial Committee for questions on European economic cooperation) to effectively follow and coordinate all the policies with a European dimension. Presidential intervention seems to weaken coordination—with the exception of cohabitation periods—but the Conseil d'Etat has become a most efficient partner in implementing the SGCI. The authors conclude that in France a distinction between the two levels of governance—European and national—can no longer be made. In many cases, the EU is used as a pretext to pursue necessary policies that are hard to "sell" to the French electorate.

Other books in this series focus on Spain and Ireland.[87] Apart from these two series, there is little literature available on the issue of members' adaptation to EU policy and the impact of European decisions on individual member states. France is possibly the most studied case. The most detailed and thorough work on the relationship between European and French decision-making processes is that of Christian Lequesne.[88]

According to Lequesne, there are three empirical approaches to analyzing relations between member states and the Community: (a) study the main national actors most involved with Community activities; (b) isolate a specific function of the administrative/political system common to some or all member states, and then make a comparative analysis; (c) select one or several member states and study the input of both governmental and nongovernmental actors. Lequesne's study follows the first line of research. He analyzed the behavior and functioning of the central political-administrative French bodies that deal with European issues for the period from May 1981 to May 1991. Lequesne focused on the evolution of both the structures and functions adopted by sectorial ministries in relation to communitarian policies: the ministry of Foreign Affairs, the coordination body (SGCI), the president of the republic and the prime minister, the Permanent Representative, the National Assembly, and the Senate. Of the two phases in the European policy cycle—devising and adopting—Lequesne chose to focus on the first. His four main findings are as follows: (a) the methods chosen by each member state to manage European policies are influenced by the national context; (b) there is a need to create an interdepartmental coordination body; (c) there is a tendency toward increased interaction between public institutions and private actors (for example, when enacting the Internal Market); (d) European policies are treated and dealt with differently than foreign policy. This last element is emphasized in the French case by the dual responsibility of the president and prime minister in solving interministerial conflicts.

Lequesne further contributed to this field of study over the years, with numerous articles published in books and journals. For example, in *L'administration centrale française et l'Union Européenne*, C. Lequesne and Y. Doutriaux retrace how French European politics are elaborated and then pursued in the EU institutions.[89] Another scholar, Michel Clamen, in 1996 used a different approach to show how French European politics are developed and how they work in the EU institutions, specifically addressing the strategies adopted in order to influence Brussels.[90]

As for Italy, the earliest comprehensive work on Italy and the European Communities is Francesco Francioni's *Italy and EU Membership Evaluated*, which examines Italy's participation in the EEC in a number of different areas, from monetary to agricultural policy, from the environment to foreign policy, and so on, mostly in terms of a cost-benefit analysis.[91] However, it very seldom covers the details of how the different policies and subpolicies were elaborated; nor does it present an overall assessment of Italy's participation in the Communities. More recently, there is Achille Albonetti's *L'Italia, la politica estera e l'unità dell'Europa*, which examines aspects of the Italian foreign policy, mostly from a European perspective;[92] and *L'Italia in Europa*, by Marta Cartabia and Joseph Weiler, is an in-depth juridical analysis of the way Italian institutions—at various levels—interact with the European Union.[93]

By far the most relevant studies on Italy and the EU, however, are those devoted to the impact of the European Union on Italy—that is, those that belong to the stream of studies on the Europeanization process. For instance, Sergio Fabbrini's *L'europeizzazione dell'Italia* is a classic case of top-down analysis: it focuses on the effect EU participation has had on the national system, both its institutions and its policies, through an analysis of the government, the regions, and several policies (competition, health, foreign policy).[94] Albeit with some nuances, the authors of the different chapters agree that, in general terms, membership and participation in the European Union has had a positive impact on both the structure of Italy's government and on Italian policies, essentially promoting efficiency. From this perspective, one might say that Italy has been "saved by Europe"—an idea that has been supported by many, starting with Joe Di Palma, Sergio Fabbrini, and Giorgio Freddi in *Condannata al successo? L'Italia nell'Europa integrata* [Condemned to succeed? Italy in an integrated Europe].[95]

Sergio Fabbrini and Simona Piattoni's *Italy in the European Union* also took this tack, looking at a number of policies ranging from the CAP to macroeconomics to social policy. For each issue under consideration, they chose a number of case studies, including examples of both success and failure. The authors conclude that "systemic variables of a political and institutional nature, as well as actor-related factors . . . determined the outcome of the policymaking process in each particular instance." [96]

In all of the above-mentioned books, though, the focus of the authors was the opposite of the focus of this volume. Instead of studying the impact of the EU on the national system, this analysis considers how the national system influences the EU decisionmaking processes. Naturally, this also means looking at how the different branches of the Italian state have adapted to this task. This book therefore aims to fill a relevant gap in European Studies and on Italy and the EU in particular.

3 | *Italy and the EU in Historical Perspective*

This examination of Italy's historical role in the European Communities considers both exogenous and endogenous variables. As regards the exogenous, European integration—while a fundamental value in Italian foreign policy—must be considered in terms of transatlantic relations, relations with Russia and the other former Soviet states (and previously the USSR), and other nearby regions, such as the Mediterranean and the Balkans. Because of the relevant impact on Italy of these exogenous variables—especially in the first twenty years of European integration—this chapter indulges in discussing them whenever necessary.

As for the endogenous variables, fascism plays a significant role: "The national interest" was long seen as taboo in Italy's public debate, owing to fascism's legacy, and it was replaced with "the European interest" as a guiding principle in policymaking. Second, but no less important, there is the question of the way political parties have perceived the process of European integration. Here, one can distinguish three periods: the origins to the late 1970s; the late 1970s to the mid-1990s; and the mid-1990s to today. The first period was characterized by the opposition of the left to European and Atlantic integration, on ideological grounds; the second witnessed a shared consensus by all political parties on integration—especially European; in the latest period, domestic political divisions have at times led parties to oppose European integration.

The End of World War II

The end of World War II essentially left Italy on the side of the losers, despite the fact that the country changed sides in 1943. The war's loss, together with the mishandling of the "liberazione" (the gradual freeing of the country by U.S. troops beginning September 8, 1943), led to the end of Italy's monarchy. On June 2, 1946, in fact, the monarchy was abolished by popular referendum; the new Republican Constitution was promulgated on January 1, 1948.

During the first years after the end of the war, the leaders of the main Italian parties—the Christian Democrat Alcide De Gasperi, the Communist Palmiro Togliatti, and the Socialist Pietro Nenni—united to form a coalition government, led by De Gasperi, which lasted from the end of 1945 to June 1947. However, the Communists and the Socialists had to leave the government for Italy to be included in the Marshall Plan—a first example of U.S. influence on Italian domestic politics. By 1947, Europe was already divided into two parts: Western and Eastern. The Italian ruling leadership (including leaders on the left) wanted to link the country firmly with the former.

This division existed before the formal end of hostilities, of course, when Winston Churchill, Joseph Stalin, and Franklin Roosevelt met to outline possible postwar scenarios. The most celebrated meeting of the three leaders took place in Yalta, February 4–11, 1945. During that conference, an agreement was reached: the Declaration on Liberated Europe stated that every European state would hold free elections and proceed to establish democratic governments. In the years 1946–1948, the Central and Eastern European countries evolved into Communist-led satellite states, orbiting around the USSR. Unable to reach an agreement with the USSR on the future of Germany, the United States, France, and Great Britain decided to create a German state uniting the three western zones of occupation. The Russian response was quick: on the night of June 23, 1948, all commercial traffic into Berlin was blocked. Thus, for almost a year, the city was supplied by a gigantic airlift, organized by American forces. In May 1949, the blockade was finally lifted, and the division of Germany into the western Federal Republic of Germany and the eastern Democratic Republic of Germany was formalized.

On September 19, 1946, at the University of Zurich, Winston Churchill spoke of the need to unite Europe: "We must re-create the European family in a regional structure called, it may be, the United States of Europe. The first step is to form a Council of Europe."[1] Churchill, of course, thought of a United States of Europe as limited to the continent.

Churchill was not the only one to call for a united Europe. Of the different voices claiming that such an entity would solve the continent's problems, the

Italian one was particularly loud. From the little island of Ventotene, where he had been confined by the Fascist regime, Altiero Spinelli (1907–1986) wrote—along with Eugenio Colorni and Ernesto Rossi—the *Ventotene Manifesto* (1943). The authors affirmed that it was "the time for new men: for the MOVE-MENT FOR A UNITED AND FREE EUROPE."[2] In September 1946, Spinelli, together with Alexander Marc, Henry Brugmans, and Henry Frenay, founded the Union Européenne des Federalistes in Paris: the subsequent Congress of Montreux (August 1947) was the first great demonstration in favor of European integration in the postwar period, reuniting federalist and Europeanist movements from all over Europe.[3] Europe-wide organizations were created in those years by different political parties and movements: the Confédération Européenne de l'Agriculture (1945), the Nouvelles Equipes Internationales (1947), the Mouvement pour les Etats-Unis socialistes d'Europe (1947), the Union Parlementaire Européenne (1947), the Conseil des Fédérations Industrielles d'Europe (1949).

All of these and other pro-European movements met at The Hague, March 7–10, 1948, at the Congress for the Foundation of the European Movement. Under the presidency of Winston Churchill, approximately 800 pro-Europeanists participated: the delegations included both political and intellectual leaders such as François Mitterrand, Salvador de Madriaga, Denis de Rougemont, Paul Van Zeeland, Paul Ramadier, Paul Reynaud, Alcide De Gasperi, Ignazio Silone, Bruno Visentini, Konrad Adenauer, Robert Schuman, Léon Blum, Anthony Eden, Walter Hallestein, and Harold Macmillan.[4] The Italian delegation included more intellectuals than politicians.

The process of European integration then developed in three successive waves: economic, with the Marshall Plan and the creation of the European Organization of Economic Cooperation (OECE); diplomatic and military, with the Brussels Pact and the signing of the North Atlantic Treaty; political, with the Council of Europe and the European Communities.

The Marshall Plan

The reconstruction process was not an easy one for Europe. Substantial aid arrived from the Marshall Plan, announced by General George C. Marshall at Harvard University on June 5, 1947. Sixteen countries participated in the economic conference, which was held from July 12 to September 22, 1947, to determine Europe's needs: France, Great Britain, Belgium, Holland, Luxembourg, Ireland, Norway, Denmark, Sweden, Iceland, Austria, Switzerland, Italy, Portugal, Greece, and Turkey. Czechoslovakia, whose government had expressed interest in participating in the conference, was forced by Stalin to retract its request. On April 16, 1948, at the Château de la Muette in Paris, a convention was signed that gave birth to the Organization for European Economic Cooperation (OEEC), the organization which—in accordance with specific U.S. requests—took charge of managing the Marshall Plan. The United States, in fact, wanted to force the European countries to decide, together, where and how to use the funds and support; in the end, the United States wanted Europeans to cooperate in creating an internal market—a condition particularly important to the U.S. Congress.

The Italian government's reaction to the Marshall Plan was quick and positive. The plan would be useful from a number of different points of view. First, it would improve the dire economic situation, thus positively influencing public opinion (also in view of approaching legislative elections). Second, the Marshall Plan and OEEC represented Italy's first chance to be reinstated in the international diplomatic game, on equal footing with other countries.[5] Furthermore, Italy seized the occasion to propose that a customs union be established with France. The treaty was signed on March 26, 1949. In principle, the customs union was then to be enlarged to the Benelux (Belgium, the Netherlands, Luxembourg) countries (and to be called Fritalux, or Finebel), but in the end, the union never saw the light of day.[6]

The North Atlantic Treaty

On March 17, 1948, the United Kingdom, France, and the Benelux countries signed the Treaty of Brussels, a defense treaty that was to last fifty years. Soon after that, the idea of a defense system between Europe and the United States started to be developed. With the utmost discretion, negotiations began among the United Kingdom, the United States, and Canada at the Pentagon (the so-called Pentagon Talks). The group was subsequently enlarged to include France, Holland, Belgium, and Luxembourg. Before the draft of the treaty was completed, other European countries (Norway, Denmark, Iceland, and Italy) became interested in what was to become the North Atlantic Alliance. Italy formally introduced its candidacy on January 1, 1949. France strongly opposed Norwegian membership, while it supported Italian participation, which it saw as a guarantee for better strategic protection of Corsica and Algeria. Great Britain, on the other hand, opposed Italian participation because of the country's fragile economic and political situation. The British suggested that Italy should belong to a Mediterranean pact, separate from the North Atlantic system.

For the United States, Italy represented a serious problem. First, geographically speaking, it was not an Atlantic country. Second, Italy was thought to contribute very little militarily to Western European security. But politically speaking, the United States saw Italy's exclusion from the North Atlantic Alliance as potentially dangerous. Given its former enemy status, an Italy without close ties to the other European countries might assume an isolationist position. Moreover, given its solid communist background, Italy might easily be influenced by the Soviets. Therefore, in the end, despite several reluctant U.S. senators, a decision was made to allow Italy to be one of the founding members of the North Atlantic security system. As part of a comprehensive deal, Norway too became an integral part of the North Atlantic Alliance.

The Council of Europe

The creation of the Council of Europe in 1949, in accordance with the political initiative of the French foreign minister, Robert Schuman, was the most important political result of action undertaken by the European Movement. The German chancellor, Konrad Adenauer, defined it as "the most important event since the end of the war." This view was shared by the Italian foreign minister, Count Carlo Sforza. The United States, Belgium, and Luxembourg all sided with the French initiative as well, while the British seemed somewhat hostile toward the proposal. A group of eighteen representatives (five English, five French, three Belgian, three Dutch, and two from Luxembourg), called the Comité d'études pour l'Union Européenne, began its work on November 26, 1948, to study the various proposals. On March 28, 1949, the committee was enlarged to include five more countries: Italy, Ireland, Denmark, Norway, and Sweden. The name "European Union," proposed by Schuman, with the support of Italy and Belgium, was rejected by the British and by the Scandinavian countries because they feared it could mean "European Federation," a supranational political-institutional structure that Euro-skeptical countries would never accept.

The Charter of the Council of Europe was signed by ten countries in the Palace of Saint James in London on May 5, 1949. For Italy, it was a diplomatic success to be included in the negotiations (unlike what had happened with the North Atlantic Treaty, when it was barely accepted as a founding member). In domestic terms, membership in the Council of Europe also gave Christian Democrat leader and Prime Minister De Gasperi needed support for membership in the Atlantic Pact. Thus did a small group of leaders, led by the prime minister and his foreign minister, Sforza, succeed in linking Italy firmly to the Western world.

Both the Communist and Socialist Parties opposed membership in the North Atlantic Treaty. The Socialists asked for a popular referendum—which was denied—and its leader, Pietro Nenni, affirmed that, with the signature of the treaty, "the Third War had been launched."[7] The Italian Communist Party was, at the time, totally subjugated to the Soviet Communist Party (PCUS). But even the left fringes of the Christian Democrats, led by Giuseppe Dossetti and Giovanni Gronchi, were in favor of keeping an equidistant relationship with the two superpowers, the United States and the USSR. They thus favored a neutral, nonaligned Italy and opposed Italy's signing of the North Atlantic Treaty.

Since the Communists and the Socialists were definitely expected to vote against the treaty,[8] De Gasperi desperately needed all of his party's votes in parliament. In this light, he used Italy's inclusion in the Council of Europe to "sell" Atlantic integration to his own party. In signing the North Atlantic Treaty on April 4, 1949, De Gasperi also underlined its political rather than military aspects. When the founding treaty of the Council of Europe was signed in May, to please the leftist parties, the Italian government also negotiated a commercial agreement with Moscow,[9] thus initiating what was to become a flourishing cooperation between the two countries.

From the Schuman Plan to the European Coal and Steel Community (ECSC)

After the creation of the first government of the new Federal Republic of Germany, Chancellor Konrad Adenauer never stopped complaining about the limitations imposed by the Allies. He was committed to fully restoring the sovereignty of Germany. In particular, he lamented the presence of the Allied Commission of Control, pointed to the International Ruhr Authority's strain on the German economy, and complained about France's control over the Saar region. At the end of World War II, the Saar had in fact become an autonomous region and had created an economic union with France. All the coal produced in the region was to be handed over to the French—a fact that raised the level of tension between the two countries.

The U.S. high commissioner to Germany, John McCloy, on behalf of the U.S. government, supported a French-German rapprochement within a European framework. Therefore, on the occasion of a meeting between French foreign minister Robert Schuman, British foreign secretary Ernest Bevin, and U.S. secretary of state Dean Acheson in Washington in September 1949, the French foreign minister was asked to draft a project for a common policy toward Germany, in which the questions of the Saar and the Ruhr were to be addressed. Yet the winter passed without any improvements in French-German relations and without any proposals from Schuman.

In April, Jean Monnet, then general commissioner of the Plan de modernisation et d'équipement, took the initiative. He delivered a note to Bernard Clapier, Schuman's assistant, containing a proposal that he had prepared during the previous weeks with the help of a team of young lawyers: Paul Reuter, Pierre Uri, and Etienne Hirsh. In the note, he affirmed that the only possible solution was to organize Europe on a federal basis. It was an old idea of his. Already on August 5, 1943, Jean Monnet—then a member of the provisional exiled French government—had written in his diary in Algeria: "There will be no peace if the [European] states are rebuilt on the basis of national sovereignty. . . . [It is necessary that] the European states form a federation."[10] In keeping with his convictions, Monnet proposed that all production of French and German coal and steel be placed under the rule of an independent international authority, open to the participation of other European countries.

Schuman appreciated the idea and, after obtaining Adenauer's assent (thanks to the good office of a common friend, Judge Robert Mischlich), officially presented to the press (at 6 p.m. on May 9, 1950, at the Quai d'Orsay in the salon de l'Horloge) what was to be known as the Schuman Declaration. At the same time, in Bonn, Adenauer officially announced his country's acceptance of the proposal to journalists gathered for the occasion. In all, six governments welcomed the proposal and began negotiations: Italy, Belgium, the Netherlands, and Luxembourg, as well as France and Germany.

For Italy, this was an important political and economic opportunity. It would help the difficult reconstruction of the country's democratic and economic systems. Furthermore, De Gasperi—aware that the Eastern markets were closed to Italy—chose to pit the Italian economy against the most competitive and difficult markets: the Atlantic and Western European ones. According to Mario Telò,[11] "De Gasperi was convinced that, in order to balance domestic instability, a strong counterweight of international dimensions was needed . . . ; Sforza saw linking Italy to Europe as the country's only hope to emerge from defeat. Italy's future development depended on Europe and the West. For Italy to succeed in being more than a simple satellite of the United States . . . [it needed] to intelligently combine the three dimensions of De Gasperi's action: bilateral relations—especially with the U.S.; bilateral diplomacy within international organizations; and commitment to new supranational organizations, linked to European integration."

Nevertheless, many people in Italy opposed this plan, for both political and economic reasons. According to Ambassador Achille Albonetti, difficulties derived from the fact that Italy "paid tribute to other countries for raw materials for the iron and steel industry and that domestic production in Italy cost more than elsewhere."[12] The Italian ambassador in Paris, Pietro Quaroni, opposed the proposal, convinced that the plan would favor French interests alone, thus threatening the Italian coal and steel industry. Also, he did not believe that Schuman would be fully engaged in defending Italian industry. Quaroni also suspected that Monnet was a neutralist and that this might work against the Christian Democrats' pro-Atlantic positions. In the words of Paolo Emilio Taviani, then head of the ECSC delegation: "Unlike La Malfa—who said Europe first, then the North Atlantic Treaty—we Christian Democrats said yes to Europe, but following the North Atlantic Treaty. We were convinced that we needed America on our side."[13]

The Socialists continued to oppose any kind of European integration—in total isolation from other European Socialist parties.[14] According to the Italian party's leader, Pietro Nenni, there was a need for a "national" foreign policy not guided by ideological constraints, but rather by the exclusive definition of the national interest.[15]

As for the Communists, the party's international political choices were subordinate to and coordinated by the USSR's foreign policy. The Communists' political discourse in this phase was centered on the need to preserve "Italian interests"—most notably geopolitical ones—against the transatlantic monopolies.[16]

Industry, in particular heavy industry—with the notable exception of Fiat—was against the ECSC for fear of the liberalization that would follow. The trade unions viewed things differently: the trade union representing Catholic groups (CISL, the Italian Confederation of Trade Unions) was in favor of European integration, and the leftist one (CGIL, the Italian General Confederation of Labor) looked upon the European Communities with some interest.

In the end, the decision to join the ECSC essentially belonged to the government or, more precisely, to De Gasperi and Sforza. The Treaty of Paris, which created the European Coal and Steel Community, was signed on April 18, 1951, with Italy as a founding member. The High Authority, presided over by Jean Monnet, was established in Luxembourg on August 10, 1951.

The European Defense Community (EDC) and the end of Alcide De Gasperi

Already during negotiations relating to the Schuman Plan, a new concern had emerged: German rearmament. The United States suggested the creation of an integrated operational structure—NATO, or North Atlantic Treaty Organization—within the sphere of the Atlantic Alliance. Within this context, a German army could participate under direct American control. The French rejected this proposal and were thus obliged, under increasing American pressure, to find an alternative for German rearmament. France's solution, born from the ideas of Monnet and the French prime minister René Pleven, was announced by Pleven at the French National Assembly on October 24, 1950. The Pleven Plan proposed the creation of a European army, to be placed under the control of a European Ministry of Defense. The soldiers from various countries—including Germany—would be integrated in a European army at the level of the smallest unit.

On February 15, 1951, Germany, Italy, Belgium, and Luxembourg met in Paris to start the talks. The Netherlands joined on October 8, while the United States, Great Britain, Canada, Norway, and Denmark sent observers. As for the Italian position, in the summer of 1951, De Gasperi received a memorandum from Spinelli, who was convinced that the construction of a European army had to be accompanied by the creation of a supranational political organism. He saw this as the first step toward realizing a United States of Europe. De Gasperi, who was also in charge of foreign affairs at the time, fully shared these ideas, which became the guidelines for Italian action: Italy accepted the creation of the EDC, provided that it would be instrumental in establishing a European political community. The result of De Gasperi's initiative was the addition, in the EDC treaty, of article 38: this stated that once the EDC was established, its parliamentary assembly would be responsible for elaborating a project for the birth of a political community, to be examined by the member states. The new treaty, founding the European Defense Community, was signed on May 27, 1952, the day after the signing of the Bonn Agreements, which returned to Germany its sovereignty rights in the realm of defense.

According to Mario Telò, Italy played a propulsive role at the European level between the years 1951 and 1953.[17] De Gasperi, who was deeply involved in the project, declared to the Christian Democrats in Naples in 1954: "Political collaboration among the countries of continental Europe represents the indispensable premise on which to build international relations of economic and social cooperation. Without these, Italy will never resolve its fundamental problems." In other words, De Gasperi's overarching belief was that without European solidarity, Italy could not safeguard it own interests at an international level.

Between 1953 and 1954, the EDC Treaty was ratified by Germany and by the Benelux countries. In Italy, the treaty was approved by the competent commission in parliament, despite opposition from both right-wing and left-wing parties. However, the Italian parliament did not vote for the treaty's ratification, preferring to wait for the French vote. The new government under

Giuseppe Pella, which took over after the 1953 elections, assumed a more nationalistic stance, trying to link the EDC question to that of Trieste, which had still not been given back to Italy. The following government, under Mario Scelba (1954–1955), was not capable of changing this political stance. According to Sergio Pistone,[18] the Italian parliament's refusal to ratify the EDC Treaty had a negative impact on French public opinion. Meanwhile, as Robert Schuman was replaced by Georges Bidault at the Ministry of Foreign Affairs in Pierre Mendès-France's new government, French public opinion was divided between the *cedistes* (favorable to ratification) and the *anti-cedistes* (who were opposed). In the end, the National Assembly, on August 30, 1954, failed to ratify the treaty.

The problem of German rearmament thus remained unresolved. A new initiative was launched, this time from the British foreign minister, Anthony Eden. In 1954 it was decided that Germany would enter NATO, that Italy and Germany would join the Brussels Pact, and that the Western European Union would be created subsequently. It was also agreed that Germany would not develop atomic weapons and that two British divisions would be stationed in Germany.

In Italy, the end of the European Defense Community also symbolized the end of Alcide De Gasperi's political life. In supporting the EDC and the progressive creation of a federal project he was, once again, ahead of his own party. His fellow Christian Democrats were still digesting the Atlantic choice at the time, and were not ready for the EDC Treaty. The old leader died just a few months after the treaty's failure.

The European Economic Community and the Euratom

Jean Monnet was convinced that collaboration on atomic energy could revive European integration. The Belgian foreign minister, Paul Henry Spaak, was also convinced of the need to revive the integration process. On April 2, 1955, he wrote to Konrad Adenauer and to his French and Italian colleagues, Antoine Pinay and Gaetano de Martino, proposing to extend the competences of the ECSC to additional sectors, such as transportation and atomic energy. Jan Willem Beyen—the Dutch foreign minister—proposed, on April 21, 1955, at the Mouvement Européen meeting, to create a supranational community that would supersede an economic union. This was followed up by the so-called Benelux Memorandum.

The reactions of France, the Federal Republic of Germany, and Italy were very prudent. Monnet—who, meanwhile, had created a "Committee for the United States of Europe," gathering the leaders of European political parties and trade unions—invited the ECSC foreign ministers to convene an Inter-governmental Conference (IGC) with the aim of drafting, in collaboration with the ECSC institutions, the international acts necessary to further European integration. The Italian foreign minister, Antonio Martino, succeeded in gaining support for the conference to be held in Messina. Italy's interests in a possible nuclear community and in a prospective common market were strong enough for it to want to join the negotiations, but the country demanded that certain specifically Italian needs be taken into consideration. Primarily, it felt that the principle of free circulation should be applied not only to goods but also to labor and capital. This first objective corresponded to the traditional Italian need to favor emigration for its laborers, while the second one revealed the government's special regard for Italy's South: it hoped that financial resources would flow throughout the peninsula, thereby contributing to the nation's overall development.

At the Messina meeting (June 1–3, 1955), the foreign ministers of the six ECSC member states established that it was time to take new steps toward the creation of a European framework, and that these new steps needed to be taken predominantly in the economic sector. In particular, progress was called for in creating a common market and partial integration in the field of atomic energy. Naturally, divergences existed: the Germans, the Italians, and the Dutch, for example, favored general economic integration, while France supported sector-by-sector integration. An intergovernmental committee, chaired by Spaak, was thus created (the Spaak Committee). The subsequent Spaak Report was presented to the ECSC foreign ministers on April 21, 1956. Negotiations then began. The country showing the greatest resistance was France. In particular, Mendès-France feared that the Italians would "export" their unemployment to France, something that Robert Marjolin defined as a "vision apocalyptique."[19] From Italy's perspective, given the country's poverty levels, the main preoccupation was indeed how to take advantage of this new initiative. The French thus posed a number of reservations, though they understood that if they wanted Euratom, a European Atomic Energy Community, accepted on their conditions, they had to accept its linkage with the common market, a key criterion for other countries. In the end, international events ended up providing the necessary impetus for the conclusion of negotiations: on March 25, 1957, after the invasion of Hungary (November 4, 1956) and the nationalization of the Suez Canal (July 20, 1956), the treaties creating the European Economic Community (EEC) and Euratom were signed in Rome (hence the name Treaties of Rome).

In Italy, the invasion of Hungary had a lasting effect on domestic politics. The Italian Socialist Party (PSI) sharply criticized the USSR's intervention and broke its alliance with the Communists for good. Although the Socialists criticized the government for the way it handled the negotiations and thus abstained from voting on the EEC, they voted in favor of Euratom.[20] The change in the PSI's approach to foreign policy then allowed the party to join the majority supporting the government in 1958 and to formally enter the government in 1963. From then on, the Italian Socialists would remain pro-European.

From Six to Nine: The First Enlargement

The United Kingdom initially participated in the works of the Spaak Committee but then abandoned it, believing that the idea of a common market would fail. Instead, it promoted the European Free Trade Association (EFTA), signed on January 4, 1960. Nevertheless, between 1958 and 1962, the process for the creation of a customs union within the new EEC proceeded well, helping the growth of intracommunity exchange. The most controversial issue was the Common Agricultural Policy (CAP), over which French and Italian interests clashed. On June 30, 1960, the commissioner for agriculture, Sicco Mansholt (a former Dutch minister of agriculture), listed a number of principles that were necessary for the CAP to function. Nevertheless, it took eight years to implement them, with interminable meetings known as the "agricultural marathons."

In the meantime, in the spring of 1958, following the Algerian crisis,[21] General Charles de Gaulle was called to lead the French government. He accepted on the condition that a new constitution be prepared. The new constitution, approved by referendum in September 1958, marked the beginning of the Fifth Republic, of which de Gaulle was elected the first president in November.

Contrary to initially pessimistic expectations, de Gaulle soon took the necessary steps toward implementing the common market. Still, he had a personal vision of Europe and of France's role in it. His "Europe Européenne" or "Europe des États," made up of national states, was to hold a leadership position at least equal to that of the United States and the Soviet Union on the international scene. In this light, a plan was elaborated by the European Commission with a view to relaunching political cooperation among the EEC member states, called the Fouchet Plan. The first draft was presented on November 2, 1961, and a redraft in January 1962. The Italian government initially felt it was a modest proposal, yet nevertheless considered it a good first step. Despite the fact that Prime Minister Amintore Fanfani was far from enthusiastic about the Fouchet Plan, the Italian Foreign Ministry worked hard to improve it and to foster consensus on a compromise text. In particular, Italy wanted any treaty to contain provisions for the direct election of the European Parliament and to give it control over defense expenses. To avoid failing in its own parliament, Italy also wanted to have the new treaty ratified at the same time as British membership—which it supported. In September 1962, Italy further stated that it would not support any plan for political union "until the British problem was resolved," a position also supported by Foreign Minister Giuseppe Saragat during his visit to London in January 1964.[22] In 1961 the British conservative government, led by Harold Macmillan, had in fact introduced a request to join the EEC.

Soon afterwards, in 1962, the U.S. administration of John F. Kennedy launched the "Grand Design"—the idea of cooperation between an enlarged European Community and the United States, including a multilateral nuclear agreement and common customs tariffs. However, the United States also offered to let the British and the French install Polaris missiles on their territory. France rejected the offer and decided to become a nuclear power on its own. Charles de Gaulle then used the U.S. proposal as an excuse to abruptly end membership negotiations with the United Kingdom, offering instead an association agreement. Macmillan, of course, took this as an offense, as it put the United Kingdom on the same level as Greece and Turkey. Italy, disagreeing with de Gaulle, chose to continue supporting UK membership.

Eventually, the crisis culminated over the Common Agricultural Policy. A Commission proposal under examination called for the establishment, by July 1967, of a CAP common market, to be financed with tariffs and customs rights, which the Community would administer as its own. On June 14, 1965, the Council began to discuss the issue. The French foreign minister, Maurice Couve de Murville, who was chairing the meeting, opposed the Commission's proposals and eventually dismissed the meeting on June 30. On July 1, France announced that it would not collaborate with Community institutions. Consequently, the French representatives refrained from participating in the Council's working groups, as well as in the COREPER meetings—the biweekly gatherings of the EEC member states' Permanent Representatives in Brussels—giving birth to what became known as the "empty chair crisis."

Also on July 1, Italy assumed the EEC presidency.[23] Emilio Colombo (the treasury minister was also the acting foreign minister, owing to Amintore Fanfani's health problems) tried to reach an agreement with France. At the heart of the problem lay French opposition to the qualified majority voting (QMV) system.[24] This system was to become the decisionmaking rule in the Council starting January 1, 1966. Colombo invited France to attend an extraordinary meeting of the Council of Ministers and then, in a bilateral meeting held in France on December 8, 1965, finally managed to convince Couve de Murville to join a January 29 meeting of the six foreign ministers in Luxembourg.[25] There, in the absence of the Commission, an agreement was reached on the question of qualified majority voting. This so-called Luxembourg compromise allowed member states to ask for unanimous decisions rather than QMV should a "vital interest" be at stake: in practical terms, this meant that, from that moment forward, consensus became the decisionmaking rule.

The year 1967 brought change to Europe. Kurt Kiesinger became the German chancellor, Willy Brandt foreign minister. The coup d'état in Greece froze the association agreement between the EEC and Greece. The Labour Party won the elections in Great Britain, and Harold Wilson became the new prime minister. Wilson soon reintroduced the UK candidacy for EEC membership (May 2, 1967); however, despite the Commission's positive view, de Gaulle again vetoed Great Britain's entrance (November 27, 1967).

Only after de Gaulle resigned (April 27, 1969) and George Pompidou was elected (June 15, 1969) did things start to move again. Pompidou, in fact, proposed a Triptique to the summit meeting in The Hague (December 1–2, 1969). The Triptique consisted of three principles: completion, deepening, enlargement. The completion of the common market by January 1, 1970, with particular attention to the CAP's financing with Community resources; the deepening of the Community, especially in the field of economic and monetary policy; and enlargement to Great Britain and other countries, conditional on the Community's adoption of a common position before the beginning of negotiations.

Consequently, on April 22, 1970, the Treaty of Luxembourg was signed, according to which the Community was to acquire its own resources by 1975 and the Parliament's powers were to be slightly expanded. The summit also commissioned a report to Pierre Werner, prime minister of Luxembourg, on economic and monetary union. The report, published on October 17, 1970, proposed the creation of a European Monetary Union (EMU) within ten years and a common system for the national central banks. The plan was never carried out. The only concrete results were the "monetary snake" (April 24, 1972) and the subsequent European Monetary System (EMS, March 13, 1979).[26] The Bali accords, which were at the foundation of the EMS, created a margin for the fluctuation of currency of +/–2.25 percent, but allowed a more flexible +/– 6 percent for the weaker Italian and British currencies.

From the Europe of Nine to the Europe of Ten, 1973–1981

The 1970s are considered a period of stagnation for the process of European integration. They were also difficult years for Italy. The country's domestic weaknesses heavily influenced the consideration of its European partners, which reached an all-time low.

On July 2, 1970, the new European Commission entered into force with the Italian Franco Maria Malfatti as its president. In a speech to the European Parliament (September 16, 1970), Malfatti expressed his hopes for the Commission to once again serve as the engine of European integration. However, less than two years later, Malfatti resigned to stand for political elections in Italy. Despite the fact that other commissioners have also resigned early, Malfatti's departure is often held up as an example of the Italians' lack of trustworthiness, undermining the role of future Italian commissioners.[27] At the time, France eventually used this argument to strip Italy of the agriculture portfolio.[28]

On October 27, 1970, the so-called Davignon Report—introducing proposals for cooperation in the field of foreign policy, called European Political Cooperation (EPC)—was approved. Italy insisted on including security and defense in EPC, thus clashing with France.[29] In response to these timid European attempts at coordination in the field of foreign policy, the U.S. secretary of state, Henry Kissinger, claimed that only the United States had global responsibilities.[30] He claimed that Europe's interests were only regional and sarcastically pronounced 1973 as "the Year of Europe" (in the sense that the United States had to take care of Europe). Unsurprisingly, this approach was not welcomed on the opposite side of the Atlantic. Italy, in particular, claimed that Europe needed to speak with a single voice.

In October 1973, the third Arab-Israeli conflict erupted. The first repercussion in Europe was an increase in oil prices: Italy was hardest hit because it was also suffering at the time from internal difficulties due to terrorism. For the first time, Italy blamed the European Community for its economic difficulties, which also conveniently offered a sort of justification for the country's lack of respect for EEC deadlines and obligations. Meanwhile, as we shall see in the next chapter, a shift in domestic politics was taking place, with the Communists changing their view of the Communities.

The Italian domestic situation was further complicated by U.S. president Richard Nixon's decision to end the dollar's convertibility into gold. The EEC member states first tried to protect themselves through the "European monetary snake," created in 1972, but this was not enough for Italy. Once the European Monetary System (EMS) took effect in 1978, Italy faced more difficulties and was forced to ask for partial opt-outs. Such weaknesses in its system were stigmatized by Italy's European counterparts—especially Germany—which called it the European Cinderella (or the "sick one"). Similarly, within the CAP debates, Italy was disadvantaged by the lack of a global agriculture strategy and by its patchwork domestic agriculture organization. Italy counted just one triumph in this period: it succeeded in establishing the European Regional Fund in 1973, thanks to British support, and despite the German refusal to fund it until Rome proved itself capable of using the financing in an efficient way.[31]

Italy was thus in a weak position when it assumed the EEC presidency on July 1, 1975. Its objectives were to speed up the process of European political union and to develop better relations with the Mediterranean area. In general terms, Italian action during its 1975 presidency was weak and unimpressive. The only positive note was the decision—taken during the Rome European Council (December 1–2, 1975)—to have the European Parliament elected directly by the citizens.[32] Yet when Emilio Colombo, in his capacity as European Parliament president, announced the date of the forthcoming elections to the plenary on March 24, 1977, the only other Italian in the room was Altiero Spinelli; the others were all in Rome for the elections of the new Italian president.[33] Nonetheless, as we shall see in chapter 4, the direct elections of the European Parliament were to have an important effect on Italy's domestic and European policies.

Last but not least, again during the 1975 Italian presidency, when the EEC was not invited to the first summit of the most industrialized countries (in the French town of Rambouillet, November 1975), the nine EEC members tried to convince Italy to participate not in an individual capacity, but as an EEC representative. Worried that this could constitute a dangerous precedent, Italy refused.

From Euro-sclerosis to the Return of European Integration

The long "Euro-sclerotic" period ended by the mid-1980s. In the first "semester" of 1980, Italy again held the presidency. The agenda looked difficult: not only was it complicated by the question of the British rebate (Margaret Thatcher's famous "I want my money back"), but it also contained the negotiation of the 1980 Community budget and a partial revision of the CAP. On the question of the British rebate, the Italian position—supported by France—was to rebalance it though the creation of new policy areas. This approach was rejected by Germany and Great Britain.

Despite intense consultations organized by the Italian government in preparing for its presidency, Italian action was less effective than hoped owing to the domestic crises of the first government of Prime Minister Francesco Cossiga (Cossiga I, which eventually led to Cossiga II). These difficulties led Cossiga to postpone the meeting of the European Council scheduled for April 27–28, 1980. After a first refusal on the part of the British prime minister to accept any compromise, an agreement was finally reached after a marathon twenty-hour meeting on May 30, 1980. This reduced the British contribution while giving the Commission a mandate to review the common policies in view of their more balanced future development.[34]

Soon afterwards, the political geography of the European member states changed. In 1981 François Mitterrand was elected president of France on the basis of a Communist-Socialist majority, and on October 1, 1982, the Christian Democrat leader Helmut Kohl became chancellor of Germany. Thanks to these two leaders, Franco-German relations remained at the heart of the European integration process. In contrast, France's relations with Italy—whose government, for the first time, was headed by a leader from a party other than the Christian Democrats, Republican Giovanni Spadolini—were at a particularly low point. Rome was accusing France of being too protectionist, while Paris was unhappy about Italy's strong links with the United States.[35] Relations improved later, however, in particular once the Italian Socialist leader Bettino Craxi assumed power in 1983. On the other hand, the arrival of the Christian Democrats led by Helmut Kohl in Germany immensely improved the country's relations with Italy. Italian and German Christian Democrat leaders would meet periodically to discuss European politics—usually at the Konrad Adenauer Foundation's villa in Cadenabbia. As a result, from the mid-1980s through the early 1990s, Italy ended up at the core of the European process, playing a key role.

When France first assumed the presidency of the Community (in the first half of 1984), Mitterrand was determined to make good use of it. Negotiations for the EEC membership of Spain and Portugal were given new impetus, for example. Still, it was thanks to the Italian presidency (in the first half of 1985) that the last remaining problems were solved and that the accession treaties were finally signed (June 12, 1985, taking effect on January 1, 1986). In particular, it took the negotiating skills of Giulio Andreotti, then minister of foreign affairs, to disengage the deadlock on fisheries and fishing quotas that was preventing the signing of the accession treaty.

During its 1984 presidency, France also took a number of steps to facilitate what was to become the Single European Act of 1987. On February 14, 1984, the European Parliament approved Altiero Spinelli's draft treaty. In addressing the European Parliament, François Mitterrand affirmed that the draft treaty—together with the Stuttgart Declaration drafted in 1981 by the German and Italian foreign ministers, Hans-Dietrich Genscher and Emilio Colombo—provided a starting point for further reform. To this end, at the European Council in Fontainebleau, he launched two ad hoc committees: the "Doodge Committee" was charged with studying institutional reforms, while the "Adonnino Committee" (chaired by an Italian member of Parliament) was charged with outlining prospects for the development of a European identity. The heads of state and government further agreed to name Jacques Delors the new president of the European Commission, as of January 1985. The Doodge Committee presented its report to the Council on March 19, 1985, recommending a number of measures to reinforce the European institutions and suggesting that an Intergovernmental Conference be called, as an instrument for its adoption. The Adonnino Committee presented its report on "a Europe of citizens" on June 20, 1985.

The Italian Presidency of 1985 and the Single Market

In the first semester of 1985, Italy again held the EEC presidency. The Christian Democrat leader and Foreign Minister Giulio Andreotti declared in a speech to the European Parliament (January 16, 1985) that the aim of the Italian presidency would be to convene an IGC to reform the EEC Treaty. However, at the European Council in Milan (June 28–29, 1985), the United Kingdom and Greece raised strong resistance. After a tense debate, the Italian presidency took the unprecedented move to ask for a vote, in which Greece, Denmark, and the United Kingdom were defeated and the IGC was called.

The IGC began work on September 9, 1985. Although difficulties emerged—especially related to the harmonization of legislation—the pragmatic approach proposed by the Commission made it possible to reach a consensus. At the European Council in Luxembourg, December 2–3, 1985, the Single European Act was agreed upon. In response to domestic pressures (primarily from the Federalists, led by Altiero Spinelli), Italy declared its discontent with the final result and stated that it would ratify the treaty only if the European Parliament did so, too. Italy therefore was present at the signing of the treaty (February 17, 1987), but did not sign it itself until February 28, 1987, together with Denmark and Greece.

In the same year, Italy gained an important victory over the "Delors Package," which introduced the idea of a fourth source of income for the EEC budget—to be calculated as a percentage of GNP—which Italy strongly opposed, as it was bound to be penalized. In September 1987, the prime minister—Christian Democrat Giovanni Goria—embarked on a tour of the European capitals to explain the Italian position, and in the European Council (Copenhagen, December 4–5, 1987) he affirmed that Italy could not overlook its objections. Though the Italian government fell once again, Italy managed to hold firm on this issue, and finally, thanks to Helmut Kohl, a compromise was reached: Italy's proposal to calculate the fourth resource on the difference between the GNP and value-added tax (VAT) revenues was accepted.[36]

However, Italy's poor implementation record for directives needed to complete the Single European Market caused the country difficulties once again. In Italy, some blamed the problem on the EEC for failing to match Italian interests. In response, the new government of Ciriaco De Mita (in April 1988) put a great emphasis on Europe and on the need to complete the Single Market. Nonetheless, Italy was forced to request (and succeeded in obtaining) a two-year delay in the liberalization of capital movements.[37]

The Fall of the Berlin Wall and the New European Union

Transformations that began in 1989 were to have lasting consequences for all of Europe and for the entire world. Their impact on Italian domestic politics is still being felt today. In June 1989, Solidarnosc (the Solidarity Party) won the elections in Poland. The iron curtain between Austria and Hungary was removed. During the summer, Eastern Europeans began flooding Western Europe through Austria. In Czechoslovakia, protesters led by Vaclav Havel and Alexander Dubček obtained the resignation of the entire Communist Party. In December, Havel was elected president of the republic. In Bulgaria, Todor Živkov was forced to resign in November; the reformist Petar Mladenov took his position and quickly announced free elections before May of the following year. In Romania, opposition forces took control of the entire country by December. The country's president, Nicolae Ceauşescu, was captured in his attempt to escape and was immediately tried and executed. The event that best symbolizes the end of the cold war, of course, remains the fall of the Berlin Wall: on November 9, the doors between East Berlin and West Berlin were finally reopened.

All of these changes inspired hope, but they also aroused fear over the prospect of a reunited Germany. As the German chancellor Helmut Kohl himself suggested, the solution was to proceed further toward the process of European integration: a larger Germany in a stronger Europe. Once again, Italy was to play a leading role. On November 28, 1989, Kohl presented a program of ten points to the Bundestag outlining steps to take in reuniting the country. Its European partners were forced to accept reunification.[38] Consequently, the European Council in Strasbourg (December 8–9, 1989), while blessing German reunification, decided to summon two Intergovernmental Conferences—one on European Monetary Union (EMU) and the other on political union.

On July 1, 1990—the day that marked the beginning of the monetary union between the two German republics—Italy again held the EEC presidency. A short time later, Giulio Andreotti was named prime minister. The Italian presidency gave top priority to the preparation of the IGC on EMU. To that end,

Andreotti proposed to hold an informal European Council meeting in Rome (October 27–28, 1990) where, notwithstanding UK opposition, the Carli Report on the EMU was approved. This eventually led to Prime Minister Margaret Thatcher's defeat and resignation at home (November 28, 1990). She was replaced by John Major. Andreotti and his foreign minister, the socialist Gianni De Michelis, used their personal and political networks to secure a successful formal meeting of the European Council in Rome (December 14–15, 1990). As we will see in greater detail in Chapter 8, the two IGCs were successfully convened at the end of the Italian presidency, and negotiated into 1992.

While the IGC on EMU, for which most details had been set during the Italian presidency, went smoothly, the one on political union was more troubled. The so-called Luxembourg non-paper, presented by the Luxembourg presidency on April 17, 1991, was short-lived. Likewise, the Dutch draft treaty, presented by the subsequent presidency at the beginning of October 1991, was promptly and abruptly rejected. There was fear that no agreement would be reached at the European Council in December: "Never has a European Council had such a surcharged agenda," wrote *The Economist*.[39] However, an agreement was finally reached and the Treaty of Maastricht was born (December 9–10, 1991).

Then, the ratification process was blocked by the Danish "no" in a national referendum (June 2, 1992). Mitterrand subsequently announced that France too would hold a referendum, to show how strongly the French supported the process of European integration. What he thought would be easy, however, turned into a nightmare. Meanwhile, the Italian lira and the British pound were attacked by speculators. On September 4, Italy was forced to raise its interest rates and had to devalue the lira by 7 percent. On September 13, the Deutsche Bank intervened by lowering rates. On September 17—three days before the French referendum—it became evident that it would be impossible to avoid a crisis of the European monetary system, which resulted in the withdrawal of the Italian lira and the British pound. Despite everything, the "yes" prevailed in France (September 20)—though by a tiny margin (51.04 percent to 48.95 percent, with 3.37 percent of the ballots left blank). Denmark too, after negotiating a number of opt-outs—notably on EMU— finally approved the treaty.

From Maastricht to Amsterdam

New enlargements then began to loom large on the horizon. On January 1, 1995, Austria, Finland, and Sweden brought the European Union's membership to fifteen, though Norway, once again, failed to join. In the meantime, the

European Council of Copenhagen (June 21–22, 1993) had established the so-called Copenhagen criteria, which candidate countries were required to fulfill. With more enlargements in sight, a new IGC was scheduled to further modify the treaties: a Reflection Group was also created, led by the Spanish minister of European affairs, Carlos Westendorp.

In light of the upcoming IGC, the Italian government had approved a number of documents, outlining its own key priorities. First, the IGC was to remedy the gaps and insufficiencies in the Maastricht Treaty and, above all, prepare the ground for forthcoming enlargements of the Union. Second, there was the need for a treaty that the public could easily understand and that would strengthen the Union's democratic character, render its institutional mechanisms more efficient, and develop its capacity to play a leading, coherent, and responsible role on the world stage. At the parliamentary debate that followed the presentation of the Italian priorities, five resolutions were approved supporting the government's position.[40] Yet, for the first time in ages, the debate was tense, a sign that domestic conditions in Italy had changed.

In the meantime, Italy's old ruling parties had been destroyed and new political actors were emerging, such as Forza Italia, the Lega Nord (Northern League), and the post-Communist and post–Christian Democrat parties. In March 1994, the right-wing coalition led by Silvio Berlusconi won the elections. For the first time, an Italian government was expressing anti-European sentiments; indeed, Foreign Minister Antonio Martino was a proud member of Thatcher's Club de Bruges.[41] The idea of preserving and promoting the national interest as a guiding principle in drafting and approving European policy was introduced into the public debate for the first time in the history of the republic. Coherently, in his first speech to parliament, Berlusconi aggressively declared that Italy would play "a leading role in the framework of the European Union,"[42] while Minister of Agriculture Adriana Poli Bortone affirmed that Italy would "play hard in Brussels."[43] The Berlusconi I government initially opposed Slovenia's membership in the EU due to reservations on the part of Alleanza Nazionale (the post-fascist party)[44] and almost created a diplomatic case when the German CDU proposed a "two-speed Europe," in which Italy was to be in the circle of "latecomers."[45] For the first time, an Italian government was isolated in Europe: none of the member parties belonged to major European political families, and a number of Italy's European counterparts objected to the presence of Alleanza Nazionale in the government. As we shall see in the next chapter, Silvio Berlusconi soon learned the lesson and devoted much of his party's energy in the following years to becoming a leading member of the European People's Party family.

At the same time, with the end of the cold war, Italy lost its international geopolitical significance. It took a long time for Italy to realize this and to redefine its foreign policy. Indeed, the process continues. Former ambassador and historian Sergio Romano wrote in 1993: "Unhappily, the regime is dying, while the position Italy has occupied for the last 45 years is disappearing entirely. That position was an element in a delicate mechanism whose counterweights were European integration, the United States, the Atlantic Alliance and the Soviet Union. . . . Italy no longer knows what it can reasonably expect and lacks the means to obtain its goals. Italy no longer has a foreign policy because its objectives and its instruments have disappeared, all at once."[46]

Yet Europe was moving on. At the European Council in Madrid, it was decided to launch a new IGC. The conference took place in Turin on March 29, 1996, during a new Italian presidency. This time, however, embedded in its domestic problems, Italy's contribution was far less relevant than in 1985 and in 1991. The Berlusconi I government had meanwhile collapsed, to be replaced by a transition government led by the former director of the Bank of Italy, Lamberto Dini. The new elections in April 1996 took place in the midst of the EU presidency and led to the formation of the government of Prime Minister Romano Prodi, a large and troublesome center-left coalition. Notwithstanding all this, the Italian parliament ratified the Amsterdam Treaty with 428 votes in favor, 1 against, and 44 abstentions (the Northern League) in the Chamber of Deputies and with the positive votes of all parties but the Northern League in the Senate as well.[47] The new treaty—know as the Treaty of Amsterdam—came into effect on May 1, 1999.

Toward the Fifth Enlargement: The Treaty of Nice

On May 2, 1999, the European heads of state and of government judged eleven countries to be qualified for the Economic and Monetary Union: Portugal, Spain, France, Luxembourg, Belgium, Holland, Ireland, Italy, Germany, Austria, and Finland. How Italy managed to participate, having previously withdrawn the lira from the process, is a complex and interesting story, to which chapter 9 gives the deserved attention.

Still, concern remained that the challenges of enlargement could not be met by the Treaty of Amsterdam. In its meeting in Cologne (June 3–4, 1999), the European Council thus decided to summon yet another IGC in 2000, with the aim of resolving the "Amsterdam leftovers": the organization of the Commission, the reweighting of the votes in the Council, the extension of the qualified majority voting system. The IGC started its work in Brussels on February

12, 2000, under the Portuguese presidency and progressed quickly. Unfortunately, during the second half of the year (under the French presidency), difficulties abounded.

Meanwhile, the European political landscape had changed. Jacques Chirac had replaced François Mitterrand as France's president, but did not equal him in negotiating abilities. Gerhard Schröder, with a Socialist-Green coalition, had taken over in Germany, further weakening the French-German dyad. In Italy, Romano Prodi was defeated in parliament and replaced first by the former Communist leader Massimo D'Alema and then by the former Socialist leader Giuliano Amato. Following Jacques Santer's resignation as head of the Commission, Romano Prodi found himself at the head of the Commission beginning in December 1998. Prodi, however, was decidedly unimpressive in the job and only seldom enjoyed strong support in his home country.

The French EU presidency was far from impressive, too. The two European Councils organized by the French presidency—in Biarritz (October 13–14, 2001) and in Nice (December 7–9, 2001)—were among the worst-managed gatherings in the history of European integration. Disagreement existed in particular over the possible "capping" of the commissioners at fifteen or twenty, over the reweighting of the votes in the Council, and over the extension of QMV as a general rule in the Council. In spite of these differences and despite many difficulties—and after almost five days of negotiations—the Union finally did reach an agreement in the form of the Treaty of Nice. On this occasion, the European Council also adopted an Italian-German proposal aimed at opening a detailed debate on the future of Europe, which would involve the Union's institutions, the national parliaments, and civil society. Slowly, Italy was regaining a prominent role.

Toward the New European Constitution

Although the Union had succeeded in reaching an agreement, and had signed the Treaty of Nice, the member states were faced once again with the realization that the treaty would not suffice in the face of inevitable problems presented by a much enlarged EU. Alternative means for revising treaties were needed to overcome this issue in the future. It was thus decided to call a constitutional convention, as had been done for the Charter of Fundamental Rights. Participants were even reminded of the drafting of the U.S. Constitution two centuries earlier. Once again, Italy's role was to be pivotal, though not as positive as in the past.

Silvio Berlusconi had regained power in Italy in 2001 and decided to name his deputy prime minister, Gianfranco Fini, as his personal representative to the convention. As Fini was the leader of the post-fascist Alleanza Nazionale, the Belgian government balked. The Belgians tried to claim that Berlusconi did not need to name a personal representative and suggested that the vice president of the convention, Giuliano Amato, also serve as the representative of the Italian government. Both the prime minister and Amato refused to consider this proposal. Political and diplomatic tension grew, until the question was finally settled with Fini's confirmation and an official explanation that the conclusions of the European Council would read differently in the Dutch and Italian versions(!). In the end, as we shall see in chapter 4, the convention experience proved fundamental in finalizing the conversion both of Fini, personally, and of his party to pro-European values. The EU member states came to accept him and his party as respected players following this experience, thus proving Berlusconi's nomination a clever one.

The Italian delegates to the convention were remarkably active during the convention. The most influential Italian was without a doubt Professor and Senator Giuliano Amato, who had previously also worked on a "consolidated version" of the EU Treaty at the European University Institute. Amato's role was pivotal, thanks to his ability to reconcile different positions—a coveted skill, considering the rather authoritarian style of the convention's president, Valéry Giscard d'Estaing—and to his deep knowledge of EU law.

Nevertheless, clouds gathered for the Italian government during the first phase of the convention's work. When the Berlusconi II government was first formed, Ambassador Renato Ruggiero was appointed foreign minister. A former top diplomat and secretary general of the World Trade Organization (WTO), his nomination was welcomed in Italy and abroad as a sign of continuity in Italian foreign policy and as a counterbalance to the presence of anti-European forces in the government.

Unfortunately, however, clashes between the foreign minister and the rest of the government emerged quickly, eventually leading Ruggiero to resign. Upon Ruggiero's resignation, Berlusconi temporarily assumed the post of foreign minister himself. He kept the position from January to November 2002. Therefore, as the convention was launched, Berlusconi was both prime minister and foreign minister. However, by the end of the first year of convention negotiations, with the Italian EU presidency approaching and the situation becoming unmanageable, Berlusconi finally named a new foreign minister— Minister of Public Administration Franco Frattini. When first named, Frattini was considered a Berlusconi yes-man who would let the prime minister keep running Italian foreign policy from Palazzo Chigi. This expectation, however, proved wrong: a former top student with an impressive (legal) curriculum in Italian public administration, Frattini soon acquired in-depth knowledge of the EU technical dossiers and foreign policy issues, quickly gained the diplomatic skills needed at the Farnesina, and developed into an excellent and dedicated foreign minister.

Nonetheless, the Italian EU presidency of 2003 started with a major incident. On July 2, 2003, Silvio Berlusconi was attending the plenary session of the European Parliament to discuss, as is custom, the forthcoming Italian presidency. In the course of the discussion, a German member of the European Parliament (MEP), Martin Schulz, aggressively attacked Italy for its immigration policies and for Berlusconi's failure to end the conflicts of interest between his own business and political activities. Berlusconi in turn overreacted, essentially accusing Schulz of being like a Nazi, creating a serious diplomatic row with Germany, which gravely endangered the beginning of the Italian presidency.[48]

On July 18, 2003, in Rome, the president of the European convention, Giscard d'Estaing, presented the "Draft Treaty establishing a Constitution for Europe" to the Italian EU presidency. In order to complete the EU reform process, it was now necessary to formally open a conference of government representatives from the member states—another IGC. Opinion diverged about how to proceed, however. Some members wanted to go back to their national parliaments before launching the final negotiations, while others wanted to take advantage of the positive impetus provided by the convention. In the end, the European Council asked the Italian presidency to launch the IGC. This suited Berlusconi, as he wanted the new treaty to be signed in Rome, before the end of the Italian semester. For this reason he put pressure on the IGC negotiations.

Negotiations were not easy. The Italian presidency sought to underscore the continuity between the convention and the Intergovernmental Conference; however, over the summer, the member states had examined the convention's proposals and it had become clear that several problematic points persisted: these would have to be discussed again, by the IGC. As we shall see in chapter 8, the IGC was followed meticulously by the Farnesina. The same can be said of the concluding European Council in Brussels, December 12–13, 2003.

With such careful planning, the first part of the European Council concluded quickly and satisfactorily. It was then time to move on to the IGC. Italy recognized that the primary remaining obstacle was the question of QMV—due, in particular, to the opposition of both Spain and Poland (though Poland was not yet an EU member state). Italy's strategy, therefore, was to reach a compromise on this point above all, hoping that the resolution of all other outstanding problems would follow smoothly. Unfortunately, however, all efforts were useless. Faced with a deadlock, the Italian presidency was unable to make a balanced proposal, one that would be acceptable to everyone. Italy was left with the arduous task of admitting that it was impossible to reach an overall agreement. The Intergovernmental Conference accordingly issued a statement declaring that negotiations had failed and asking the Irish presidency to continue consultations.

As chapter 8 discusses in more depth, the 2003 Italian presidency lacked the support of both France and Germany, whose backing had been fundamental in the previous Italian presidencies (1984 and 1990). This, ultimately, led to the failure of the IGC.

Before finishing its term, the Berlusconi government was trapped in yet another problem of both domestic and European dimensions. In June 2004, a new European Parliament was elected and a new president of the Commission was chosen: the conservative Portuguese former prime minister José Manuel Durao Barroso. When the Berlusconi II government was initially formed in 2001, one of the party leaders joining the government coalition—the former Christian Democrat Rocco Buttiglione—had accepted a post perhaps below his standing and expertise: that of minister for EU policies. Fluent in several languages, Buttiglione in fact had one political ambition—that of becoming European Commissioner. In his mind, the post of EU minister was a stepping stone toward that goal in 2004. Indeed, Buttiglione got the Italian government's designation. However, the Italians had not taken carefully enough into consideration the fact that the European Parliament had acquired significant power in confirming the governments' choices, and that it would wield that power as a political tool.

With the Socialist leader Josep Borell Fontelles leading the protest, the Parliament expressed its disapproval of Barroso's choice to give Buttiglione "Justice and Home Affairs"—a portfolio also including civil liberties. Until then, the Portuguese socialist and brilliant lawyer Antonio Vitorino had been in charge of this portfolio. Buttiglione, in contrast, was known for his intransigent Catholic stance and for his close relationship with the late Pope John Paul II. Questioned about gay rights during the formal hearing by the Civil Liberties Committee in the European Parliament, he eventually mentioned his personal moral opposition to homosexuality. In an unprecedented move, and with a vote of 26 to 27, the parliamentary committee rejected his nomination to the Commission (October 11, 2004). Borrell hence informed Barroso that the Parliament would veto his appointment of Buttiglione to the Commission if Barroso did not withdraw it. Barroso, in turn, told Berlusconi that it was an Italian domestic problem, one that he could not resolve. Once again Franco Frattini was chosen by Berlusconi to save the day. And, again Frattini turned out to be the right man in the right place: he did an excellent job and was much praised as Justice and Home Affairs commissioner.

After five years in power—completing a full parliamentary mandate for the first time in the history of the Italian Republic—Berlusconi was narrowly defeated in the legislative elections. The first move made by the subsequent Prodi II government (2006–2008) was to follow José Luis Zapatero's new Spanish government's lead and to withdraw Italian troops from Iraq.[49] Second, Prodi sought to relocate European integration at the center of Italian foreign policy. In so doing, however, he followed the tradition and the strategic approach of the Christian Democrat governments of the past: that is to say, he equated the European interest and the national interest, thereby somehow taking a step backwards. The discussion of the national interest, in fact, had progressed over the years (especially under Massimo D'Alema, prime minister from 1998 to 2000), leading to a substantial shared consensus that eventual national interests must be defended in Brussels by the Italian representatives. In an early speech in front of the Italian parliament (May 18, 2006), Romano Prodi affirmed: "We will be guided by precise choices in our foreign policy: we choose Europe and the integration process as the best environment for developing Italian policy. . . . Europe represents the map on which Italy—a country destroyed by war—bet its future. As long as Italy honors this bet, it wins. Naturally, Europe too has its crises, which we do not ignore or underestimate. Indeed, Europe needs us. Europe needs an Italy that dares to take up the mantle of its long tradition, that dares to relaunch an integration process—through new initiatives and concrete actions—that offers tangible answers to the demands of millions of Europeans. . . . We are convinced that the Italian national interest and the European interest are one and the same. We are convinced that Italy will count—even in relations with its greatest ally—only if it counts in Europe. We will work to put Italy back among the leaders of a new Europe."[50]

The case of the redistribution of seats in the post-2009 European Parliament, however, shows a gap between words and reality when dealing with the promotion of Italian national interests within the EU. Under the new Lisbon Treaty (2009), the number of Italian MEPs will be cut. This cut was elaborated in the European Parliament on the principle that the number of MEPs should be calculated according to the number of residents in a given country, rather than the number of voters. According to this system, Italy would have six fewer MEPs than with the previous system, and, most important, fewer MEPs than France. The Lamassoure Report (named for the rapporteur in the European Parliament, French MEP Alain Lamassoure) was approved by the European Council meeting in Brussels on June 21–23, 2007, but when word reached the Italian press, people protested vehemently and called for Italy to use its veto.

There was general outrage again when the European Parliament approved new provisions in the Lamassoure Report on October 11, 2007. Yet, according to a witness at the meeting, the two Italian representatives in the European Council—Romano Prodi and Foreign Minister Massimo D'Alema—were not even present: apparently, while the new numbering was being approved, they were momentarily outside the meeting room, trying to resolve a domestic political problem. Eventually a diplomatic solution was found: one more MEP was added to the final number—the formula being "750 plus the president"—and that extra MEP was promised to Italy.

The greatest achievement of the Prodi II government in European (and foreign) policy, however, was the production of the first-ever comprehensive reflection on the future of Italian foreign policy. A paper referred to as "Italia 2020" was the result of work by a number of Italian stakeholders. In it, Europe again plays a central role: the paper questions how best to preserve national interests in an enlarged European Union. The EU policy areas that are identified as most strategic for Italy are EMU, defense, immigration, and home security. It clearly calls for more coherent action, claiming: "The effort to build a more coherent, concrete, and continuative image for Italy in Europe demands first greater solidity on the domestic level. From many points of view, in fact, European policy is no longer 'foreign' or 'international,' but rather 'intermestic.' If the old theory of 'external constraint' [*vincolo esterno*] was based on the assumption that Italy would derive inner strength from its association with Europe, today that constraint appears inverted: only through greater domestic stability will Italy carry any weight in Europe. Only thus will Italy have the capacity to influence decision-making on policy, which, as it is European, is also necessarily domestic."[51]

Prodi's tiny majority in parliament did not create the foundation for a long reign, and the Prodi II government fell after less than two years. In May 2008, Silvio Berlusconi was back in power as prime minister, this time with a more comfortable majority than in the past. Determined to undertake those changes he had been unable to enact during his previous stints in government, he seems to be concentrating more on domestic politics, substantially delegating European policy and most foreign policy to Franco Frattini, the now experienced foreign minister. Berlusconi thus lately tends to appear on center stage just in the brightest foreign spotlights (such as G-8 summits).

In his speech to the Italian parliament to present his program (May 13, 2008), Berlusconi only briefly mentioned the future of Italian foreign policy and Europe in particular: "Italy's role in Europe and in the world . . . will serve as a compass for our work, as founders of the European project and as a great

Mediterranean nation. We will be called upon to enhance relations between the two shores of our sea and to act as a pillar in the friendly relations between Europe and the United States of America."[52]

In presenting the specificities of his foreign policy to the Italian parliament (July 2, 2008), Frattini confirmed the impressions of those who had noticed how strongly his time spent as European Commissioner had influenced the minister's actions and values. While he touched on Italy's role in the rest of the world—in transatlantic relations and relations with the Middle East, Russia, and various international multilateral forums—most of Frattini's speech was devoted to the future of European integration and to the role Italy was to play in it. Frattini defined European integration as the first axis around which Italian foreign policy would revolve, the other being transatlantic relations. He made a point of explaining that these two were not in contradiction with each other. Frattini also revealed his intention to use a bipartisan approach to foreign policy, and this has so far met with the approval and support of the opposition.

The new course in Berlusconi's government and in Italy's European policy was confirmed, on July 31, 2008, by a unanimous vote, when the Italian parliament ratified the Lisbon Treaty.

4

Parties and Public Opinion Regarding Europe

The Italian party system has been, and to a certain extent still is, a peculiar case among Western democracies. In many ways, Joseph Di Palma's and Joseph La Palombara's classic works on Italy remain valid even today.[1] And when Leonardo Morlino compares the Italian and the Spanish cases, for instance, he finds that the democratic regime in Spain has succeeded in becoming comparatively more consolidated than the one in Italy.[2] One needs, however, to distinguish between two periods: from the beginning of the Republic to the early 1990s (the so-called First Republic) and the period since then, often called the Second Republic.

The Italian Party System, between the First and Second Republics

In the postwar period, Italian parties developed along the lines of at least two different models. The Christian Democrats (DC) emerged as a confessional or denominational party, very close to the catch-all party model. The communist PCI, in contrast, became the classic party of mass integration. The Socialists (PSI) attempted to imitate the PCI, but with limited success. A similar mass party model was adopted by the neofascist Movimento Sociale Italiano (MSI). In contrast, the Liberals (PLI) and Republicans (PRI) could be regarded as opinion parties and, at the same time, elite parties. Giuseppe Saragat's Social Democrats (PSDI) occupied an intermediate position between the mass party and the party of "notables" (the elite party).[3]

The electoral system that was initially chosen for the new republic—and that lasted until the early 1990s—was a proportional system. This helped create a fragmented, unstable party system, with at least eight national parties represented in parliament at any given time. The republic had more than fifty cabinets between 1948 and the early 1990s: all were rather large and unstable, supported for most of the postwar period by four- or five-party coalitions (the so-called *pentapartito*). Coalition governments normally included the DC, PLI, PRI, PSDI, and, from the early 1960s, the PSI. As long as the possibility of a government including the PCI was perceived as risky, the DC played the role of the ruling party, granting stability to the system.[4] Jean Paul Frognier, for example, showed that governmental instability was counterbalanced by the existence of a pivotal group of sixteen ministers who were present in most governments.[5] Although that system allowed the democratic system to survive, it also cost a lot in terms of efficiency.[6] It led to an incoherent legislative pattern characterized by an overflow of insignificant laws, known in Italian as *leggine* (little laws).[7]

The gridlocked political situation—which characterized Italy in its first forty years of history as a republic—first began to be challenged in the early 1990s. According to Steven Gundle and Simon Parker, what happened in Italy between 1992 and 1994 was a true political earthquake.[8]

Following the fall of the Berlin Wall in 1989 and the end of the communist regimes in Eastern Europe, the PCI, led by Achille Occhetto, was transformed into the new Democratic Party of the Left (PDS). The end of the "communist threat" then allowed for new political scenarios and, eventually, a redistribution of power. Meanwhile, in a wave of antipolitical sentiment, two referendums modified the electoral law: in 1991 a vote expressing one single preference in legislative elections was introduced; in 1992 the electoral law itself was revoked.

In the April 1992 general elections, the Christian Democrats' share of votes fell below 30 percent, and the steady growth of the PSI came to a halt. The president of the republic, Oscar Luigi Scalfaro, was nevertheless expected to offer the post of prime minister to the PSI leader, Bettino Craxi. Meanwhile, however, starting with a local investigation of bribery in Milan, a huge network of corruption came to light. Led by Judge Antonio Di Pietro, the investigations of bribery (known as *Tangentopoli*, that is, "bribe city") would come to represent a major challenge to the political establishment (namely to the DC and PSI). It literally destroyed the old party system and led to the creation of a new one. In the event, the president of the republic offered the top governmental job to the law professor and past undersecretary of state Giuliano Amato. The Amato I government marked a major break from its predecessors for its structure and operation. As we shall see in chapter 5, it was one of the very few governments in Italian history not to be dependent upon the political parties. Amato had to sail in difficult waters, as in September 1992 the Italian lira had dropped out of the EMS and experienced a spectacular decrease in value.

In hopes of reducing the number of parties, a new electoral law (known as Legge Mattarellum) was introduced in 1994. It injected elements of majority rule into the Italian electoral system: in the Chamber of Deputies 75 percent of the members of parliament (MPs) were now to be elected on a first-past-the-post majority system, while only the remaining 25 percent were to be distributed on a proportional basis.

In April 1993, at the height of the Tangentopoli investigations, the majority parties' positions were defeated in eight referendums in what was described as "the end of a regime."[9] A major opportunity for reforming the Italian system presented itself at that point, though it was not adequately seized. Therefore, as we shall see, most of the chronic problems of the Italian political and bureaucratic system persist. In any event, in Italy today, the term "First Republic" is used to indicate the period before Tangentopoli, and "Second Republic" to refer to what has followed.

In March 1994, legislative elections were held once again: the left-wing parties (renamed for the occasion Progressisti) were defeated by the right-wing "dual" alliance created by Silvio Berlusconi's Forza Italia, with the Lega Nord (Northern League) in the North and Alleanza Nazionale (successor to MSI) in the South. Welcomed by many as the supposed victory of "anti-partitocrazia,"[10] the coalition rapidly proved its inefficiency and by the end of 1994 had already collapsed. Lamberto Dini, minister of the treasury in the Berlusconi I government and a former director general of Banca d'Italia, was named prime minister and formed a "nonpartisan" government. Ironically, Dini eventually governed thanks to the support of the center-left parties, which had, in the meanwhile, created a new coalition (Ulivo, or Olive Tree) and won the April 1995 administrative elections. At the end of 1995—once the annual financial bill was passed in parliament—discussions took place over the future of the government, in view of the forthcoming Italian presidency of the EU (January–June 1996). At first it seemed that the government would stay in power until the end of the semester, despite the fact that it was unable to get a comprehensive parliamentary resolution about the incoming EU presidency. Five different documents were in fact approved,[11] a division that was in itself a sign of the changing times in the Italian political scenario.

In the end, legislative elections were called again for April 21, 1996, right in the middle of the Italian EU presidency. They were won by the Ulivo coalition, and thus, on May 17, 1996, just one month before the Florence European Council, the Prodi I government was formed.

However, while the coalition had enough votes to support its government in the Senate, that was not the case in the Chamber. The government thus became dependent upon the external support of the new communist party, Rifondazione Comunista (RC), a fact that was to harm the government's European and foreign policies on several occasions.

Since then, two opposing coalitions have alternated in power: Berlusconi's Polo delle Libertà and Prodi's Ulivo (and their respective successors). Berlusconi's center-right coalition has been formed by conservative post–Christian Democrats, northern separatists (Northern League), post-fascists (Alleanza Nazionale), and Berlusconi's own party (Forza Italia). The center-left coalition has been made up of progressive post–Christian Democrats, various post-communist parties, Greens, and a number of minor, more or less "personal" parties (ex Di Pietro's, and others).

For the first time since 1968, the late 2000s brought parliamentary stability to Italy. In 2006 the legislature ended its natural five-year cycle. Also, for the first time since 1953, a prime minister (Berlusconi) remained in power for the full five-year term (though his term was technically divided into two distinct governments, Berlusconi II and Berlusconi III).

Despite these developments, it took many years for the number of parties in parliament to start decreasing: the 1996–2000 legislature featured some forty different political groups in parliament and an eight-party government coalition. In 2006 yet another new electoral law was approved by the parliament (Law 270/2005). This law introduced, among other things, "blocked" lists of candidates (that is, lists in which a block of candidates is preselected by each party rather than by voters) to be presented in each of the twenty-six electoral constituencies. Hence, today voters can only choose the party to vote for—not the individual candidate. In turn, the parties choose whether to be formally linked to one of the running coalitions and the other parties that constitute it. The parties can also indicate the name of the person they wish to govern in case of victory (though this is not formally binding, because the Constitution says that the prime minister is chosen by the president of the republic).

The new system is a proportional one, with two correctives: a minimum threshold has to be reached (4 percent for electoral lists that are not linked to any coalition and 2 percent for those having established a formal link with one of the running coalitions); a majority reward is offered the winning coalition if it does not gain 340 seats in the Chamber of Deputies. Since the Constitution says that senators are to be elected on a regional basis, the majority bonus in the Senate is redistributed on a regional basis, thereby accentuating the difference in political composition between the two chambers.[12] The first time the law was used, in 2006, it resulted in a (still) highly fragmented parliament, with sixteen political groups in the Chamber and ten in the Senate. Consequently, as we shall see in chapter 5, the Prodi II government (2006–08) was composed of a coalition of nine parties whose political differences often forced the prime minister to resort to votes of confidence, even for the adoption of bills.

Yet things changed substantially with the elections held on April 21, 2008, following an early fall of the Prodi II government. Credit must be given to Walter Veltroni, the leader of the new Democratic Party (PD was created in the fall of 2007 from the ashes of the Democratic Party of the Left, the remains of the leftist post–Christian Democrats, and various others), for his decision to run his campaign without allying his party with the small leftist parties. This initiative toward disaggregation was, to a certain extent, mirrored on the right. During the electoral campaign, both Veltroni and Berlusconi repeatedly appealed to the electorate to cast a "useful vote." The Italian people overwhelmingly responded to the call, thereby simplifying the existing political system. It is an important call for change that must not go unacknowledged. In a country that, historically, is quite fragmented and polarized, the voters' choice to back away from the smaller parties is a remarkable one. The first immediate result was the winnowing of the number of parties in the parliament to six—thirty-five had contested the elections but most failed to reach the 4 percent popular vote threshold. In the end, the parties present in parliament included the progressive Democratic Party and its ally Italia dei Valori; the centrist Union of Christian Democrats; the center-right Popolo della Libertà (born from the fusion between Forza Italia and Alleanza Nazionale) and its allies the Northern League and the Autonomy Movement.

In 2009 the elections for the European Parliament—where a 4 percent requirement was also added to the otherwise pure proportional system—confirmed the trend. The next important step in Italian party politics will come when Silvio Berlusconi steps back from his party leadership position. If enough time is given then to a new center-right party to consolidate and to a newer "truly melted" generation to emerge—so that no splits occur alongside the lines of the old parties at the time of the change of leadership—a historic political transition will have been completed in Italy. The still divided Democratic Party will be forced to face up to the fact that a German type of political party system has replaced the old one and act accordingly. Without a charismatic leader, the Democratic Party needs a generational turnover more than ever. The "older" politicians—anyone who was politically active during the First Republic—tend to feel a strong allegiance to the party they once belonged to and to the people they worked with at the time. Hence, if at the time of Berlusconi's departure from politics the "new" leadership still belongs to that world, it is likely that the ancient Guelfi and Ghibellini Italian habit of dividing and fighting will be revived, leading the Italian political system once again into chaos. As this book goes to press, political rivalries have emerged within the main political parties, suggesting that old habits and divisions are still well alive in Italy, to the detriment of much needed political stability.

Attitudes toward European Integration

Italians are known to be among the most convinced supporters of the process of European integration. This is consistent with their vision, their interpretation of history, and their reading of the role the peninsula is to play on the continent.

The Romans perceived themselves as pivotal in securing the peace and civilization of the continent. Their cosmopolitan values and their contribution to the spread of civilization throughout the then-known world (the ideas of Pax Romana and *romana civitas*) are highlighted in Italian schoolbooks. Ancient Rome is considered one of the most glorious periods in the country's long history. Centuries later, Dante—the most important Italian writer and the first to use the Italian language (in *The Divine Comedy*)—underlined, in *De Monarchia* (1310–13), that the only way to achieve true justice was through world unity (the "world" as he knew it, of course). In such a process of unification, the Roman people were to play the pivotal role: it was their birthright.

During the Risorgimento period, the claim for a "united Europe" was considered within the context of freeing Italy from foreign rule. Unity, indeed, was seen as a way to reach that goal. The most influential philosophers and politicians of the Risorgimento supported the idea of a better and more peaceful future for the peninsula within the context of a (united) Europe. Thus, in *Rinnovamento* (1851), Vincenzo Gioberti advocated a "social-democratic" renewal throughout Europe, in which the Italian national resurgence could take place. Cesare Balbo's *Le speranze d'Italia* (1844) stressed that an Italian federation (without the Austrians) would have contributed enormously to the stability of all Europe. Other people, like Giuseppe Ferrari, promoted the idea of broader federalism as the result of the free will and action of the people (*La rivoluzione e le riforme in Italia*, 1851). According to Carlo Cattaneo, only a United States of Europe could ever secure peace and prosperity on the continent (*Considerazioni in fine del primo volume dell' "Archivio triennale"*).

Giuseppe Mazzini, a major promoter of a united (and republican) Italy and founder of La Giovine Italia—the movement in favor of Italian independence—was a strong supporter of a United States of Europe, too. Mazzini, who also founded La Giovine Europa (Young Europe), conceived of the nation as a means by which to achieve a better life for all people. Europe would be shaped by thirteen or fourteen nation-states (with "nation" having a spiritual and historical meaning, rather than territorial or racial one), each with a mission of its own, in the view of achieving overall improvements.

Owing to this historical background, the Italian people today feel that a more integrated Europe follows a logical continuum in their history. They still believe it is the best way to secure democracy and peace. Moreover, as the EEC made its firsts steps during the "economic miracle" period, membership in the Communities came to be associated with better socioeconomic conditions. This was true even to the extent that when financial restraint became necessary to join the European Monetary Union (EMU), Italians did not complain too much about paying an ad hoc tax to get rid of their lira and its troubles for good. In fact, as the Italian system was entering into a deep crisis, the EC began to be perceived as the only chance to bring order to the national system: thus the demand for supranational structures also came to represent a demand for a solution to the inefficiencies of the Italian system.

For Italians, the EU mainly represents the freedom to travel, study, and work anywhere in the European Union. Italians think that the EU gives Europeans a stronger say in the world and protects common values such as democracy and cultural diversity, as well as economic prosperity. The level of knowledge among the populace about the institutions of the European Union, according to Eurobarometer surveys, is higher in Italy than in other EU countries, although it declined in the 2000s: in 2009, 51 percent of Italians acknowledged their ignorance about how the EU functions;[13] 49 percent consider their country's membership in the EU to be positive, compared to 32 percent who hold a neutral opinion, and 13 percent who judge it as negative. However, trust in the EU remains strong: 52 percent of Italians trust the European Union in general; 54 percent have confidence in the European Parliament, 51 percent in the Commission, 47 percent in the Council, and 45 percent in the European Central Bank.

During the economic crisis that began in 2007, Italian support for the common European currency increased. In 2009, 63 percent of Italians favored the monetary union and the euro compared to 61 percent in 2008. The euro is thought to have mitigated the negative effects of the financial and economic crisis, according to 53 percent of those interviewed. The European Union is seen as best suited to face the crisis (25 percent); it is widely viewed as better than global bodies, such as the G-20 (11 percent) and the International Monetary Fund (11 percent), at solving international financial and economic problems.

The Italian Political Parties and the Process of European Integration, from the Origins to the Early 1990s

The decision to link Italy firmly to the process of European integration was essentially the decision of a small group of leaders, led by the prime minister and head of the Christian Democrats, Alcide De Gasperi, and his foreign minister, Carlo Sforza. This choice was intrinsically linked to the decision to join the North Atlantic Pact in 1949. The DC—a party that would later become a champion of Europeanism—was at the time divided over the issue. Vera Capperucci talks about three periods in the early DC years: 1948–49, the Atlantic choice; 1950–54, the Euro-Atlantic strategy; and 1954–58, neo-Atlanticism.[14] In the very early years of the republic, the left fringes of the DC leadership, led by Giuseppe Dossetti and Giovanni Gronchi, were in favor of keeping an equidistant relation between Italy and the two superpowers: the United States and the USSR. They welcomed the prospect of a neutral, or nonaligned, Italy. Though Italy's terrible economic conditions made it clear that the country needed American support—namely via the Marshall Plan—they felt it was important to show "dignity" in receiving it. The left wing of the DC thus opposed signing the North Atlantic Pact. As the Communists and the Socialists too were expected to vote against the pact, De Gasperi desperately needed all his party's votes in parliament. In this light, he used Italy's inclusion in a European integration process (at the time represented by the Council of Europe) to sell Atlantic integration to the DC. In signing the North Atlantic Pact (April 4, 1949), De Gasperi underlined its political rather than military aspects. Also, soon afterwards (May 5, 1949), he signed the founding treaty of the Council of Europe. Last but not least, his government negotiated a commercial agreement with Moscow. These links and ambiguities were to have an impact on Italy's foreign policy.[15]

One year later, in 1950, the decision to join the European Coal and Steel Community was, once again, essentially a De Gasperi–Sforza one. De Gasperi's idea was that Italy could better defend its national interests only within a policy of European solidarity.[16] In addition, involvement in supranational European institutions would help strengthen the domestic political system and the new democracy.[17] European integration was seen as a fundamental opportunity for the peninsula. Joining the ECSC, once again, was a political decision. Indeed, there were several reservations about technical issues. Piero Craveri talks about an external bond in relation to De Gasperi's vision of European integration: he says that, thanks to Italy's participation in the European Communities, De Gasperi aimed to make up for what he could not achieve on the national institutional level.[18]

Despite some internal divisions in the 1960s and a new anti-European crisis in the 1970s, the European choice—strictly linked with the Atlantic one—came to represent a widespread and founding principle shared by the whole Christian Democratic Party. In particular, in the late 1980s and the early 1990s, the party undertook a marked activism at the European level, also thanks to leaders like Giulio Andreotti and Emilio Colombo. However, as Niccolò Conti and Luca Verzichelli point out, the style was more "reactive" than "proactive"; there was a distinct lack of continuity and strategy in the DC's European policy, especially as foreign policy was considered a minor issue in comparison with domestic politics.[19]

As for the other parties of the governing coalition during De Gasperi's time, the two smaller ones—the Liberals (PLI) and the Republicans (PRI)—were convinced supporters of the process of European integration. In particular, PLI leaders like Luigi Einaudi (first as governor of the Bank of Italy, then as a minister, and finally as president of the republic) and Gaetano de Martino (as foreign minister) were De Gasperi's fundamental allies. Craveri compares Einaudi and Sforza with De Gasperi: unlike the prime minister, they shared the classical vision of foreign policy in terms of power politics.[20] The Liberals' Western choice was a basic one—indeed, one of the pillars of the party's identity. The situation with the Republicans was similar: Ugo La Malfa, the party's historical leader, felt European federalism was an ideal to pursue; each step in that direction (for instance, signing the European Defense Community) was thus to be encouraged.[21]

The two major parties of the left—PCI and PSI—felt differently. Since the very early days of the republic, both the Communists and the Socialists were very negative toward Atlantic and European issues, perceived as a form of "submission" to the United States.[22] The Socialist leader Pietro Nenni considered foreign policy a dependent variable in domestic politics and felt that, as such, it should be used solely to serve Italian national interests. In his mind, that meant that Italy should not enter the North Atlantic Treaty—which he perceived as a threat to the USSR and a number of other UN member states—or any European community, including the Council of Europe.

This strict loyalty to the USSR isolated the Italian Socialist Party from its fellow European ones. Indeed, so strong was Nenni's opposition to European integration that in May 1950 the party explicitly forbade its members to join the European Federalist Movement(!). Nevertheless, with the gradual easing of tensions in East-West relations in the following years, Nenni began to think that new room to maneuver was available to the PSI and slowly came to acknowledge the European status quo.

The definitive break with USSR foreign policy came with the Suez and the Hungarian crises of 1956. Nenni thus decided to name a party commission to study the question of the two new communities: the EEC and Euratom (the European Atomic Energy Community). Though not without criticizing the government for the way it handled the negotiations, the commission recommended abstaining on the EEC and voting in favor of Euratom.[23] Meanwhile, Nenni had been co-opted into Jean Monnet's Comité d'Action.[24] The change in the PSI's approach to foreign policy then allowed the party to join the majority supporting the government in 1958 and to enter the government in 1963. From then on, it would remain pro-European.

The conversion of the Communist Party to support for Europe was slower and less linear. Today, in the national political culture, a myth surrounds the party, as if the PCI had always been pro-European. However, the recent opening of the Moscow archives has allowed for a more accurate reconstruction of the facts by historians. The files in Moscow confirm the PCI's long dependence on the USSR—from both a policy and a monetary point of view. Italian communist political discourse was centered on the defense of the Italian national interest—first and foremost, the geopolitical one.[25] The PCI demonstrated several times against the Americans and against the European Communities. The party had a fierce aversion to any form of European or Atlantic integration.

Some isolated communist leaders—such as Giorgio Amendola and Gian Carlo Pajetta—showed a timid interest in some of the ideas of Christian Democrat leaders like Amintore Fanfani or Giovanni Gronchi (with his *Ostpolitik)*—but that was about it. The events of 1956 and the brutal repression of the Hungarian uprising was a difficult moment for the PCI. Yet unlike the PSI, the party remained staunchly allied with the USSR.

Though the PCI leader, Palmiro Togliatti, was quick to suppress any idea that departed from the party's official one, the first cracks in the party line were nevertheless starting to appear: the communist trade union (CGIL), for instance, felt that the EEC would speed Italian economic recovery. Finally, after the 1962 Cuban missile crisis and the subsequent changes on the world scene, the PCI started to change too. When, in 1969, the first Communists were appointed to the European Parliament, the PCI began to overhaul its foreign policy.[26] By the time of the first direct election of the European Parliament in 1979, the European Federalist leader, Altiero Spinelli, was elected as an independent on the lists of the PCI, thus completing the party's reversal, from rejection to acceptance of pro-European values.[27]

Still, alignment on pro-European values by the various Italian parties did not result in a more proactive Italian European foreign policy; rather, a "depoliticization" of Italian foreign policy started to take place. Gradually, the EC became a nonissue in the Italian political arena. According to former ambassador Sergio Romano, Europe is an icon before which Italian politicians quickly kneel before moving on to other things. Seldom has strong political leadership emerged on European policy. There are some exceptions, but they were the result of individual action on the part of a few leaders rather than of a concrete policy underwritten by the Italian parties. Only since roughly the turn of the twenty-first century have things begun to change more concretely.

It is the Italian dimension rather than the European one that appeals to national politicians. Too many times they—using a pure party-based logic—tend to consider "Euro-jobs" as (well-paid) retirement or interim positions. Such jobs are just meant to tide them over until they can get back into the national political arena. The EC/EU has also been used by Italian politicians to legitimize their own actions.[28] In fact, European constraints are often cited to justify otherwise unpopular fiscal and monetary measures. Some headlines from leading Italian newspapers make this clear: "The Twelve ask for blood and tears";[29] "Privatization? It is imposed by the EC."[30] Several parties have also warned of the dangers of the euro, as we shall see in chapter 5.

The Italian Political Parties and the Process of European Integration from the Early 1990s to Today

Have things changed with the arrival of the so-called Second Republic? Has the political turmoil experienced by the Italian party system had an effect on European policymaking?

The Italian political system underwent an upheaval in the 1990s that had consequences for both the national debate about Europe and European decisionmaking. At the European level, the most important changes have been a shift in the membership of the European political families and in their internal alliances—the most visible concerning the European People's Party (EPP). Within the EPP, two parties had long been stronger than the others: the Italian DC and the German CDU-CSU (Christian Democratic Union and Christian Social Union). The two parties held biannual consultations (often at the CDU-CSU villa in Cadenabbia on Lake Como) where they confronted their positions. The Adenauer Foundation in Rome, together with the Italian Christian Democratic Foundation, were also sites of ongoing dialogue.

A good example of the Italian-German entente is the Genscher-Colombo Plan, submitted to all the member states on November 6, 1981, which led to the Solemn Declaration on European Union of June 17–19, 1983. Important collaboration also took place during the Italian presidencies of 1985 and 1990. A number of satellites revolved around the Germans and the Italians, including a core group of Benelux Christian Democratic parties. This group of parties was able to impose its pro-federalist views on the others within the EPP.

A first crisis within the EPP appeared with the inclusion of the Spanish Partido Popular, which the Italians fiercely opposed. Then, at the first signs of the impending collapse of the DC, other EPP parties felt they could benefit by gaining a greater share of power. When the first split took place within the DC in 1993, it was the new Italian Partito Popolare (PPI, Italian Popular Party) that inherited a seat in the EPP. The party's transformation, and most of all its center-left orientation, was neither understood nor welcomed by an EPP that was becoming progressively more conservative. The new party leader, Mino Martinazzoli, instead of assiduously lobbying other parties at EPP meetings, missed most of those meetings altogether: it turned out he was afraid to fly. In a typically parochial yet arrogant Italian manner, the leadership completely underestimated the impact of its changes on the other EPP members and continued to rely on its alliance with the German and Benelux parties. But circumstances had changed.

When the heir to the DC, the PPI, split again in 1995, the EPP promoted an agreement between the old leadership and the new: in a meeting in Nice, the secessionist Rocco Buttiglione was "awarded" the old Christian Democrat symbol, while the remaining leadership kept the (newer) name of PPI. Complete collapse was just around the corner.

Meanwhile, in 1994, Silvio Berlusconi, the new leader of the center-right coalition, had become prime minister. His nine months in office clearly showed him that isolation at the European level was a potential threat to his possible future governments. Therefore, Berlusconi devoted tremendous effort to bringing his own party, Forza Italia, into the EPP. That was done through both traditional political channels (members of the European Parliament, Claudio Azzolina and Antonio Tajani were instrumental in this process) and Berlusconi's own "personal diplomacy." José Maria Aznar's former personal assistant Alejandro Agag—at the time EPP's deputy secretary general and then secretary general—was invited to vacation on Berlusconi's boat and at his villas in Sardinia, for example. Berlusconi also occasionally invited Aznar's son and daughter. Legend has it that, during a romantic holiday on Berlusconi's boat, young Alejandro fell in love with Ana, Aznar's daughter. Berlusconi was hence rewarded with EPP membership (indeed, Forza Italia is today a major actor within the EPP) as well as an invitation to act as best man at the wedding.

PPI put up a fight, but it was far too late. The Italian Popular Party had no negotiating force left to oppose Forza Italia's entrance, and its opposition only contributed to its further relegation to a corner. Meanwhile, Pier Ferdinando Casini's small party (Union of Christian Democrats, UDC) had become a member of the EPP too. For some time, Lamberto Dini's and Mario Segni's tiny parties were part of the EPP as well, and in 2001 Clemente Mastella's essentially southern party (Union of Democrats for Europe, UDEUR) was finally accepted too. And to make matters worse, this plethora of Italian parties—in itself a phenomenon difficult to understand from abroad—tended to seize the occasion of EPP meetings to fight over domestic matters.

Today three Italian parties belong to the EPP: Popolo della Libertà (People of Freedom), UDC, and the regional party Südtiroler Volkspartei. The People of Freedom Party was founded in 2009 by the fusion of Forza Italia, Alleanza Nazionale, and other Italian parties. The only UDEUR representative, Clemente Mastella, is also part of the People of Freedom Party.[31] Though Forza Italia enjoyed relative strength within the EPP due to its size, the prestige and power of the former DC are lost forever. Forza Italia itself, with its special relations to the Spanish and other conservative parties, has contributed to a genetic change in the EPP leadership: no longer social, Christian, and pro-European, the party has become conservative and more skeptical about the EU.

The story of Italian membership in the socialist family of parties in Europe (SOC) is only a little easier. The new Democratic Party of the Left (PDS)—born, as mentioned, in 1990, out of the ashes of the former PCI—quickly applied for membership in the socialist family. The declining Italian Socialist Party (PSI), at first fiercely opposed to the move, came around in November 1992, at the Berlin Congress, when the PSI leader Bettino Craxi was faced with the fact that he could no longer delay its entrance. From then until 2008, both Italian parties were members of the European Socialists. Then, once the Italian Partito Democratico (PD) was created, the party suffered long agony concerning its affiliation in the European Parliament. Most parts of the former Christian Democrats within it were understandably averse to joining the SOC. Nevertheless, after the 2009 European Parliament elections, they did end up in the Socialist group, which, for the occasion, was renamed "Group of the Progressive Alliance of Socialists and Democrats in the European Parliament."[32]

As for the other parties, once the European liberal family of parties (ELDR)—previously the third strongest in the European Parliament—lost the two small but active Italian parties PLI and PRI, it began to decline, leading to what is now a much more heterogeneous group. Since the 2009 elections, the only Italian party in ELDR is Italia dei Valori (former "Tangentopoli" judge Di Pietro's party).

In the domestic arena, from the 1970s to 1990s, unlike in other European countries, EU issues were not used as a tool of domestic political confrontation. With the 1990s things changed.

In his first speech to the Italian parliament outlining his goals and agenda, Silvio Berlusconi declared that Italy would play "a leading role" in the European Union.[33] His government featured an aggressive minister for agriculture, Adriana Poli Bortone, who affirmed that Italy would "play hard in Brussels,"[34] and even a proud member of Margaret Thatcher's Club de Bruges, Foreign Minister Antonio Martino, who favored a position of "qualified integrationism" and was critical of the nascent European Economic and Monetary Union.[35] A number of confrontational episodes took place in this phase. For example, Italy opposed Slovenia's EU membership bid[36] and almost created a diplomatic incident when the German CDU proposed a two-speed Europe, placing Italy in the circle of "latecomers."[37] This, together with the international political isolation of the Berlusconi I government, relegated Italy to a lesser role in the European arena. According to Gianni Bonvicini, the first center-right government, between 1994 and 1995, was thus characterized by a greater assertiveness in foreign policy that affected the balance between Europe and the United States.[38]

In 1996 national elections were won by the center-left Olive Tree coalition. The Prodi I government made a concerted effort to relocate Italy in the European arena, in particular by focusing on economic reforms needed to successfully fulfill the requirements of the EMU. Yet Prodi's handling of the EU presidency in 1996 was far less successful than that of his predecessors. Also, the Prodi I government suffered from the anti-European stance of its ally, Rifondazione Comunista. Rifondazione's votes in the Chamber of Deputies were necessary to Prodi's survival, but the party—born of a split in the PDS and still believing in communism as a viable solution—had reverted to the original communist opposition to both European integration and NATO. The positions of the Rifondazione Comunista therefore made it difficult for Italy to effect the economic reforms necessary to follow the path toward EMU. In this sense, the Rifondazione aligned itself with the Northern League—a far-right party—in opposition to EU integration, thus definitively breaking the consensus on European integration that had characterized the Italian political system since the early 1980s.

In 2001 Silvio Berlusconi regained power, this time with a solid parliamentary majority, which allowed him more freedom in foreign policy than any Italian government had enjoyed before. In search of international recognition, after the isolation of the 1994 experience, Berlusconi opted to "go American," and better, he forged a strong personal friendship with U.S. president George W. Bush, thus importing his own "personal diplomacy" operations (which had, after all, proved rather successful in settling the issue of Forza Italia's membership in the EPP). According to Filippo Andreatta, that led to an "unbalanced foreign policy in which bilateral relations with the Bush administration took precedent over multilateral relations with Europe, leading to frequent tensions with EU institutions and partners. . . . Most prominent was the support given to the Bush administration's global war on terror after 9/11, which implied significant and unprecedented positions."[39] Berlusconi also invested much of his "personal diplomacy" into building preferential relations with Russian president Vladimir Putin. According to Elisabetta Brighi, the government seemed to believe that "a more assertive Italian foreign policy passed from Washington, thus equating Atlanticism with nationalism . . . [while] a significant number of influential ministers . . . have professed a particularly complex brand of Euro-skepticism, which the Prime Minister has qualified as Euro-realism."[40]

The Prodi II government (2006–08), on the contrary, had among its objectives that of relocating European integration at the center of Italian foreign policy. However, the troublesome coalition he was leading allowed him little room to maneuver.

In the 2008 electoral campaign, for the first time since the early 1990s, Europe no longer constituted a divisive issue—indeed, it was hardly mentioned in the parties' programs or in the debates. Berlusconi's Polo delle Libertà (the electoral merging of Forza Italia and Alleanza Nazionale, transformed in 2009 into the new PDL [People of Freedom, or Freedom Party]) mentioned the need to respect the obligations deriving from the EU treaties, while safeguarding Italian interests in the EU. The Democratic Party (PD, the new post-Catholic and post-Communist party) manifesto affirmed its belief in the rather vague slogan "as much Europe as possible" (*Europa massima possibile*).[41]

Once elected, the Berlusconi IV government largely continued the foreign policy (and specifically the European policy) of the previous Italian government. The new course in Berlusconi's government and for Italy's European policy was confirmed by a unanimous vote on July 31, 2008, when the Italian parliament ratified the Treaty of Lisbon.[42]

IN SUM, FROM the early 1990s to the late 2000s there were differences in the perception of European integration by the two main political coalitions. At times, these have been used in the domestic political debate as a means of confrontation, in a stop-and-go argument over European values and Italian interests and over who is best fit to preserve them.[43] The Berlusconi I government (1994–95) represented a break with the past with its lack of support for the European integration process. Later on, the Berlusconi II and III governments (2001–2006) used their good relations with George W. Bush to gain respectability and influence at home and in Europe. The various center-left governments (1996–2001 and 2006–08) stressed European integration as the foundation of Italian foreign policy, but at times had a more strained relationship with Washington.

In both cases, however, the anti-European parties—the Northern League on the right and Rifondazione Comunista on the left—made significant trouble for their respective coalitions, at times using the EU as a scapegoat. But Alleanza Nazionale—a former Euro-skeptic party—was "converted" to Europe during its years in government. It is not surprising, therefore, that in his first speech as president of the Chamber of Deputies on April 29, 2008, Gianfranco Fini, the Alleanza Nazionale leader, promoted the acceptance of European values and the importance of the EU integration process.[44]

After the 2008 elections eliminated the smaller parties, the only Euro-skeptic party remaining in parliament was the Northern League. But, as the vote on the Lisbon Treaty also shows, even it has downscaled its rhetoric against the EU, focusing instead on problems that are more important to the party: first and foremost, illegal immigration.

Hence, in his speech to the parliament on April 29, 2008, setting forth his governing agenda, Silvio Berlusconi left behind the old rhetoric of Italy's power politics in favor of a speech of a rather "ecumenical" flavor. In fact, he only briefly mentioned foreign policy and Europe in particular: "Italy's role in Europe and in the world . . . will be the navigator of our policy; we are one of the Fathers of European integration and a great Mediterranean nation, naturally fit to foster cooperation among the two sides of that Sea and to act as a pillar of transatlantic relations."[45] Indeed, in Berlusconi's mind, foreign policy has two main connotations, which became particularly evident in his last government. First, the content of the policy: foreign policy is primarily seen as economic diplomacy, having as its supreme goal that of selling Italy and Italian products abroad. As such, it is seen as part of the economic policy of the country. Second, the way foreign policy shall be conducted: the prime minister maintains personal relationships with a number of his peers and deals directly with those themes he considers most relevant at particular times. All the rest—that is, the task of laying out the specifics of the Italian foreign policy—is in the hands of the foreign minister, who today is his close colleague Franco Frattini.

Indeed, Frattini shows how the years he spent as EU Commissioner have left their mark. His policy is profoundly pro-European and thus skeptical of the way the EU is evolving in the post-Lisbon phase. Not by chance in his first speech to the parliament (July 2, 2008), he defined the future of European integration as the first priority of Italian foreign policy. The second pillar of Frattini's foreign policy is transatlantic relations, and he has devoted particular energy to improving a relationship that was perceived to be shaky, first after the previous Prodi government and then after the election of Barack Obama. The third pillar is the large Mediterranean area, including the Balkans (historically a priority for Italy) and the Middle East. The Middle East possibly represents the main difference from his predecessor, former communist leader Massimo D'Alema, who was known for his more pro-Arab stance, while Frattini is comparatively more pro-Israel. Last but not least, there are relations with Russia, and the engagement in international multilateral forums.

In any case, for the first time since the early 1990s, Italy's European policy has remained coherent from one government to the next.

5

The Italian Parliament and the EU:
A Slow and Gradual Europeanization

The growing involvement of the national parliaments in EU policy-making has passed through three phases: limited or no involvement was the trend until the 1980s; after the Single European Act (SEA) in 1987, national parliaments started to be interested in European affairs and to set up specialized committees; following the Maastricht Treaty (Treaty on the European Union, or TEU) in 1992, the involvement of national parliaments in EU affairs became a response to the question of "democratic deficit" in the EU.[1]

The growing number of policies dealt with at the EU level, the consequently increasing influence of EU law on national legislation, and the new powers of the Union all worked together to push national legislators to seek a "scrutiny role" in the drafting of EU legislation. Once the TEU was signed, a more parliamentary climate prevailed.[2] In recent years, national parliaments have distinguished themselves by their greater role in the scrutiny of EU legislation;[3] more specialized members of parliament (MPs) sit on the Committees on EU affairs; the amount of work for EU specialists has increased. Also, parliamentary scrutiny, initially only optional and ex post, is now increasingly ex ante and/or mandatory.[4]

Also, though national parliaments are not mentioned in the first ten para-constitutional articles of the TEU, they were the object of specific declarations and protocols: Declarations No. 13 and 14, attached to the Maastricht Treaty; and the Protocol on the Role of National Parliaments, attached to the Amsterdam Treaty (1996), which focused on the role of national parliaments. According to the protocol, for example, national governments agree to send all Commission documents and legislative proposals to their parliaments. The new Treaty of Lisbon further enhanced the role of national parliaments:

if one-third of the parliaments oppose a Commission proposal it will have to be reexamined. As we shall see, the Italian parliament participates in this trend of growing involvement.

Basic Features of the Italian Political System

The 1948 Constitution of the Italian Republic—written and approved in 1947, after the fascist period—is a long (139 articles), rigid, programmatic text. It is the result of many compromises, all aimed at reuniting the country despite its many cleavages. Italian society was, and still is, a pluralist one, and the Constitution reflects that. Indeed, the Constitution was not the result of a comprehensive and harmonious agreement, but rather of a number of partial agreements among ideologically distant political forces.[5]

Nevertheless, in most areas, and specifically as regards the form of government, the Constitution essentially represented an agreement between the Communist Party (PCI) and the Christian Democrats (DC) to impose their will on all the others. Leaders chose a parliamentary system rather than a presidential one for this reason. A strong executive was, in fact, perceived by many constituent fathers as risky for the newborn democratic system. The Italian system of checks and balances, as it were, is granted by the primacy of the parliament over the executive; the latter's work can be scrutinized or vetoed at any time.[6]

In particular, the political parties were to play the central role in the democratic game: in the minds of the founding fathers of the Italian republic, the system would work thanks to the strength and the authority injected from outside by the parties. This had already begun toward the end of the war. As the Allies began their invasion in July 1943, German troops occupied the main strategic points of central and northern Italy, including Rome. To escape the Nazi penetration, the government of Pietro Badoglio and the royal family took refuge in Brindisi. In doing so, the government and the king left the nation in complete turmoil. In the absence of any legitimate governing authority, the political parties reentered the political arena. Together they formed the National Liberation Committee (CLN). The CLN did not benefit institutionally from any governing prerogative, yet it filled the power vacuum: as the only visible and recognized authority, it set about confronting the numerous problems the country faced. The parties appointed the political and administrative authorities of the municipalities so that they could take care of public services. Thus the CLN got into the habit of nominating its members to take charge of the public administration when no one else was in a position to do so: the so-called "lottizzazione" began in that period.[7]

Not only were the parties involved in policymaking, but they also played the role of gatekeepers, both politically and socioeconomically.[8] They appointed the ministers, they chose undersecretaries, and they named the chairs and board members of public companies and important public bodies—including the top executives of state-owned or partially state-owned companies.[9] The centrality of the parties, together with the choice to adopt a proportional electoral law, opened doors to what is known as *partitocrazia*: that is, the rule and supremacy of the parties. It also encouraged a continuous negotiation between the ruling majority and the opposition rather than direct confrontation.[10]

The Italian parliament is thus "a highly polycentric institution not easily amenable to majoritarian decisions and to firm leadership by the Cabinet."[11] The legislature is based on equal bicameralism, with the Senate (upper house) and the Chamber of Deputies (lower house) performing identical functions and sharing legislative power (art. 70 of the Italian Constitution).

It has a committee-centered structure and is in many ways a "working parliament." In particular, vertical committees are empowered, under certain conditions, to adopt laws without a vote in the plenary session. Parliamentary procedures also assign a marginal role to the government in parliamentary works. On the other hand, opportunities for individual deputies and minor groups to influence the agenda and/or the legislative process are maximized by a prevailing consociative attitude. All this tends to shape a recognizable organizational and procedural model whereby the parliament acts as a legislator and neglects control and scrutiny functions.[12] In the beginning, this was meant to reduce confrontation and involve opposition parties in the democratic system. Over the years, however, it has weakened the parliament's performance and reduced its effectiveness.

The Italian Parliament and the EU to the Early 1990s

The participation of the Italian parliament in domestic decisionmaking on EU affairs emerged gradually. From the early Community years until the Single European Act, the Italian parliament maintained a "low level of Europeanization" because of its weak structural adaptation, the minimal time and energy it devoted to the scrutiny of EC law, and its general lack of interest in a greater role.[13] Initially, Community affairs were seen as a component of foreign policy and therefore considered primarily a matter for the government. The Chamber of Deputies and the Senate did not establish standing committees for European affairs or set up a specific scrutiny procedure. In both houses, EC legislation and policies were reviewed, sporadically, by the committees for foreign affairs, through the normal parliamentary procedures.

In 1968 the Senate established an ad hoc body for dealing with European affairs—the Giunta per gli affari delle Comunità europee. This decision can be seen as a signal of change in Italy's approach to EU affairs. However, because the Giunta was an ad hoc body, not a standing committee, and had only fact-finding and consultative functions, it had a small impact on parliamentary activities.

Over this period, a significant backlog developed in the implementation of EC directives. More and more frequently, the European Court of Justice condemned Italy for its failure to implement EC law correctly or in a timely fashion. As EC directives were implemented mainly through legislative acts, the parliament and its cumbersome lawmaking procedures were often fingered as the main reason for incomplete implementation. The Single European Act and the expected wave of directives for the completion of the Internal Market finally provided the catalyst for a radical reorganization of internal decision-making on EU matters.

Between 1987 and 1989 the Italian parliament adopted two laws providing the framework for domestic decisionmaking on EU affairs: Law 183/1987, otherwise known as the Fabbri Law, and Law 86/1989, also knows as the La Pergola Law. Taken together, the two laws introduced a number of innovations: they redefined the government's structures for coordinating the national position on EU policies; they made it the government's duty to transmit EC draft legislation to parliament; and they formalized the parliament's right to adopt resolutions on EU matters. Finally, the La Pergola Law also set up the Annual Community Law, a mechanism for the systematic and timely implementation of EU legislation.

As a result, both the Senate (in 1988) and the Chamber of Deputies (in 1990) adapted their internal rules of procedure to take advantage of the opportunities offered by the new legal framework. First, special procedures were established to deal with EC policies. Second, standing committees were empowered to express their position on EC proposals, in a resolution addressed to the government. The Italian parliament came to see participation in decisionmaking on EU affairs not as a way to assert control over Brussels, but as a "temporary extension" of its traditional lawmaking and scrutiny function at a national level, justified by the so-called democratic deficit at the European level.

In organizational terms, the development of specific structures and procedures to deal with EC matters was a smooth process. Since the tasks and competencies entrusted to specialized committees were new, they did not threaten the position of the powerful standing committees. In practice, the reforms had a limited impact and the parliament's influence on EU affairs remained marginal. The parliament's information on EC business was usually insufficient and irregular. The government often failed to fulfill its duty to transmit the Commission's proposals and presented its written reports with significant delays. Even the most significant innovation brought about by Law 86/1989—the power to examine proposals for EC legislation—remained underused. Parliamentary committees examined and debated only a few EC proposals, and the number of resolutions on EC affairs it adopted was even smaller.[14]

On the other hand, the parliament actively developed formal and informal relationships with other national legislatures, as well as with the European Parliament. The first two gatherings of the EU national parliaments—respectively the "Assises" in July 1990 and the first formal meeting of the COSAC (Conference of Community and European Affairs Committees of Parliaments of the European Union)—were hosted by the Italian parliament in Rome. And while contacts between national MPs and Italian MEPs were unsystematic, disorganized, and irregular, the standing committees did communicate frequently with their counterparts in the European Parliament, both bilaterally and multilaterally.

Reforms since the Mid-1990s

Unlike in other countries, such as France, Portugal, and Germany, in Italy the Maastricht Treaty did not raise a debate over parliamentary sovereignty. Nor did it prompt a revision of the domestic framework for EU decisionmaking. However, the Amsterdam Treaty, and subsequently the Constitutional Treaty, did trigger a new wave of reforms, a sign of significant progress in the Europeanization of the Italian parliament. In a context dominated by the national effort to ensure entry into the euro area, the rationale behind the reforms was to promote greater and more proactive national participation in EU decisionmaking, and to adapt the domestic institutional framework to the need to compete and cooperate effectively with partner member states in a more integrated Union.

Although the reforms were driven by a common aspiration, they were fragmented over a series of amendments to the Fabbri and La Pergola Laws. With regard to the parliament, these reforms—embodied in the ratification of the Amsterdam Treaty (Law 209/1998) and in the changes introduced by the "Community Laws" for 1995–1997 (Law 128/1998); 1998 (Law 25/1999); 1999 (Law 526/1999); 2000 (Law 422/2000); and 2001 (Law 39/2002)—expanded the scope of parliamentary scrutiny, obliging the government to forward all draft EU legislation, including second and third pillar acts. They also served to simplify and rationalize the presentation of government reports on EU affairs (Law 25/1999) and they introduced a "soft version" of "parliamentary scrutiny reserve" (Law 422/2000) (discussed later in this chapter).

As during the first wave of reforms after the SEA, the changes in the general institutional framework for relations between Italy and the EU were followed by a revision of the domestic parliamentary rules of procedure. The Chamber of Deputies significantly revised its internal rules of procedure in 1997 and in 1999; the Senate did so in February 2000 and 2003. These changes addressed a number of issues left unresolved by the post-SEA reforms as well as some newly emerging issues. More important, they signaled a qualitative change in the Italian parliament's approach to EU matters. They drew on ideas and suggestions raised in the international debate on better regulation, and they often referred to best practices in the scrutiny of EU affairs as developed by other EU members' parliaments. The circulation and exchange of best practices in interparliamentary forums (such as the COSAC or the Conference of Speakers of European Parliaments) played a significant role in shaping the reformers' ideas in this phase.

Meanwhile, in 1990 the Chamber of Deputies had finally set up an ad hoc Committee for European Affairs, which a few years later was given important powers.

A number of converging factors have led to another wide-ranging revision of the legal framework for Italian participation in EU decisionmaking, with direct implications for the role of the parliament. First, at the European level, the Nice Treaty (and the Constitutional Treaty) brought about important institutional changes. Second, the Italian constitutional reform adopted in 2001 substantially modified the competencies and powers of the regions, giving them a greater role in EU decisionmaking and in the implementation of EU law, as we shall see in chapter 7 (Constitutional Amendment Act no. 3 of October 18, 2001, and Law 131/2003). Third, the accumulation of amendments to the Fabbri and La Pergola Laws fragmented the legal framework into a plurality of sources, thus raising some issues of clarity and consistency. In response to these factors, the parliament adopted Law 11/2005 (also known as the Stucchi-Buttiglione Law), which consolidates and clarifies the legal framework for Italian participation in EU decisionmaking. This law replaced the Fabbri and La Pergola Laws and all of their subsequent amendments.

The Stucchi-Buttiglione Law provides for a comprehensive definition of the domestic decisionmaking process on EU affairs, on the basis of the principles of "subsidiarity, proportionality, efficiency, transparency, and democratic participation." While the major changes concern the role of the regions, the law also introduces some important innovations regarding parliamentary participation. These might provide the basis for a more effective and influential role of the Italian parliament in European affairs. Yet, in the framework of the government's and the parliament's enhanced activism (see chapter 6), a discussion is taking place on whether to amend the Law 11/2005 in order to further enhance the parliament's role.

Standing Committees on EU Policies (or EU Committees): The First Phase

As mentioned above, the Senate created the Giunta per gli affari delle Comunità europee in 1968, entrusting it with fact-finding and consultative functions. However, the Giunta was to have a minimal impact on parliamentary activities. The Chamber of Deputies only set up its Commissione speciale per le politiche comunitarie in 1990. The structure, membership, and modus operandi of the two organs were similar: they were both ad hoc committees, equal to the standing committees in size, structure, and function, but without full legislative power. The Giunta was made up of twenty-four members and the Commissione speciale of forty-eight, all of whom also simultaneously served as full members of a standing committee.

The two committees were relatively "open" structures. The Commissione speciale, with the consent of the president of the Chamber of Deputies, was able to invite Italian members of the European Parliament to attend its meetings, with the right to speak but not to vote.[15] The Chamber of Deputies rules of procedure provided, in addition, for a periodic meeting of the Commissione speciale with a special delegation from the European Parliament (EP) composed of members of the Bureau of the EP presidency, heads of EP political groups, and the president of EP committees at the opening and closing of the rotating EC presidency. This provision was deleted, however, in the reform adopted in July 1999.

The Senate rules of procedure were slightly more restrictive: the attendance of MEPs was limited to a single representative for each political group present in the European Parliament, chosen by common agreement by the president of the Giunta and its European counterparts.[16]

The Commissione speciale and the Giunta usually met two days a week. But because all of the members were also members of another standing committee, regular attendance at the meetings was spotty, as was the continuity of their work. Meetings, in fact, had to compete for space and time with those of the standing committees.

The two ad hoc committees had horizontal functions, but they were vested with a greater role in the area of EC norm implementation than in the scrutiny of government positions within European negotiations. The powerful standing committees had the primary responsibility for reviewing proposals for EC legislation in their respective subject areas. The specialized committees were entitled to receive all Community documents and could adopt resolutions or reports on the institutional aspects of EC activities. It was not their duty to review all European proposals and report to the standing committees, but they could adopt an opinion on a specific proposal being examined by a standing committee. In implementing EC law, the specialized committees played a full coordination role. All draft legislation for the implementation of Community directives and regulations—as well as any proposals for new legislation that fell within the purview of Community competencies—were to be referred to the Giunta and the Commissione speciale with a view to receiving an opinion on their consistency with existing Community law.[17]

While the specialized and the standing committees shared the power to monitor government conduct within European negotiations, only the specialized committees were empowered to review the twice-yearly government report on Community policy before it was debated in the plenary session. In addition, the specialized committees were responsible for reviewing Community legislation after its adoption and, in the Chamber, the rulings of the European Court of Justice. Finally, they could question ministers about draft proposals for EC legislation, as well as on general EC policy issues. These committees were also allowed to invite high-ranking public officials to testify before them, with the assent of the competent minister. Members of the Chamber of Deputies could also employ traditional control and information procedures to spark a debate on Community issues. Usually the two committees had a consensual working style, kept conflict low-key, maintained a nonpartisan attitude, and engaged in dialogue with the executive in an informal and cooperative atmosphere.

The scope of parliamentary scrutiny included the full range of Community legislative activities. According to Law 183/1987, the government was to transmit all proposals of regulations, directives, and decisions within thirty days of their reception, as well as the legal acts adopted by Community institutions, together with a short assessment of their impact on the domestic legal order. Furthermore, Law 86/1989 provided for greater parliamentary access to written information on Community developments. Every six months, the government was to present to both houses a report on Italy's participation in Community policy and, every year, a general report focusing on the progress made by the European Community toward the achievement of the Internal Market, with special attention to the effects of regional policies and to the national management of Structural Funds. The latter report was also to cover the activities performed by the WEU (Western European Union) and the Council of Europe (articles 7 and 8, Law 86/1989).

The Giunta, the Commissione speciale, and the standing committees (in their respective subject areas) could review draft EC legislation once the proposals were published in the Italian Official Journal and adopt a resolution. In most cases, the review of EU proposals could be accomplished in one meeting. Should the political relevance of the issue require it, it could be debated over one or more supplementary meetings, allowing members to ask for oral or written evidence before deliberating. The scrutiny could end with the adoption of a resolution—carrying only a politically binding value—or, indeed, without any formal decision. Whereas the Senate rules of procedure (art. 143 c. 6) expressly stated that the Giunta and the standing committees could vote on a resolution at the end of the scrutiny process (describing in detail the structure of the resolution), the Chamber of Deputies rules (art. 127) made no reference to a formal parliamentary act, simply indicating that the competent committees "may express, in a final report, their opinion on the opportunity of future initiatives." When the committees debated resolutions on EU affairs, the government was to be present and could propose amendments, ask for the postponement of the vote, or request to defer it to the plenary body. The scrutiny procedure was decentralized, in line with the parliament's purpose as a "working parliament." The plenary body was not permitted to debate and/or vote on a resolution if it was scheduled to be discussed in a committee.

Nevertheless, the practice in the 1990s was a mixed one. The parliament's information about EC business was insufficient and irregular. The government failed to fulfill its duty to transmit Commission proposals and often forwarded the written reports with significant delays—usually in a generic and superficial manner—so that any detailed parliamentary debate was rendered meaningless. Not surprisingly, the parliament's participation in EC policymaking was marginal. Most of the work was carried out by the specialized committees, while standing committees and the assembly were, to a great extent, isolated from the European arena. Only a handful of deputies were active and knowledgeable in European affairs.[18]

The case of the EC directive on the legal protection of biotechnological inventions provides an example of the many contradictions inherent in the role played by parliament in those years. The Italian parliament began considering the issue many months before the proposal reached the Council for a final decision. In 1997 the standing committee on agriculture undertook an inquiry that lasted until October, and ended up recommending that the proposal be rejected. Meanwhile, in August 1997 the European Commission had submitted to the Council and parliament a modified proposal. On November 26, 1997, the Committee for Agriculture in the Chamber of Deputies passed a resolution calling on the government to delay adopting the directive; on November 27 the Council reached a political agreement on a common position. On February 16, 1998, the Committee for Social Affairs in the Chamber of Deputies began debating a draft resolution recommending that the government oppose the directive; further, it requested a moratorium on the production and use of genetically modified organisms in Europe. While the draft resolution was waiting to be voted on, the Council adopted its common position; the Italian government abstained. A couple of weeks later, the Committee for Social Affairs formally adopted the resolution to oppose the directive. On the same day, the Senate passed a motion requesting the suspension of the directive and promoting the elaboration of a new directive with more stringent requirements for the patentability of biotechnological inventions. Nevertheless, the Council approved the directive on July 6, 1998; again, Italy abstained. Later on, the Italian government decided to take part in the action for annulment brought before the European Court of Justice by the Dutch government. Pending the court's judgment, the Italians, given their diverging views on the matter, excluded the directive from the Annual Community Bill and introduced to parliament a specific piece of legislation to implement the directive. The bill met with the resistance of a large coalition of parliamentary forces, which sought to force the government to ask that the directive be rewritten or that concessions be made in the implementing legislation. Parliamentary obstruction prevented the timely implementation of the directive, thus leading to tension with the European Commission.

This case illustrates not only how little input the parliament usually had in Italy's EU decisionmaking, but also how woefully uncoordinated its attempts at intervention were. Such a pattern has led observers to describe the Europeanization of the Italian parliament as protracted and insufficient. Some authors have even described the slow adaptation to EU dynamics as a deliberate effort to protect the specific organizational and functional characteristics of the Italian parliament from the pressures for change coming from the European arena.[19] By the mid-1990s, Italy's lack of Europeanization was widely perceived as unsatisfactory and dysfunctional. Changes at the European level and internal developments then provided the catalyst for a second and comprehensive process of reform, which took place after the negotiation of the Amsterdam Treaty.[20]

The Standing Committees on EU Policy: Changes since the Late 1990s

In the years 1998–1999 a number of significant reforms took place. The first step was taken on August 1, 1996, when the ad hoc committee in the Chamber of Deputies was transformed into a standing committee, "XIV Committee—EU Policies." The objective of this change was to raise the political profile and authority of the committee, to facilitate the meetings, and to make the standing committee an engine for all activities in parliament linked to EU affairs.

In 1997 and 1999 the procedures concerning European affairs were also significantly revised in the Chamber of Deputies itself. All of the reforms had two broad goals (which went hand in hand with the reform of the government's structure for EU policy management that is described in chapter 6): first, to update the instruments for dealing with European affairs, so as to promote a proactive and anticipatory style of policymaking and to establish a stricter link between the negotiating and implementing phases in EC policymaking; second, to modify the parliament's philosophy when dealing with European affairs by introducing the issues of quality and of coherence in legislation, in accordance with OECD guidelines.

On the whole, four main directions were set in reorganizing the role of the parliament in European affairs: (a) to revise the institutional setting, at least in the Chamber; (b) to reinforce access to EU information; (c) to update the rules allowing for the scrutiny of EC legislative proposals and for political control over government action within European institutions; (d) to introduce a policy that would enhance the quality of legislation implementation.

The Senate was slower to follow suit: the Senate's internal rules were not changed until February 2000, and only in 2003 was the old Committee on European Affairs finally replaced by the Standing Committee on EU Policies, also called "XIV Committee"

The Senate and the Chamber committees have similar terms of reference and powers, though they differ somewhat in size and membership. The Chamber of Deputies' XIV Committee has, on average, forty members, who are not allowed to be full members of any other standing committee at the same time. The Senate's XIV Committee usually has thirty members; they, on the contrary, can also sit on other committees.[21] The latter approach is to ensure that members of the EU affairs committee combine knowledge of EU affairs with an expertise in issues dealt with in the sector-specific committees. This practice also ensures a bridge between the work done in the "horizontal" EU committee and in the "vertical" sector-specific committees. In fact, the

Senate Rules of Procedure state that, when standing committees are reviewing a legislative proposal, the senators who are also members of XIV Committee have to report on its compatibility with EU law in light of the opinion adopted by the committee. The downside is that double membership can negatively affect attendance at meetings; to help, meetings are often organized during lunch time or early in the morning.

Members of the two committees are appointed at the beginning of each parliamentary term by the presidents of the two houses, reflecting the indications given by parliamentary groups and their balance in the plenary body. Committees are renewed every two and half years, but members can be reappointed and usually are. The committees elect a chairman, usually drawn from the parliamentary majority, two vice chairmen, and two secretaries, collectively known as the Bureau. The chairman represents the committee in its relations with other committees and outside the parliament; he or she convenes the meetings, presides over the orderly conduct of business, and has an influential role in shaping the agenda. The Bureau sets up the calendar of meetings. The committees usually meet two or three days a week. Committee meetings are closed to the public; however, the minutes of the debates and the relevant documents under consideration are published shortly after each meeting. In addition, the chairman may authorize the broadcast of a session for the press or for visitors through the internal television channel.

The committees can rely on backup from parliamentary services. Special departments in the Senate and Chamber of Deputies provide assistance to the secretariat of the meetings and also monitor EU legislative developments, draft legal opinions, and prepare background documents. Both houses have also opened an office in Brussels, located within the building of the European Parliament.

The two committees are still "open" structures. With the consent of the president of the Chamber of Deputies, the committees may invite members of the European Parliament or the European Commission to present evidence on the activities and policies of EU institutions.[22] Both committees may hold hearings of public officials from the national administration, with the consent of the competent minister, and of representatives from economic and social groups or nongovernmental organizations (NGOs). They may also acquire all documents necessary for the conduct of their fact-finding or scrutiny activities.

With regard to their powers and responsibilities, the primary responsibility of the EU committees is to check on the compatibility of national legislation with EU law and to ensure that EU treaties are incorporated into national legislation.[23] The primary responsibility for the scrutiny of Commission proposals or of draft domestic legislation aimed at implementing EU secondary legislation normally lies with the powerful standing committees. Still, as before, the committees on EU policies are entitled to receive all relevant documents; they may call in ministers to discuss a Commission proposal and they may adopt an opinion addressed to the competent standing committee, but they do not have the general function of sifting through European proposals and reporting to the standing committees. However, if the standing committee does not take a position on the proposals assigned to it for review, the EU committee may request to take a position on it by itself. A stronger role is foreseen in the review and discussion of the government's report on EU affairs, where the EU committees can present a report to the plenary body, after consulting the sector-specific committees. When they deal with institutional issues or the politics of the EU, the committees are also responsible for reviewing resolutions adopted by the European Parliament. Deputies may also avail themselves of normal control and information procedures to initiate a debate on EC/EU issues.

On matters related to the implementation of Community rules and to the compliance of domestic rules with EU law, the powers of the committees on EU policy are stronger. Each committee has the lead role in its house's examination of the Annual Community Law. This marks a sharp difference with the past: in the Senate, until the 2003 reform, this role was a prerogative of the powerful Committee for Constitutional Affairs. In addition, today's committees must be consulted on government proposals for the implementation of EU secondary legislation as well as on proposals that might raise issues of conformity with EU legislation. They can make observations or adopt an opinion on these texts, which are then addressed to the relevant standing committee for that subject matter. The rules of procedure in the Chamber of Deputies and the Senate provide that when XIV Committee issues a negative opinion on draft proposals, the proposal cannot be adopted by the standing committee (in a so-called decentralized adoption procedure), but has to be discussed and voted on in the plenary session. In connection with the constitutional reform of 2001, which assigned a greater role in EU affairs to the regions, article 23 of the Senate Rules of Procedure demands that the EU Committee examine the compatibility and coordination of any proposed measures with regard to regional competencies, as set out in article 117 of the Constitution. The committee must also examine the proposed measure's compatibility and coordination with the subsidiarity principle, as set out in article 120 of the Constitution. The Committee on EU Policies thus assumes the crucial role of ensuring the smooth coordination of various layers of legislation and competency—European, national, and regional.[24] Finally, the EU committees have the right to appoint a rapporteur when standing committees review the "most important" rulings of the European Court of Justice. This scrutiny can eventually lead to the adoption of a resolution by the government.[25]

The EU committees are also responsible for interparliamentary relations, and in particular for cooperation with the European Parliament and the COSAC.

Like their predecessors (the Giunta and Commissione speciale), the two committees are still characterized by a consensual working style; their conflicts are normally low-key and nonpartisan, and they engage in dialogue with the executive in an informal and cooperative atmosphere.

Control over the Government's Participation in EU Decisionmaking: Fact Finding and Policy-Setting Activities

The Italian parliament has gradually developed a wide range of instruments to acquire information on EU policy developments and to discuss the government's orientation on EU affairs. This is a prerequisite for exercising its role in the scrutiny of EU draft legislation and in the subsequent implementation of EU law.

Under article 3 of the Stucchi-Buttiglione Law, before each European Council, the Italian government has to provide both houses of its legislature with the agenda for the meeting and inform them of the position it intends to adopt. The government is then obligated to report on the results of the meetings of the European Council within fifteen days after the meeting. Also, upon request from the competent standing committees, the relevant minister must brief the committee on the forthcoming meetings of the Council of the Union. In addition, in twice-yearly reports, the prime minister or the minister for European policy must keep the houses abreast of the main issues and the most politically sensitive initiatives planned or under discussion at the EU level.[26]

The second major source of information on EU affairs for the parliament is the government's annual report on the EU. Since the enactment of Law 25/1999, this report has replaced a number of written reports that the government was previously required to submit throughout the year. It is meant to provide a comprehensive overview of the state of play of EU affairs, reviewing both what happened in the previous year and the government's priorities for the next twelve months. According to article 15 of Law 11/2005, the report should cover the following: (a) the state of play of EU policies, including security and defense policy as well as justice and home affairs; (b) the main guidelines of the government's position on negotiations in future EU legislation; (c) the implementation of cohesive regional policies in Italy, with particular reference to the use of funds allocated to Italy, referring, when appropriate, to the reports adopted by the European Court of Auditors; (d) the follow-up given to the resolutions and observations adopted by the legislature and by regional authorities; (e) the list of cases in which the government has decided to challenge, before the European Court of Justice, a decision adopted by the Council or by the European Commission.

The report should be presented to both houses every year before January 31, together with the government's draft proposal for the Annual Community Act. However, this has not always happened. The correlation between the presentation of the annual report and the tabling of the Annual Community Act—in a "Session on Community Affairs"—is designed to provide more focus and prominence for the parliamentary debate on EU affairs. The idea is to concentrate the discussion on a range of aspects regarding national participation in EU decisionmaking, combining the forward-looking discussion of trends in EU policymaking with the implementation of EU legislation on a domestic level. The model chosen was that of the budget session in which, in the second semester of each year, the parliament examines the budget and sets guidelines for future economic legislation.

The Senate and the Chamber of Deputies have put in place similar procedures for the joint discussion of the annual report and the draft Community Act that require the participation of both the committees on EU affairs and sector-specific standing committees. In short, the committees for European policies examine the annual report and present an opinion to the plenary body, taking into account the comments received from the other standing committees. This opinion, together with the Annual Community Act, is then considered by the plenary body. MPs may table resolutions on the annual report. These are voted on after the final vote on the Annual Community Act.[27]

Since the year 2000, the two houses of the legislature also discuss the Commission Legislative and Work Program (CWLP) and the Council's Annual Program. The aim here is to enhance the Italian parliament's ability to identify future issues in the EU system. The procedure, introduced on a trial basis in March 2000, follows the one prescribed for the annual report, involving the standing committees, the EU committees, and the plenary session, and ending with a vote on a resolution. The committees for EU policies review the program and adopt a report, which is then discussed and adopted by the plenary session. While in previous years the debate on the CLWP had not had a significant impact (it took place too late in the year owing to late transmission by the government and scheduling problems within the houses), in 2006 both houses succeeded in examining the programs in the first months of the year. The Senate adopted its resolution on the CLWP and the Annual Program of the Austrian and Finnish Presidencies on January 26, 2006. The Resolution on the 2005 CLWP had been adopted on November 9, 2005. This allowed the parliament to take part in the pilot project "Raising European Awareness" launched by the Conference of Speakers of the EU Parliaments, aimed at encouraging national parliaments to hold coinciding debates on the CLWP.

Existing rules prevent representatives of private interests or organizations from appearing before the EU committees. Thus the committees have turned to a wider use of inquiries to gain access to outside sources of expertise. Inquiries allow them to exchange views with business and trade unions, NGOs, and other organized interests. Usually, inquiries are launched without reference to a single proposal for EU legislation. Rather, they deal with broad issues, which remain on the EU agenda for a longer period of time, or aim at evaluating the implementation of existing regulations in order to suggest amendments or new initiatives. During the XIVth legislature (2001–2006), in the Chamber of Deputies, major inquiries were held on the EU decisionmaking process, on EU initiatives for strengthening competitiveness, and on 2007–2013 financial perspectives (jointly with V Committee on Budget, Finances, and Programming). During the same period, the Senate carried out two inquiries on the objectives of the Lisbon strategy and on the proposal for a directive on services in the Internal Market (jointly with the Committee on Industry, Trade, and Tourism). Furthermore, a joint Senate/Chamber inquiry was conducted on the future of the EU.

In the short XVth legislature (2006–2008) the EU committees of the two houses conducted a joint inquiry into the reform of the EU treaties. And since November 2008, the EU committee in the Chamber of Deputies has been working on possible reforms of Law 11/2005, while the Senate EU committee is inquiring into the use of EU funds.

Scrutiny of EU Draft Legislation

Since the end of the 1980s, the Italian parliament has gradually developed a "document-based" system for scrutinizing EU draft legislation. In practice, however, the parliament's influence on the government has remained limited. Parliaments' opinions are sent to CIACE, the government's interministerial coordinating body for European affairs, but they are too general (and often too late) to be usefully employed in defining the Italian position. Indeed, one result of the inquiry the Chamber's EU committee set up in 2009 is that the parliament is still very slow to provide input, a practice that does not suit the fast EU decisionmaking and lawmaking procedures. Also, the recommendations of the Italian parliament tend to be very generic, in contrast with the detailed and technical character of most EU directives.[28] Although some reasons for this limited input can be found in structural factors (a focus on legislation rather than on control functions, the lower importance attached to European affairs than to domestic issues, general pro-European feelings), parliamentary control over EU affairs has in fact suffered from more practical and concrete weaknesses. Four major problems have emerged in the recent past: incomplete and late transmission of draft legislation by the government; lack of access to technical information clarifying the background and impact of EU legislation; bad timing of parliamentary scrutiny; and absence of feedback on the follow-up given to parliamentary resolutions. The Stucchi-Buttiglione Law addresses these unresolved issues. The lawmakers had hoped it could lay the groundwork for a more effective use of scrutiny powers. But since the problems remain, there are now talks of revising the law further. To speed up the parliamentary process, the parliament's own rules of procedure might need to be adapted, and this, paradoxically, is not so easy to achieve.

The prime minister or the minister for European policies is to transmit to the parliament (and also to the regions) all proposals for EU legislation and their subsequent modifications, together with an indication of their likely date of discussion or adoption. This obligation extends to the transmission of any green and white papers produced by the Commission, as well as any official communications or other consultative documents (Law 11/2005, Law 128/1998, Law 209/1998, and Law 422/2000). In addition, the Department for European Policies of the Presidency of the Council of Ministers is charged with keeping the houses regularly informed of the state of play on proposals forwarded to them. This department is also charged with informing the houses—without delay—when these proposals are put on the agenda of a meeting of the Council of the Union.

The houses' standing committees can then examine those acts and adopt resolutions or forward their opinions to the government. The precise mechanisms for parliamentary scrutiny are further spelled out in the two houses' rules of procedure.[29]

In order to perform their scrutiny, the standing committees can request additional written information from government departments on the state of play of Council negotiations on a proposal. They may also request information on the views and opinions expressed by stakeholders, on compliance costs for the administration, and on the estimated impact on the domestic legal system, on businesses, and on citizens. Indeed, article 13 of Law 128/1998 requests that the transmission of EU acts that have already been adopted be accompanied by a short assessment of the internal regulations that will need to be amended in order to implement those acts. However, such information applies to future implementation rather than to the scrutiny of EU proposals in the earliest stages of discussion.

This provision is meant to facilitate more substantial scrutiny of EU proposals. As the government usually has on hand a wealth of material and information to which the parliament does not have access, it makes more sense for the parliament to request that information from the government than to try to replicate it. Once the parliament has reviewed all of the evidence, it can decide whether the government position is justified or not.

Parliamentary Scrutiny Reserve

One of the most important innovations brought about by the Stucchi-Buttiglione Law was the introduction of the "parliamentary scrutiny reserve." Previously, the Italian parliament had often voiced its dissatisfaction at not being able to keep up with the pace and schedule of discussions on proposals within the Council of the Union. In some cases, the parliament voted on a proposed EU measure only to discover that the proposal had been adopted by the Council a few days earlier. The introduction of a scrutiny reserve similar to that in the UK system had come to be seen as the best remedy to such situations. Briefly, parliamentary scrutiny reserve allows government representatives in the Council not to take an official position on an issue until the national parliament has examined it.

The government was reluctant initially, but it finally accepted a "soft version" of the principle, as set out in article 6 of Law 422/2000. When forwarding EU draft legislation to parliament, the government was required to indicate its expected date of adoption explicitly. If the houses had not expressed their opinion by that deadline or, at the very least, before the meeting of the Council during which the proposal was to be adopted, the government was free to vote.

If this provision aimed at ensuring at least some synchrony between the EU legislative process and the agenda of parliamentary committees, the new provisions introduced with article 4 of the Stucchi-Buttiglione Law (Law 11/2005) marked a further step forward. As the law exists today, once the parliament starts considering a draft EU legislative act, the government has to wait for it to conclude its scrutiny before exercising its own powers within the Council. The only exception is if parliament has not issued an opinion within twenty days. This time limit runs from the day the government informs the houses that it has put a parliamentary scrutiny reserve in the Council. Scrutiny reserve may be requested by the parliament, but can also be issued by the government on its own initiative. For legislative proposals or other measures of particular political, economic, or social importance, the government may decide to put a parliamentary scrutiny reserve on the text under discussion within the Council or on some parts of it and inform the parliament of this decision, implicitly inviting it to offer its views on the subject matter. If after twenty days the parliament has not issued an opinion, the government can proceed to exercise its powers.

This "dual nature" of parliamentary scrutiny reserve shows how the government's approach to parliamentary control in EU affairs is changing. It shows, in fact, a greater understanding of the parliament's need for time and information as a prerequisite to effective scrutiny, as well as a more positive view of parliament's role in domestic decisionmaking on EU affairs. The parliament is no longer seen as an antagonist but as an ally, and its control is not an unwelcome interference but a tool to reinforce the quality and effectiveness of the Italian position within Council negotiations. Legend has it that Rocco Buttiglione (when he was minister for EU policies in the Berlusconi II government and thus in charge of the Single Market Council) noticed at a certain point that the wise use of certain forms of parliamentary scrutiny reserve could be very useful for the negotiating delegations; he thus began acting as if Italy had one too, and then began working on a law that would actually allow Italy to use the parliamentary scrutiny tool.

The new system of scrutiny reserve, however, has yet to be employed effectively. The success of this instrument requires both the parliament and the government to use it. It also requires the parliament to complete the scrutiny quickly. To this end, the Senate and the Chamber of Deputies rules state that the likely calendar of adoption at the EU level of relevant legislative proposals should be taken into account by standing committees when preparing their own agendas, but the committees have yet to implement this provision much in practice.[30]

Finally, two instruments have been introduced to ensure that the government is held accountable for following up on the parliament's resolutions. First, the prime minister or the minister for EU policies (or the foreign minister) is to inform the parliament of the outcome of Council negotiations within fifteen days after the Council meeting. This statutory provision reinforces what is already possible under the parliament's rules of procedure, by which standing committees may always call in ministers to provide information on the outcome of negotiations or on the follow-up given to parliamentary resolutions. Scarce at the beginning, such post-Council sessions are now routine. Second, in the annual report on EU policies, the government has to report on the follow-up given to parliamentary resolutions and to observations made by regional authorities. The annual reports, therefore, are now very detailed documents describing government action in the EU.

Overall, the available data highlight a steady increase in the parliament's attention to European affairs. Nevertheless, it is interesting to note that a significant part of this increased attention is channeled through procedures other than formal scrutiny—primarily through oral hearings. In fact, deputies as well as ministers find oral evidence procedures speedier than formal scrutiny and more suitable to an informal and cooperative exchange of views. Such hearings are not only organized with members of the executive branch but also with a variety of subjects, from European Commissioners to Commission officials, from members of the European Parliament to officials dealing with EU affairs in the various branches of the Italian public administration, from the governor of the Bank of Italy to the director of the special coordination unit for the management of Structural Funds, and so on. In many cases, therefore, hearings on EU proposals have replaced legislative scrutiny.

The Italian Parliament's Role in the Implementation of EU Legislation: The Annual Community Law

For a long time, the discussion and adoption of measures implementing EU legislation represented the main access point to the EU policy process for the Italian parliament. The focal point for the parliament's involvement in the implementation phase was the Annual Community Law, set up in 1989 with the La Pergola Law, and subsequently amended several times. It is currently regulated by Law 11/2005. The purpose of the Annual Community Law is to ensure the regular, systematic, and timely incorporation of EU legislation into the national legal order. The discussion and approval of a given bill is conducted in parallel with the discussion of the government's annual report on EU affairs, thus creating a sort of "Community session," during which the parliament focuses exclusively on EU policies.

By virtue of the mechanisms introduced with the Community Law, the parliament can have a complete picture of the measures to be incorporated in the national legal order, and then decide on the most appropriate legal tool for doing so (law, delegated legislation, regulation, etc.). The rationale behind the Community Act is therefore to strike a balance between efficiency and democratic control. On one hand, by combining several implementing measures in a single package, the government can speed up adoption and reduce the chances of having an individual measure held up by parliament. On the other hand, parliament obtains information and oversees a number of measures that would normally be adopted by the government or the regions without its participation.

Every year, by January 31, the government must submit to the parliament a bill containing all EC regulations, directives, decisions, and EU framework decisions adopted in the previous calendar year and that need to be implemented in the national framework.

The bill is to be accompanied by a report providing an overview of the state of compliance of the national legislation with the Community Law. This report should fulfill the following requirements: cover pending infringement procedures and decisions adopted by the European Court of Justice;[31] provide a list of directives already implemented or to be implemented by government agencies or through administrative acts (thus not included in the bill); explain the reasons for the exclusion from the bill of any EC/EU legislative acts whose deadline for implementation expires within the reference year; and finally, list the regulatory measures through which regions and autonomous provinces may implement directives on matters within their competence. The 300-plus annual regulations are comprehensive and important documents for understanding Italy's participation in the EU.

The Annual Community Law may provide for the direct implementation of EU legislation by amending or abrogating national provisions that conflict with Community obligations or that are subject to infringement procedures. Alternatively, it may authorize the government to adopt implementing measures: these can be in the form of delegated legislation (which must respect the principles and guidelines laid down by the parliament in the Community Law itself) or in the form of regulations in areas previously controlled by other primary legislation, but where an act of parliament is not constitutionally mandatory. In addition, the Community Law sets out the following: principles that should guide regions and autonomous provinces in defining implementing measures in their own fields of competence; provisions that enable the national government to pass legislative measures if a region is unable to implement the EU legislation within the set deadlines.

In principle, the Annual Community Law covers all EU legislation to be implemented by individual countries. However, for acts of particular importance, or when implementation is urgent, the government is free to present to parliament a separate, specific implementing measure.

The discussion and approval of the bill is conducted in parallel with the discussion of the government's annual report on EU affairs, thus creating the "Community session" described above, during which the parliament focuses exclusively on EU policies.

While at first the Community Law made halting progress at best, the system is now working. Statistics show that the Annual Community Law has helped to significantly reduce Italy's previously poor implementation record. However, the anticipated legislative elections of 2008 prevented the consolidation of Italy's performance; they slowed down the implementation of the 2007 and 2008 Community Laws. Therefore, while a few years ago Italy was performing in line with the member states, in 2007 the country failed to incorporate 1.5 percent of the European directives, and by 2009, 1.7 percent of European directives.[32] Parliament continues to work too slowly: by the time the Community Law is ready there are many more directives to be enacted. It has been suggested that one way to mend this problem would be to have two Community Laws each year.

Great effort has been made to prevent infringement procedures or to resolve existing ones. Indeed, there were 213 pending infringement procedures against Italy in September 2007, 181 in June 2008, 155 in June 2009, and 127 as of September 2010.[33] However, that effort is almost useless if one of the sources of infringements is the enacting body itself! It is also worth noting that, in the past, a significant share of the infringement procedures against Italy related to incorrect implementation or to inconsistency of national legislation with Community standards rather than to an outright failure to adopt specific measures.

Apart from the Annual Community Act, the two legislative chambers are involved in the implementation of EU law through other channels. The standing committees can review and adopt resolutions on the acts adopted by the EU institutions and on decisions of the European Court of Justice. Most important, for each legislative proposal discussed by the parliament, the committees on EU policies offer an opinion on its conformity with EU law.

Accordingly, several measures have been introduced by parliament to enhance the quality of implementing legislation and to ensure greater coherence between domestic and EU regulations. As things stand now, one of the mandatory parameters to be considered by the Chamber of Deputies' standing committees when conducting the pre-legislative evaluation of domestic bills is their consistency with EC legislation. The opinion of the Committee for EU policies on the consistency of internal legislation with EU norms has also been given greater weight. In short, this means that the standing committee may overrule a negative opinion issued by another committee only after obtaining a favorable vote from the plenary session.

The Chamber has also included the Community Law among the instruments to be evaluated by the Committee for Legislation, an ad hoc body established in 1998 and composed of ten representatives of the Chamber of

Deputies. The Committee for Legislation provides the other standing committees with "neutral" advice concerning the quality of legislation, some categories of bills, and schemes of governmental regulations: in certain cases, this is obligatory; in others it can be requested by a minority of members of the committee. Its opinion may only be overruled by a vote of the plenary session.

As regards the simplification of legislation, the most noteworthy innovation is the shift from fragmented initiatives to an organic and periodic program within the framework of the annual simplification law introduced with Law 50 of March 8, 1999. This system envisions that each year the government will present both houses with a program for the simplification and reorganization of existing legislation in a set of areas listed therein. On the basis of guidelines set out by the parliament, the government adopts—within a fixed timetable—consolidated texts. These repeal obsolete provisions, amend and coordinate norms, and systematically identify legislative rules, administrative regulations, and relevant EU legislation on the same subject. Parliamentary committees monitor the enactment of consolidated texts.

Participation in COSAC's Activities and Other Interparliamentary Bodies

The Italian parliament takes an active part in COSAC meetings—the gathering of EU committees from the various EU member states' parliaments. The Italian delegation is composed of representatives from the Bureaus of both of the houses' committees for EU policies. Participation in COSAC debates provides Italian deputies with an important opportunity to share best practices with their EU counterparts and to acquire first-hand information about other parliaments' experiences with the scrutiny of EU affairs. COSAC debates played an important role, for example, in shaping the ideas that drove Italy's reforms of parliamentary participation in EU decisionmaking mentioned above. Indeed, the Italian parliament favored the further development of COSAC and supported the proposal to establish a permanent secretariat. The Italian parliament also actively participated in the meetings of the EU parliament's Conference of Speakers.

Conclusions

Any independent observer, looking at the Italian parliament's role in EU affairs, should remain impressed by the improvements made in the twenty-first century. In a short span of time the Italian parliament has successfully addressed many issues that had remained unresolved for years, thus greatly reducing the gap between itself and the national parliaments that were best organized in the scrutiny of EU affairs. While maintaining its traditional model of "paper-based scrutiny," the parliament now has in place a full-fledged scrutiny system based on the leading role of permanent committees specialized in EU affairs. It has expanded the scope of its scrutiny of EU policies; it is regularly informed of developments in EU affairs; it has developed clear procedures for scrutiny and fact-finding; it is even protected in its prerogatives by the introduction of a scrutiny reserve system. This progress is also matched by further developments within the executive branch: the government has finally created a coordinating body for EU affairs, CIACE (described in the next chapter).

Moreover, recent legislative changes signal a significant evolution in the way relations between Europe and the Italian parliament are perceived. In the 1980s, scrutiny of EU legislation was considered a matter for the European Parliament. The national parliaments were then called on to scrutinize EU policies as a way of compensating for the democratic deficit at the European level. The Italian parliament's action on EU affairs thus focused on implementing EU directives.

In the wave of reforms that followed the signing of the Amsterdam Treaty, the parliament's role in EU affairs moved away from the implementation of EU directives and toward a more positive and proactive role in shaping the national position on draft EU legislation. This reflects the idea that the EU and Italian political systems are no longer two "separate legal orders"; they are rather deeply interconnected. Consequently, the national parliament's participation in EU decisionmaking is also essential to the quality of domestic legislation; the parliament must consider EU policy priorities when legislating. Conversely, parliamentary input can be instrumental in assessing the likely impact of draft EU legislation on the domestic system, thus contributing to the preparation of a stronger and better argued national position in negotiations within the Council. In this way the Italian government and parliament become allies, not rivals, in the formulation of national positions on EU policy.

Still, despite this positive trend, there is room for improvement. Parliamentary work needs to be speeded up; the parliament's opinions should become less generic and more specific; and, last but not least, there is a need to improve the implementation record and the compatibility of national law with EU law.

6

Adapting the State Machine: The Executive

In most of the European Union's member states, national executives tend to dominate their legislatures in EU affairs. Vincent Wright, Hussein Kassim, and Guy Peters write about "institutional convergence" in the member states:[1]

—Prime ministers' roles and resources in EU affairs have grown significantly since the mid-1980s.

—Foreign ministers still play a central role, yet their dominance has eroded. Most often they act as coordinators of EU affairs, not least because the Permanent Representatives in Brussels respond to them.

—Virtually every national minister is affected by EU policymaking, and all of them have some sort of support unit for dealing with it.

—Almost every member state has a minister of EU affairs, but they are often junior figures.

—Relations between the legislative and executive branches have been affected by EU affairs, generally resulting in a weakening of the legislature.

Yet there are also a number of dissimilarities:

—The role and powers of each foreign minister and of other ministries differ significantly from country to country.

—Members' coordinating mechanisms vary significantly in shape and goals. Some states (France, the United Kingdom, Portugal, Denmark) use them to define their national positions, while others have more modest aims.

—The connections between formal and informal coordination, administrative procedures, and political decisionmaking vary too, from well integrated (in France, Denmark, and Germany) to disconnected (in Italy).

Naturally, not all results can be traced back to interministerial coordination; however, the literature stresses the importance of efficient coordination in policymaking. The lack of such coordination, as we shall see below, represents a major weakness for Italy.

The Italian Form of Government

The Constitution of the Italian Republic, drafted in 1948 after the troubled fascist period, was the result of many political compromises. Indeed, the Constitution limited itself to outlining a grand design for the nation, leaving the details to future lawmakers. For example, it mentioned Italy's government in articles 92 to 96, but did not attempt to regulate the details—something that took a long time for the law to do. Until the late 1980s, in fact, the government's work and structure were based on a juxtaposition of old laws—almost century-old laws like the Decreto Zanardelli of 1901 and the Legge Rocco of 1925—and customs. Law 400/1988 aimed to order things more clearly, reorganizing the Presidency of the Council for instance. Yet because this task was only partially achieved, a number of new laws were issued in the 1990s, culminating in a major reform of the government in 1999 (Law 300/1999).

The Italian government is entrusted with providing political and administrative direction. It does not have autonomous legislative power, as is the case in Portugal, for example. Only in "urgent" cases can it issue decrees that have the force of law, but even those must be transformed into actual laws by the parliament within sixty days. In truth, because the parliament is not particularly efficient, practice differs widely from theory: the distorted and repeated use of decrees and confidence votes (to force the parliament to approve problematic laws) has led to a de facto dominance of the executive in lawmaking.

In constitutional terms, the prime minister (juridically, Italy has a president of the Council, not a prime minister, but for the sake of simplicity, we shall call him prime minister here) is a particularly weak actor. He is *primus inter pares* (first among equals), while most of his European counterparts are *primus supra pares.*[2] He is appointed by the president of the republic and can take office only after receiving a vote of confidence from the parliament. In principle, he selects his ministers. However, in doing so, he has to respect the "suggestions" of party leaders. Only the Amato I government (1992–93) broke this unwritten rule,[3] followed, to some extent, by the Berlusconi II and III governments (2001–06) and the Berlusconi IV government (2008–present). The Council of Ministers—in principle a collegial body—has in fact never been considered an effective center for policy coordination. Indeed, the level of collegiality is usually quite low, while interministerial competition is generally high. The mechanism allowing for the easy use of the "no-confidence vote" further weakens the Italian government. In Giuliano Amato's words: "Italy is an excellent example of the theory of involution expounded by Mancur Olson: a vital system that becomes progressively rigid, incapable of correcting its increasing entropy, and unable to keep up with the need for change, is finally destroyed by the impact on its corrupted tissues of newly emerging counterforces."[4]

Whereas in countries like Portugal the "importance" of a minister is determined by his or her ranking—as listed in the law giving birth to each government—in Italy there is no formal ranking of the ministries. There is nevertheless an important informal ranking, as laid out in the *Manuale Cencelli*, a sort of political manual about how to share power in a complex coalition setting. In it, Massimiliano Cencelli, a Christian Democrat official, not only ranked the ministries but also assigned a "value" to the undersecretaries of state, as well as to all the different chairmanships that exist within and outside the parliament.

When a new government comes into power in Italy, for instance, the governing bodies of every state-owned or partially state-owned enterprise or agency are inevitably carefully named with respect to the political balance of forces. In practical terms, this means that a minister cannot really trust his undersecretaries if they belong to a different party (or to a different faction within his own party); the consequence is a low level of cohesion and a high level of competition within each ministry. In the Berlusconi IV government, for example, a strategy has been not to attribute any official (or relevant) tasks to the undersecretaries of state, thus leaving all of the substantial power to the ministers themselves.

According to the 1999 reform, the number of ministries was to be reduced to twelve; however, that change has never been enforced. On the contrary, if we compare the governments under the so-called First Republic (1948–1992) with those of the Second Republic (from 1992 on, when the old political system collapsed), we see little true change. While in 1992 Giuliano Amato sharply cut the number of people sitting in his government (to twenty-five ministers and thirty-five undersecretaries of state), subsequent leaders have consistently added to that number, quickly reaching figures that characterized the most extreme edges of the First Republic's *partitocrazia* (that is, party-based rule). In particular, the number of junior positions (for example, undersecretaries of state) reached record numbers under the Prodi II government (2006–2008), with sixty-four undersecretaries of state, ten deputy ministers, and twenty-six ministers. The Berlusconi IV government (2008–present) has thirty-three undersecretaries of state, five deputy ministers, and twenty-two ministers.

In the Second Republic, the number of parties composing the government coalitions has also remained very high, ranging from the four of the Amato I government to the nine of the Prodi II government. The Berlusconi IV government, enjoying a comfortable majority in parliament, reduced the coalition parties to three (PDL, Northern League, DC), after the fusion of Forza Italia and Alleanza Nazionale into the People of Freedom Party; yet intra-coalition tensions still exist and are at times quite high. Indeed, less than three years into the legislature the old practice of Italian politicians creating their own personal party was back, with a number of secessionist mini-parties being formed on both ends of the political spectrum.

The prime minister's powers, as well as his operative tools, have been sensibly extended over the years. Berlusconi, in particular, tried to extend the powers provided the office of the prime minister by the Constitution and by the law; however, his government suffered from interministerial and inter-party competition as much as its predecessors. Possibly because of this past experience, in his latest government, Berlusconi created a sort of unofficial "inner cabinet." The Berlusconi IV government is led by a restricted number of ministers—of finance and foreign affairs, and the Presidency of the Council's undersecretary of state (Gianni Letta)—who work in concert and usually prevail over the others.

Where a real difference can be registered is in government turnover: while the first fifty years of the Italian republic produced more than fifty governments, the twenty-five years from 1985 to 2010 produced only ten.

The Ministry of Foreign Affairs

In Italy, the Ministry of Foreign Affairs (MAE, also known as the "Farnesina," for the building that houses it) has always played the main role in EU affairs. There are a number of explanations for this: the initial idea that the European Communities were a classic international organization; the supremacy of the Council in EU decision-making; the uncertain distribution of tasks among ministries until the reforms of the 1980s and 1990s; and the Farnesina's technical superiority—especially in its linguistic and negotiating skills. The centrality of the Foreign Ministry is also consistent with the coordination tasks given by the founding fathers to the General Affairs Council (GAC, formed by the foreign ministers); the "Villa Marlia procedure" of 1975—according to which the other Councils were to send a short note to the GAC after their meetings—confirms this.

Guidelines concerning the organization and the tasks of the Italian Foreign Ministry, as for other Italian ministries, are to be found in a number of documents. The oldest of these dates back to a Royal Decree of 1850, supplemented by Presidential Decree no. 18 and Presidential Decree no. 200 of 1967. Despite attempts to change this situation—proposals for reform have been presented by many different members of parliament: Edoardo Speranza (1981), Gilberto Bonalumi (1984), Valdo Spini (1985), Giorgio Napolitano (1985), Giulio Andreotti (1987), Gianni De Michelis (1989), Susanna Agnelli (1995 and 1996)—not until 1998 was the reform of the Foreign Ministry finally launched. Today its duties are regulated by articles 11 and 12 of Legislative Decree no. 300 of July 30, 1999. The Ministry of Foreign Affairs is charged with implementing the government's foreign policy. It is thus responsible for the following: carrying out the functions and tasks of the state in matters concerning Italy's external political, economic, social, and cultural relations; representing, coordinating, and protecting Italian interests at the international level; analyzing, defining, and implementing Italian action in international policy matters; maintaining and developing relations with other countries and with international organizations; drafting and reviewing treaties and international conventions and coordinating the activities involved in executing them; studying and resolving questions of international law, as well as international legal cases; representing the Italian position regarding the implementation of provisions connected with the Common Foreign and Security Policy as envisaged by the Treaty of the European Union; maintaining and developing the external political and economic relations of the European Union; handling development cooperation; dealing with issues of emigration and protecting the Italian community and workers abroad; and finally, following European integration activities regarding claims and negotiating processes in connection with the treaties of the European Union.

In carrying out these tasks, the Ministry of Foreign Affairs must ensure that the international and European activities engaged in by other government departments remain consistent with the country's international policy objectives, and in particular with those functions connected to Italy's participation in the European Union, which remain the responsibility of the Prime Minister's office.

Until 2000, the Ministry of Foreign Affairs was divided into six Directorates General (DGs)—Economic Affairs, Political Affairs, Culture, Emigration, Personnel, Cooperation and Development—each having its own "European desk." However, most of the EC work was traditionally done by the Economic Affairs and Political Affairs DGs. Following the 2000 reform, the MAE was subdivided into five geographic and seven thematic DGs, including a "European Countries DG" (DGEC) and a "European Integration DG" (DGIE). While the DGEC deals with bilateral issues, the DGIE handles multilateral European questions (chiefly, but not exclusively, related to the European Union). The DGIE is also charged with spreading information from the COREPER (Committee of Permanent Representatives) and the European Commission to the other branches of the Italian public administration.

As the 2000 reform of the MAE was also aimed at making EU policies more effective, the DGIE now has eighty-six people on its staff (as of August 2009), and they coordinate all aspects of EU affairs. The DGIE is divided into six offices: Office I deals with sectoral political and economic matters within the European Union framework; Office II focuses on EU external relations (relations with third countries and regional organizations), the EU enlargement process, accession negotiations, pre-accession programs, transatlantic relations, the regulatory framework for assistance programs to third countries, EU trade policy, and the preparation of common positions in international trade negotiations and European Community trade disputes; Office III follows all issues concerning financial cooperation and development cooperation between the EU and third countries, as well as the implementation of local internationalization policies; Office IV covers the area of Common Foreign and Security Policy; Office V is responsible for the third pillar of the EU (cooperation in justice and home affairs); and Office VI deals with legal and institutional affairs related to Italy's participation in the EU.

This latter portfolio covers a broad spectrum of responsibilities, including the following: relations with the European Parliament, with the jurisdictional institutions of the EU, with the Ombudsman, and with the legal services of the Council and the Commission; the Italian staff within the EU; statutes governing Community staff; the juridical analysis of Community legislation and the national legislation to implement it; preparatory inquiries and activities before legal action in Community disputes, in liaison with the Diplomatic Legal Advisers and Treaties Office; and cooperation with the Diplomatic Institute and the relevant government departments in the training of public officials to deal with EU matters.

Notwithstanding the extent of its duties and responsibilities, the DGIE, with its eighty-six employees, remains small in comparison with the other thematic DGs. For example, the DG for Economic and Financial Cooperation counts 156 employees; the DG for Cultural Promotion 243 employees and the DG for Administrative Affairs 198 people; the DG for Cooperation and Development has 373. The staffs working in the geographic DGs on other continents are usually smaller (data as of August 2009).

Apart from the thematic and geographic DGs, the Ministry of Foreign Affairs also consists of the following structures: the General Secretariat; the

State Diplomatic Protocol Department; the Office of the Inspectorate General of the Ministry and Posts Abroad; the Press and Information Service; the Diplomatic Legal Advisory Service; the Historical, Archival, and Documentation Service; the Information Technology, Communications, and Encryption Service; and the Diplomatic Institute. There are also the offices directly under the minister of foreign affairs: the Private Office (Cabinet); the Minister's Secretariat; the Legal Affairs Office; the Office for Relations with Parliament; the Internal Control Service and its support office; and the secretariats of the undersecretaries of state.

In 2011, yet a new comprehensive reform will be implemented, supposedly inspired by similar reforms abroad. The overall number of DGs will be reduced by dismantling the preexisting thematic and geographic DGs and regrouping them into a smaller number of macro-areas: Political and Security Affairs; Globalization and Global Issues; Promotion of the Italian System; European Union; Italians Abroad; Resources and Innovation; Development Cooperation; and Administration, IT, and Communications. While it is difficult to say whether the reform was conceived to increase the effectiveness of the Foreign Ministry or also to rejuvenate it (with a small number of top posts in Rome, the most senior top diplomats will have the choice to either go abroad or retire), in European Union affairs it does represent a step forward. The new General Directorate for the European Union will in fact deal with both bilateral and multilateral European affairs (with the exception of security affairs), thus facilitating and simplifying the circulation of information on European affairs.

Yet the minister himself often delegates the specific conduct of European policy to his diplomats, preferring to concentrate on transatlantic relations and other grand issues. Italy thus has had a core group of high-level diplomats—Rocco Cangelosi, Vanni D'Archirafi, Ferdinando Nelli Feroci, Silvio Fagiolo, and Umberto Vattani are some of the most relevant names—who have guided Italian EU policy from various posts (Minister's Cabinet, DGIE, Permanent Representative in Brussels). Relevant exceptions to this rule—Alcide De Gasperi, Giulio Andreotti, Gianni De Michelis, Massimo D'Alema and Franco Frattini—are described in detail in chapters 3 and 8.

The Undersecretary of State for Foreign Affairs Charged with European Affairs

Politically, the DGIE answers to the undersecretary of state for foreign affairs in charge of European affairs (Sottosegretario agli Esteri con delega per gli Affari Europei). This latter has, on paper, many tasks. He is charged with European bilateral relations and with participation in the EU, OECD, and the

Council of Europe. Unlike in other EU countries, however, undersecretaries of state in Italy are junior figures: they must strictly follow guidelines given by "their" minister and cannot act independently. They do not report directly to the prime minister. Also, unlike in other countries, they are excluded from sitting in on meetings of the Italian Council of Ministers. Although they may be part of the delegation to the European Council, they seldom get to sit at the meeting table. Likewise, the undersecretary of state for foreign affairs charged with European affairs is not entrusted with representing the government in any council of the EU, whereas his Portuguese colleague, for example, is responsible for the Single European Market and can substitute for the minister if necessary. These limitations cause considerable frustration among the Italian undersecretaries of state, which can be reflected in their work. A relationship of complete confidence with the minister might help, given this state of affairs, but as mentioned above, this seldom exists. With very few notable exceptions (Piero Fassino in the Prodi I government, for instance) the undersecretary of state for EU affairs is destined to remain in the shadows.

The President of the Council

Today's most important EU institution—the European Council—was not foreseen in the original treaties. The European Council's establishment and subsequent affirmation as a leading political actor did not happen suddenly, but was rather the result of a progressive trend. Events like the fall of the Berlin Wall offered important occasions for heads of state to act and to assume direct responsibilities in European policymaking rather than delegating to their foreign ministers. As time passed, the heads of state and government discovered the usefulness of the European Council as a major source of domestic legitimization in the framework of Putnam's classic double-edged diplomacy scheme.[5] The European Council's role peaked during the French EU presidency of 2008, for example, when crises erupted in the financial world and in the former Soviet republic of Georgia. In any event, the European Council's increased role in EU policymaking took place as part of a general expansion of the European prime ministers' tasks and resources.[6]

As of 1999, the Italian president of the Council took on a large share of responsibility for Italy's participation in the EU (Laws 400/1988, 300/1999, 59/1997). Acting in coordination, the Presidency of the Council and the Italian Foreign Ministry are meant to promote Italian positions within the European institutions. The 1999 reform enhanced the prime minister's powers in relation to European affairs by formally entrusting him with the coordination of the Italian Council of Ministers, relations with other institutions (such as the parliament), relations with EU institutions, and others.

The Presidency itself has also been reformed: several departments have been established (including one for EU affairs), and a general secretariat has been created (Law 303/1999). In reality, the prime minister himself tends to concentrate on the most relevant dossiers and on the European Council activities, delegating the day-to-day work to the minister for EU policies, especially with respect to the incorporation of EC law into national law.

Yet despite the reform, the ability of Italy's prime minister to coordinate his colleagues over EU affairs has long been limited, especially the stronger ministers (such as the minister of finance). Therefore, the temptation to use the EU in other ways—for instance, as a major source of legitimization at home—is stronger than elsewhere. Silvio Berlusconi, for instance, used this political weapon widely in his second government, especially during the period in which he was acting minister of foreign affairs as well as president of the Council. As mentioned in earlier chapters, when the clashes between Foreign Minister Renato Ruggiero and the rest of the Berlusconi government led to Ruggiero's resignation, Berlusconi temporarily assumed the position of foreign minister (January 2002 to November 2002). He tried to use his dual role to achieve his own "revised" double-edged diplomacy strategy. Not only did he intend to strengthen his international image, but, most of all, he aimed to deprive the Farnesina of its functions and powers in an effort to strengthen those of the prime minister. Further proof of this is the fact that when Berlusconi finally gave up his double mandate, in November 2002 (the work of the European Convention had already begun and the Italian semester of presidency, from July 1 to December 31, 2003, was about to start), he left the seat to the then minister of public administration, Franco Frattini.

When first named, Frattini was perceived as a Berlusconi yes-man who would let him continue to lead Italian foreign policy from the Presidency of the Council. This turned out to be a false expectation: a high achiever with an impressive (legal) record in Italian public administration, Frattini soon acquired an in-depth knowledge of the EU technical dossiers, honed his diplomatic skills, and proved to be an excellent and dedicated foreign minister, thus contributing to the relaunching of the Farnesina's role in EU policymaking.

The Minister for EU Policies

As mentioned, the prime minister tends to delegate day-to-day duties to the minister for EU policies, especially with respect to the transposition of EC law into national law.

The minister for the coordination of EC policies, as he was initially called, is a minister "without portfolio" and thus is attached to the presidency of the (Italian) European Council. The position of minister for European affairs in reality first appeared in the De Gasperi VII government, in the person of the former minister of foreign affairs Carlo Sforza (1951–52), but was not reconfirmed afterwards. Thus it is correct to say that the position was created in 1980. Its lack of resources was such that it was defined by Grottanelli de Santi as the "Cinderella of the Italian ministries."[7] The first "Cinderella" was the Christian Democrat Vincenzo Scotti in the second government of Prime Minister Francesco Cossiga (April 4–September 28, 1980). He was also reconfirmed in the following government. From then on, however, with few exceptions, the ministry has been attributed to rather secondary political figures, in a pure party-based logic. The rapid turnover of the governments, and thus of the ministries, has not helped to strengthen the EU minister's role. Indeed, the position was suppressed in 1995 by the Lamberto Dini government, its tasks assigned to the undersecretary of state for economics. In 1996 (in the Prodi I government) the EU minister's tasks were farmed out to the undersecretary of state at the Presidency of the Council and to the undersecretary of state for foreign affairs charged with European affairs, after a first period in which Prodi kept those tasks to himself.

In 1998 the minister for EU policies was reintroduced by the government of Massima d'Alema and given enhanced means and a political role. D'Alema actually turned his choice to reintroduce the ministry into a major political issue by inviting EU Commissioner Emma Bonino to fill the post. When Bonino declined (though she would accept a similar invitation from Prodi ten years later, in 2006), and owing to a question of reciprocal vetoes within the Popular Party between Rocco Buttiglione and Beniamino Andreatta, the person who was finally chosen for the post was the young assistant to Professor Andreatta, Enrico Letta. Despite being a weak political figure at the time, Letta proved extremely competent from a technical point of view. Letta had, at least according to Italian standards, broad experience in Europe: he had attended primary school in Luxembourg and was fluent in French; he spoke decent English; and for a few years, he had been the president of the European Young Christian Democrats.

A "young old man," Enrico Letta was a typical Christian Democrat in that he generally avoided confrontation. Thanks to this quality, to the good personal relationship he enjoyed with Prime Minister D'Alema, and to the government reform that allowed him to staff the new Department for EU Policies with competent people from outside the public administration, Letta managed to transform Cinderella into a working princess—at least as far as the

Table 6-1. *Italian Ministers for EU/EC Policies*

Name	Government	Year	Party
Scotti, Vincenzo	Cossiga II	1980	Christian Democrat
Scotti, Vincenzo	Forlani	1980	Christian Democrat
Abis, Lucio	Spadolini I	1981	Christian Democrat
Abis, Lucio	Spadolini II	1982	Christian Democrat
Biondi, Alfredo	Fanfani V	1982	Liberal
Forte, Francesco	Craxi I	1983	Socialist
Fortuna, Loris	Craxi I	1983	Socialist
Fabbri, Fabio	Craxi II	1986	Socialist
La Pergola, Antonio	Goria	1987	Socialist
La Pergola, Antonio	De Mita	1988	Socialist
Romita, Pier Luigi	Andreotti VI	1989	Socialist
Romita, Pier Luigi	Andreotti VII	1991	Socialist
Costa, Raffaele	Amato I	1992	Liberal
Ciaurro, Gian Franco	Amato I	1993	Liberal
Spini, Valdo	Ciampi	1993	Socialist
Paladin, Livio	Ciampi	1993	Nonaffiliated
Comino, Domenico	Berlusconi I	1994	Northern League
Letta, Enrico	D'Alema I	1998	Popular
Toia, Patrizia	D'Alema II	1999	Popular
Matteoli, Gianni	Amato II	2000	Green
Buttiglione, Rocco	Berlusconi II	2001	Post–Christian Democrat
La Malfa, Giorgio	Berlusconi III	2005	Republican
Bonino, Emma	Prodi II	2006	Radical
Ronchi, Andrea	Berlusconi IV	2008	National Alliance/PDL

incorporation of EC law into national law is concerned. For the first time in years, Italy was able to avoid delays in enforcing EC law.

Since then, Italian governments have maintained a Ministry for EU Policies. Seldom, however, has the role of EU minister gone to people with Letta's technical competence and passion for the issue—with the notable exceptions of Giorgio La Malfa in the Berlusconi III government (2005–06) and Emma Bonino in the Prodi II government (2006–08), a past EU Commissioner and a major political actor in Italy who, at the time, was also minister for international trade. For a list of all those who have held the position of minister for EU policies since 1980, see table 6-1.

Formally, the minister for EU policies' tasks have not changed significantly since the 1980s. This is rather surprising since the EEC of the early 1980s is only a distant relative of today's EU. The main task of the minister for EU policies concerns the incorporation of EC law into national law. As described in chapter 5, this is done by means of the Annual Community Law. Created in 1989 by the La Pergola Law, the Annual Community Law has subsequently been amended several times. It is currently regulated by Law 11/2005. The purpose of the Annual Community Law is to ensure the regular, systematic, and timely incorporation of EU legislation into national law.

In addition, the ministry deals with European Court of Justice cases concerning issues of national interest; promotes the professional training of public officials in EU affairs; disseminates information about the EU both to other national and regional institutions and to the public; promotes the careers of Italian citizens in the EU institutions; represents Italy in the Council for the Internal Market; coordinates other sectors of the public administration and social parties in the formative phase of EU laws. These appear to be broad tasks on paper, as Giacinto Della Cananea once affirmed: "If all the powers just mentioned were to be taken seriously, one might be tempted to conclude that the ad hoc minister is now the steering authority. However, there are several reasons to suspect that a more skeptical interpretation is appropriate."[8] Among those reasons, he included the fact that the EU minister's powers are not "owned" but rather "delegated" by the Presidency of the Council. He also pointed out that the EU Ministry had proved incapable of coordinating the other members of the government and that the Foreign Ministry has been unwilling to give up its powers over EU affairs. Interestingly, the minister for EU policies is not part of the delegations attending the General Affairs Council (CAGRE) or the European Council, a fact that has at times undermined its role both domestically and at the European level.

The Department for EU Policies

The minister for EU policies has the logistical support of the Department for EU Policies. Located at the Presidency of the Council, this department was introduced in 1987 by the Fabbri Law (Law 183/1987) under the name "Department for the Coordination of EC Policies." Its role was further specified in Law 139/1990, especially in relation to its coordination functions. Its fortunes have varied over the years, but the initial extreme lack of resources certainly contributed to the difficulties it experienced in responding to its assigned tasks.[9]

The aim of the department—operative only since June 1990 and reformed several times—was to make the Italian government's actions more effective, especially with respect to the implementation of EC directives and the completion of the Single Market. It was also meant to develop better relations with European institutions and to supervise the implementation of EC law and the use of EC funds.

The department is responsible for the following: coordinating (in agreement with the Foreign Ministry) the relevant sectors of the public administration, private interests, civic actors, and local and regional authorities, in the formative phase of EU law, with a view to defining the Italian position; supporting the work of the interministerial coordination body (CIACE) and of the permanent technical committee; monitoring the making of EU legislation so as to be able to modify the Italian position whenever relevant; maintaining relations with the EU Commission in its areas of competence; coordinating action in the EU with the regions and municipalities, in agreement with the Department for Regional Policies and the Secretariat of the State-Regions and State-Cities Conference; preparing the meetings of the Single Market Council and other relevant councils—with the specific exclusion of the General Affairs Council—for which no other government unit is specifically responsible; preparing the annual report on Italy's participation in the EU and following the making of the so-called "Community Law" as well as the actual implementation of EC law into national law; monitoring the correct application of EU law by the different branches of the Italian public administration, as well as by the regions and the autonomous provinces; following the progress of cases in which Italy is brought before the European Court of Justice; promoting the candidacy of Italian citizens for EU institutions; spreading knowledge of EU affairs among public and private officials; and promoting the diffusion of information about the EU.[10]

The department's internal organization and tasks have been redesigned several times, in particular in 2000 and in 2006. Staffed by about seventy people, in addition to some twenty-five reporting directly to the minister, the department is still understaffed if compared with similar units in other countries. Yet it is undoubtedly much better off than it was in the early 1990s, when its staff amounted to only a dozen or so. The department is divided into four "offices" (*uffici*) and 13 "units" (*servizi*). Office I is the CIACE Secretariat. CIACE is the interministerial coordinating body. Office I is divided into three additional offices, each charged with following several areas of EU competence. Office II deals with the Single Market and competitiveness; Office III follows competition policy, state aid, and cohesion policies; Office IV is called "European citizenship" and is charged with disseminating information about the EU and with training public officials about EU affairs. The department also provides logistical support to the Italian branch of SOLVIT, the Commission pilot project charged with solving problems linked to the Single Market and with preventing appeals to the European Court of Justice. In addition, the department has a unit (*nucleo*) of the Fiscal Police (Guardia di Finanza), which investigates fraud against EU funds. This unit responds directly to the head of the department. Last but not least, the department hosts a special unit (Struttura di Missione) that was created to help avoid litigation over EU law and to facilitate the resolution of existing procedures against Italy.

The Other Ministries: Intra- and Interministerial Coordination

While initially only the foreign affairs ministers were to be involved in European affairs, as other ministries were affected they too came to play a significant role. The ministers of agriculture and of economy and finance were among the first to get involved, and they are now considered among the most powerful members of the Council. Today, virtually no national ministry can avoid dealing with the EU. In Italy, the importance and involvement of the economy-related ministries is second only to that of the Foreign Ministry. Tables 6-2 and 6-3 show how tasks are distributed across the Italian public administration.

Most striking in the Italian case, however, are the different ways in which branches of government deal with European affairs. Unlike in other EU countries, there is still no uniformity in their practices. Most Italian ministries lack "European offices" or "units" charged with negotiating and implementing EU law; indeed, this is possibly the major point of weakness emerging from the hearings held by the EU Committee of the Chamber of Deputies in 2008–09.[11] For example, in the formative phase of EU law, the offices for international relations tend to dominate; in the incorporation of EU law into national law, it is the legislative offices that take the lead. Rarely is a "European unit" charged with distributing Europe-related news and information among the various departments of the ministries. (One notable exception is the Ministry of Economy and Finance, which set up an EU unit—Unità di indirizzo—in 1999 at the DG level.) In general, while the transmission of EU directives is often coordinated by the legislative offices, the negotiating phase—if it is dealt with at all—is coordinated in any number of ways. In the end, it often ends up in the hands of the diplomatic advisers (which most ministers employ).

For years, the lack of intraministerial coordination together with the typical Italian interministerial rivalry have prevented any real chance of creating an efficient system of interministerial coordination on EU affairs. And this is despite the fact that one of the tasks of the minister for EU policies was precisely to coordinate *with* the different sectors of public administration and social partners on EU policy. This task was initially to be addressed by means

Table 6-2. *Who Deals with What: EU Policies in Italy*

Issue	Ministry
EC policies (coordination)	Foreign Affairs; EU Policies
Single European Market	EU Policies
Article 36 (police cooperation and criminal law	Justice
Common agricultural policy	Agriculture; Economic Development (for international negotiations)
Competition	Economic Development
Fiscal issues	Economy and Finance
Harmonization of legislation	EU Policies
Economic and monetary policies	Economy and Finance
Euro 16 (members of the Eurozone)	Economy and Finance
Trade policy	Economic Development
Social policy	Health; Social Affairs and Labor
Education	Instruction, University, and Research
Professional training	Social Affairs and Labor
Youth	Youth
Public health	Health; Social Affairs and Labor
Consumers	Economic Development
Trans-European networks	Transportation; Foreign Affairs
Industry	Economic Development
Economic and social cohesion	Economy and Finance
Structural funds	Economy and Finance; Social Affairs and Labor
Research and development	Instruction, University, and Research
Environment	Environment
Cooperation and development	Foreign Affairs
Common foreign and security policy	Foreign Affairs
European security and defense policy	Defense
Justice and home affairs	Interior; Justice

of an ad hoc meeting of the State-Regions Conference (Sessione Comunitaria della Conferenza Stato-Regioni). However, the use of the word "with" was not casual: the ministry did not have the authority to coordinate its colleagues. In reality, there was seldom anything to coordinate. Unlike in France (with its Secrétariat général du Comité Interministériel pour les questions de coopération économique européenne, or SGCI), in Britain (with its European Secretariat in the Cabinet Office), or in Portugal (with its Commission on European Affairs), in Italy nobody has ever been charged with the interministerial coordination of European affairs. Slowly, however, things are starting to change.

Table 6-3. *What the Italian Ministers Do in the EU*

Minister	Task
Foreign Affairs	EU policies (overview, definition of the Italian position and main negotiator via the Permanent Representative); European security issues; institutional reforms
Home Affairs	Justice and domestic affairs (immigration, police, asylum, visas, etc.)
Justice	International cooperation in both civil and penal matters; Eurojust
Defense	Cooperation in the field of defense; European armaments cooperation
Finance and Treasury	Fiscal policies; macroeconomics; Ecofin; Euro 15
Economic Development	Energy; sustainable development; trade policies; consumer policies; tourism
Agriculture	CAP
Environnent	Environment; energy
Labor and Health	Social policies; job market; worker mobility; social security; safety at work; health issues (people, animal, food, water, and so on); European health agencies
Instruction, University, and Research	Education; structural funds related to education; Bologna Process
Public Administration	Represents Italy in the European Institute for Public Administration
Equal Opportunities	Equal opportunities; women's rights

In 1960 Italy created two committees, one at the political level and one at the technical level. The first one was then abolished in 1967 and its functions moved to CIPE (the Interministerial Committee for Economic Planning). Law 183/1987 then established a Fondo di Rotazione charged with collecting and redistributing all EC subventions to Italy. When this experiment was not successful, a new interministerial task force (formed by the ministers for industry, budget, and EU policies) was created and charged with coordinating EU funds. In 1989 the La Pergola Law introduced a special session of the State-Regions Conference, to be devoted to European affairs. For many years, however, it existed only on paper. Owing to a scarcity of funds at the Department for EC Policies, this solution was eventually turned down in favor of an interministerial task force to be located within the Budget Ministry and to be composed of representatives from the Budget, Industry, and EU Policies Ministries. This solution too was later turned down in favor of the creation of the Cabina di Regia ("director's box"), located within the Budget Ministry, which was to coordinate with the other regional Cabine di Regia (Law 341/1995). It now remains to be seen whether the Cabine system will succeed in responding to the tasks assigned to it, something that appears unlikely so far.

In January 2000, a meeting jointly organized by the Foreign Ministry and the Ministry for EU Policies took place at the Farnesina. It was attended by the diplomatic advisers of the two ministries and by the directors general in charge of EU affairs from the Presidency of the Council and from the following ministries: Interior, Justice, Budget, Economy and Finance, Defense, School, Public Works, Transportation, Communications, Industry, Labor, Foreign Trade, Health, Culture, Environment, University and Research, and Agriculture. Saluted by Undersecretary of State for Foreign Affairs Umberto Ranieri as the beginning of efficient interministerial coordination, it nevertheless languished afterwards. The coordinating exercise was in fact spoiled on the day of its first meeting, when a furious foreign minister, Lamberto Dini, found out that Prime Minister Massimo D'Alema had agreed to a text being drafted by the Portuguese prime minister, Antonio Gutierres, without consulting him.

The more serious problem, however, was twofold. On one side, ministers have stubbornly (and successfully) resisted being coordinated; they are jealous of their competencies and suspicious of any minister not belonging to the same wing of their own political party (which has been rather difficult given the large coalitions). On the other side, the Foreign Ministry, in principle in favor of coordination, was in truth reluctant to undertake any effort that it did not initiate. Indeed, as explained below, the persistent lack of formal coordination in Italy has led to the Permanent Representative in Brussels—part of the Foreign Ministry—picking up the slack. Over the years, this situation became increasingly untenable.[12] Eventually, the Farnesina was forced to make the most of a situation it could no longer avoid, becoming a leading actor in the process of coordination, as we shall see shortly.

In 2005 the so-called Stucchi-Buttiglione Law (Law 11 of February 4, 2005, or 11/2005) created a coordinating body at the Presidency of the Council of Ministers called CIACE (Comitato Interministeriale per gli Affari Comunitari Europei). The idea was to create a sort of "Cabinet for EU Affairs" and to locate it at the Presidency of the Council, as other countries had done (notably France). Staffed by some twenty people—individually chosen for their commitment and expertise and drawn partially from the Department for EU Affairs, CIACE was given the specific task of finally enabling the government to coordinate and deepen its actions on issues of relevance to Italy. Regions and local communities can also be invited to participate when appropriate. One year after the law was adopted, a decree by the prime minister and another by the minister for EU affairs further specified how CIACE would work in practice. The squaring of the circle—from the Foreign Ministry's point of view—came with the decision to name a high-level diplomat as CIACE's coordinator who is also serving as diplomatic adviser to the minister of EU policies (this has been Massimo Gaiani since the CIACE was set up). In addition, both the DGIE and the Permanent Representative are deeply involved in coordination, thereby securing the Farnesina's hold on EU affairs.

CIACE, like its 1960 predecessor, is to function at two levels: the political level and the technical level. At the political level, it is to organize one meeting every two months, according to the needs of the EU political agenda. The first such meeting was held under the Berlusconi III government: chaired by Minister Giorgio La Malfa on March 29, 2006, it was attended by a head of department or director general from all of the ministries. Several more meetings then took place under the Prodi II government, all chaired by the energetic and skilled minister Emma Bonino. These meetings have benefited from the involvement of a number of ministers—also thanks to the fact that they are held immediately before or after the Council of Ministers. In principle, all ministers are invited to take part in the meetings. In some cases they attend themselves, in others they delegate an undersecretary, and sometimes they send a high-level official, though the latter does not have the right to intervene in the debate.

Under Bonino, meetings were devoted to the Lisbon agenda and the incorporation of EC law into national law (July 4, 2006); to the adoption of the National Program of Reforms (October 19, 2006); and to the second report on the National Program of Reforms (July 13, 2007). During this latter meeting, attended by Prime Minister Prodi and ten other ministers, a decision was made to enhance the role of the Presidency of the Council and of the Ministry for EU Policies in coordinating the definition of the Italian position in the most relevant dossiers. Minister Bonino especially urged her colleagues to define the Italian position in the field of energy and climate change in view of the adoption of the EU directive on the "Emissions Trading System," an interesting case that is examined in chapter 9. The document defining the Italian position on energy was eventually adopted in the CIACE meeting of September 7, 2007. A subsequent meeting, on October 23, 2007, was then devoted to the Lisbon strategy.[13] During the first half of 2008, activities slowed down because of the anticipated legislative elections. The change in government, however, did not alter what appears to have finally become a routine. Gaiani was kept in place as CIACE's coordinator and as diplomatic adviser to the minister of EU policies, and during the second half of 2008 four meetings were held (September 17; October 28; December 1; December 10: Relazione Annuale sulla Partecipazione dell'Italia all'Unione Europea 2008). Since then, the minister for foreign affairs, the minister for EU affairs, and the minister for regional affairs have been meeting on average four times a year, and their meetings have been joined regularly by other ministers with relevant competencies.

At the technical level (*comitato tecnico permanente*) the objective has been to gather one member from each ministry (one delegate plus a substitute for each). The idea, indeed, was to hold a meeting every two weeks. In reality, attendance has followed a "variable geometry scheme" dictated by need and the issue. In general terms, CIACE selects those issues that not only are considered most relevant for Italy but that also involve the contribution of several departments. Over the years, three themes have received the most attention: innovation and research; energy and climate change; and immigration. In all cases, working groups have met according to the demands of the issue and of the EU agenda (sometimes they meet for a whole week). In 2008, for instance, CIACE discussed the following items: Lisbon strategy; energy and climate change; immigration; intellectual property and innovation; the directive against discrimination; the European Fund for Globalization; genetically modified organisms (GMOs); the excise tax; and wildlife protection. In some cases, the initiative came from other ministries when they needed to define a national position but could not do so without interministerial coordination.

Attendance at the meetings also varies, as it does in many other countries. Originally, participants were to be either directors general of European and/or international affairs, diplomatic advisers to the ministers, or other high-level officials in a minister's cabinet. In such cases, they were accompanied by another official who was responsible for the specific technical issue under discussion. These people, in turn, were in charge of disseminating information about the meeting within their own ministries. However, in most cases, working groups tend to meet at the level of chief of office.

Often, the specialized working groups are also joined by nongovernmental actors: stakeholders, experts, and representatives of associations, private industry, state agencies, and the like. Furthermore, for important issues like energy, the coordinating and negotiating role of the Presidency of the Council is larger. The undersecretary of state for the Presidency of the Council, for example, was involved in negotiations over energy issues, and at times the prime minister has named a personal representative in negotiations. Decisions are by consensus, so mediation takes place until all departments can agree. Then the CIACE's secretariat draws up the conclusions that are (electronically) circulated to all ministries. It is binding on the administrations that have participated, and "morally binding" on the other members. In the event that it is impossible to reach consensus on an issue, it is moved to the political level—as in EU negotiations. The regions are supposed to participate at all levels of coordination, although in practice that does not always happen, as we shall see in chapter 7.

As interministerial coordination has become a working reality, and given the greater involvement of parliament, discussions are now being launched about whether to amend law 11/2005 in order to further enhance intraministerial coordination and make it even more effective. Indeed, a number of weaknesses remain. For a start, the CIACE's opinions are not binding on the government; furthermore, the law does not mention whether coordination shall prioritize certain areas—it is very general in its terms. Last but not least, there are no extra resources (financial or human) devoted to the CIACE's coordinating tasks.

The Permanent Representative

As we have seen, intra- and interministerial coordinations have long been important unresolved problems. Over time, by default, responsibility for coordination has resided with the Ministry of Foreign Affairs, and most notably with its Permanent Representative in Brussels. The Permanent Representatives (Perm Reps, or REPERs) are the instruments through which the member states' governments interact with the EU institutions and with each other. Their role is to ensure that the national interests and positions of their home countries are given adequate attention at the EU level. Therefore, Perm Reps should ideally be the negotiators of positions elaborated at home by the respective member state administrations. In the past, however, these representatives occasionally not only defended the national position but defined it as well, particularly in the Italian case. Some countries, such as Portugal, have given their Permanent Representatives a greater official role in shaping national positions, in order to improve efficiency—that is, to shorten "reaction time." The greater role of Italy's Perm Rep, however, was due more to faults in the system than to any affirmative decision.

The founding regulations concerning the Italian Perm Rep date back to 1958 (DPR no. 16/1958). At that time, the office was considered a decentralized unit of the Foreign Ministry, and since it was up to the Farnesina to deal with Community issues, the Perm Rep was to be its *longa manus* in Brussels.[14] From the mid-1980s, following the changes introduced by the Single European Act, many other sectors of the national public administration began to be involved in Community policymaking. This made it increasingly difficult for the Farnesina to coordinate efforts. At this time, the new Ministry of EC Policies and the related Department for EC Policies at the Presidency of the Council were also introduced into the government.

In 1998 Romano Prodi, then president of the Council, issued a directive according to which the Perm Rep was to send all information to the Department for EU Policies at the Presidency of the Council rather than to the Foreign Ministry. According to Prodi's directive, the Perm Rep was to undertake three tasks: (a) transmit any EU documents to the Department for EU Policies; (b) receive input from the department within thirty days of transmitting information to the department (within that timeframe, the department was to consult the relevant national actors); (c) maintain relations with EU institutions and the other member states.

Interestingly, however, at the same time, Prodi chose not to name a minister for EU policies, but rather to assign his tasks to the undersecretary of state for European affairs at the Foreign Ministry—at the time, Piero Fassino. The Perm Rep thus was charged with maintaining a dialogue with two different institutions, while belonging only to the Foreign Ministry. This gap between the letter and the substance of the directive ended up worsening rather than improving relations between the two branches of government. To offer just one example of the problems that emerged: the Farnesina did not immediately transmit the COREUs (Corespondance Européenne, telexes sent among EU capitals) to the Presidency of the Council.

As time passed, however, and despite a further attempt to relieve the Foreign Ministry of its EU competencies under the Berlusconi II government, the office of the Perm Rep managed to reposition itself as a participant in most EU negotiations. Today it is considered a prestigious post, staffed by Italy's most brilliant diplomats.

The office of the Perm Rep is organized around different sectors. The Permanent Representative him- or herself is charged with the works of the General Affairs and External Relations Council, ECOFIN (the Economic and Financial Affairs Council), and Justice and Home Affairs. His deputy is charged to ensure coherence for the "technical" formations of the Council, including Transportation, Energy, Research; Instruction; Culture; Environment; Competitiveness; Labor, Social Policies; Health; and Consumer Policies.

The Perm Rep has also launched ongoing consultations with the most relevant and engaged Italian MEPs: vice presidents, committee presidents, heads of delegations, and the like, in addition to eventual rapporteurs.

This trend is shared by many member states. The increasing complexity, velocity, and sheer volume of issues considered at the EU level is in fact pushing member states to grant their Permanent Representatives—formally or informally—an ever more proactive role.

Yet in the Italian case, as mentioned, this was not the outcome of a specific policy choice. It was rather a result of the Italian system's inadequacy and inefficiency. Often national departments were—and in part still are—too slow in responding to requests for information; sufficient elements were often lacking with which to create complete dossiers for the Permanent Representatives. Seldom was there an overall analysis of the consequences of a determined position.[15] The result was that often it was left to the office of the Perm Rep—sometimes even to the individual diplomats!—to define the positions to be negotiated in the Council. In order to do so, Italian diplomats in Brussels used their access to relevant information and their ability to network with both private and public actors—Italians and foreigners alike. Their success in this is widely acclaimed by actors in Brussels and elsewhere. As one experienced Italian diplomat who wishes to remain anonymous put it: "It is quite fun to be an Italian diplomat in Brussels, as you get to decide much more than your peers, though I admit that this, at times, presents some pitfalls, especially in the case of very technical negotiations." It is said that, when at a loss, the last resort of Italian diplomats is to vote against the Dutch delegation. Far from being a joke, this commonplace is rooted in experience: the Dutch delegations are usually well informed, and the economic, social, and cultural circumstances in the Netherlands are usually the opposite of those in Italy.

Another peculiarity of the Italian Perm Rep has been its staffing. For a long time the Italian office in Brussels was staffed almost exclusively by diplomats, whereas the majority of people in the other Perm Rep offices were officials from departments other than the Foreign Ministry. Now, however, a growing number of public officials are being seconded from departments other than the Foreign Ministry. In 2010 Italy's Permanent Representation included twenty-two diplomats, thirty-six officials from other departments (including four from the Italian regions), and one from the Bank of Italy.

EU Affairs and the Italian Public Administration

For a long time, Italian public officials were comparatively less well trained on EU issues than most of their European peers. Other member states have launched specific training programs on EU issues and negotiating techniques, but no such programs exist in Italy. The National School of Public Administration (SSPA) provides some training with regard to the EU (usually, one-week classes), but a recent attempt to introduce ad hoc modules and simulations in English failed, despite many calls for it. The D'Alema I government did issue a plan for a program, called "Project Italy 2002," that would have educated a large number of Italian public officials about EU issues,[16] but it never saw the light of day. Soon afterward, Minister for EU Policies Enrico Letta proposed a similar program to be organized in collaboration with the University of Bologna, but it was opposed by an influential member of Letta's cabinet who hailed from a different university, and the program was subsequently canceled. The minister's authority was evidently not sufficient to impose the plan anyway.

More recently, the EU Department has begun training officials in regional and local bodies. In 2009 an online course on EU affairs for Italian public officials was also launched.[17]

Likewise, for many years, little if any effort was made by the Italian government to promote Italian candidates and Italians in general for positions in the European institutions. Only in 2010 was a directive of the prime minister, promoted by Minister Frattini, approved in order to support Italian applications for jobs in international organizations.[18] The British, French, and Spanish, on the other hand, excel at this. In general terms, Italy has preferred to deal with the issue in a rather opaque way in order to keep it as a possible redistributive option for the government: posts in Brussels are in fact often considered a sort of reward (due to the high salaries paid there in comparison with those at home). At the same time, for public officials there has been no real incentive to go to Brussels: once back in Italy after serving in such a post, they often find themselves with nothing to do, and their expertise is rarely taken advantage of. Indeed, they risk finding themselves delegated to obscure and irrelevant jobs.

But that situation may be changing as well. For a start, returning ENDs (National Detached Experts) can find an interesting workplace in CIACE if their own departments do not provide them with jobs that utilize the expertise they have acquired in Brussels. In 2009, 93 Italian ENDs were working at the European Commission—ten more than in 2007—as compared to 148 French men and women and 131 Germans. Yet the lack of financial resources prevents the serious and more systematic use of returning ENDs. In addition, the Italian system offers no incentives for the administrations to send their employees to Brussels for a term. In countries like Spain, for instance, there are financial incentives to encourage departments to send their best people to Brussels.

In addition, a joint effort by the Perm Rep, the EU Department, and the Foreign Ministry is monitoring and supporting the careers of EU permanent officials. In the past, responding to the indifference of their own government, Italians in Brussels were known to seek "sponsors" from other countries— the Germans being particularly good at doing this with foreign nationals. Today, however, the tendency to go to the Italian Perm Rep to seek a position or a promotion is much more common than in the past. In fact, there is now a person in charge of following Italians in their European careers at the Office of the Permanent Representatives. In 2010 Italy had four directors general (for economic and financial affairs; health and consumer protection; development; and interpretation) and four deputy DGs (for agriculture; external relations; regional affairs; and energy).

In comparison, at the level of director general, Germany has seven, the United Kingdom five, France three, and Spain also three. At the level of deputy DG, Germany has one, Spain one, France five, the United Kingdom two. There are also two Italian DGs in the European Parliament and one in the Council. In addition, with the cooperation of the Department of EU Affairs at the Presidency of the Council and the Foreign Ministry, a (voluntary) database has been created of Italian *lauréats de concour*. Seminars are then organized for these people, to train them and to help them establish networks, with the goal of securing a place in the EU institutions.

Conclusions

According to Giorgio Freddi, the characteristics of a nation's public administration explain the ability (or inability) of the branches of government to respond to the tasks assigned them.[19] A nation's public administration is a relevant actor in all policy processes—a fact that is widely accepted in political science—and this includes, of course, the European policy process. Italy's public administration was and in part still is one of the variables explaining the country's low score in day-to-day management of EU policy. Without an internationally skilled public administration, the Foreign Ministry diplomats have served by default. They are, as mentioned, highly trained and skilled. The downside, however, was that it thus took a long time for the country to understand that EU policies were to be treated as domestic ones, not as foreign ones. Also, however skilled, Italian diplomats form a closed circle, impermeable to external input and very protective of their prerogatives and powers. Their careers are generally thought of in terms of preventing outside influence, with the risk of the diplomats becoming self-referential. The permeability and interchange that exist in other European countries in dealing with EU affairs, therefore, are ideas that are absent in Italy. And that has meant that EU culture and EU skills have only just begun to spread across the whole spectrum of the public administration. Today, it is possible for diplomats to be detached—to serve in other branches of government or even in the private sector—but there is still no possibility to enter the diplomatic service from outside the Foreign Ministry, and even less so from the private sector.

Another factor in explaining Italy's past weaknesses in the EU is Italian politics. The high number of parties composing government coalitions and the litigious nature of these parties and their leaders have long prevented inter- and intraministerial coordination on EU policy. Also, Italian politicians tend to be concerned principally with local issues, or at most national issues, with just a few notable exceptions. They consider Brussels either a remote place—malign or benign according to the moment—or a mere source of funds and jobs for their acquaintances. Few consider it a place in which to invest time or means.

Nevertheless, these long-held practices have begun to change for the better, and most important, the change appears to be irreversible. In analyzing the Italian government and the EU, it becomes clear that for the first fifty years the country's decisionmaking model closely resembled a garbage can. After a period of muddling through, however, Italy has now achieved—if not yet a fully rational model—at least a sound one.

7 | *Territorial Politics and Organized Interests*

Regional policy was not addressed in the original EC Treaty in 1957, although the Preamble did refer to the need to narrow the differences with the less-developed regions. Some common policies (the Common Agricultural Policy, the reconversion of the steel and coal industry, the harmonization of economic policies) did have a regional connotation in the implementation phase. The need to introduce a regional policy therefore emerged in the years that followed. In 1975 the European Regional Development Fund (ERDF) was established, followed in 1987 by the incorporation of regional policy among Community policies. The reform of the Structural Funds[1] and the innovations introduced by the Single European Act (1986) prompted the regional authorities to give closer consideration to the European dimension.[2] With the establishment of the Single Market (1986–1993) regional (or local) issues had begun to be negotiated in Brussels rather than in the national capitals. This gradual shift of powers was often viewed by the regional authorities as an economic, political, and legitimizing opportunity, and they therefore began going to Brussels directly.[3]

The Commission, furthermore, welcomed the regions because it saw them as an instrument for enhancing its own legitimacy. In 1989 the Commission established the Consultative Council of Regional and Local Authorities in the EC with forty-two members, mainly civil servants.[4] Also in 1989, looking ahead to the work on the new treaty, the Conference of Minister-Presidents of the German *Länder* set up a working party whose main remit was to work out proposals for the political participation of the states and regions in Europe at the European level. Germany's proposals were supported in particular by the Autonomous Communities of Spain, by the Belgian regions, and by such countries as Denmark and Italy, while the other states that did not have a regional governance system were more lukewarm toward it. Indeed, some member states were initially opposed to the creation of the Committee of the Regions, fearful of the "regions lobby."[5] It was also thanks to such pressure that the Committee of the Regions was established with the Maastricht Treaty in 1991.

The Regions in the Italian Constitutional System

Europe has a wide and varied array of subnational constitutional systems. We can imagine the relationship between central and regional governments as a continuum ranging from unitary states (Greece, Ireland, Luxembourg, Portugal, and France) to federal states (Belgium, Germany, and Spain), with, in the center, a group of states that are decentralized or devolved to varying degrees, such as the United Kingdom, Denmark, Sweden, Finland, Italy, and the Netherlands.[6]

Italy is divided into twenty regions, of which five are Special Statute Regions (one of them, Trentino-Alto Adige, is further subdivided into the two autonomous provinces of Bolzano and Trento). But decentralization was a long process that took more than fifty years to complete. Unlike other European states, such as Germany or the United Kingdom, Italy was not the product of a federative process, but was the outcome of the gradual merging of the pre-unitary state entities with the original kingdom of Sardinia. The states were first incorporated into the Piedmont constitutional system with its typical French centralist rationale, which was subsequently heightened under the fascist regime. It was for this reason that after the fall of fascism, and in order to prevent secessionist movements from emerging, four of the present five "autonomous" regions were established: Valle d'Aosta, Sicily, Trentino-Alto Adige, and Sardinia (the fifth region, Friuli-Venezia Giulia, was not created until 1963).

During the deliberations of the Constituent Assembly (which wrote the Italian Constitution and sat from 1946 to 1948) the idea gradually took shape of dividing up the country into regional units, giving rise to a wide-ranging debate on the substance and degree of autonomy to give them and the powers to be conferred on these new entities. While it originally seemed acceptable to strike a compromise under which all the regions would be given three types of legislative power (exclusive, concurrent, and supplementary), opposition by the anti-regionalists resulted in the decision to vest the "ordinary" regions (then fourteen, and subsequently fifteen) only with concurrent and supplementary legislative powers, subordinate to the national government. The regional question arose once again over the composition of the Senate:

having opted for perfect bicameralism, it became necessary for the Constituent Assembly to decide on the composition of the second legislative chamber, and hence on its very nature: in other words, whether to make it the representative of the regional governments. But this idea was then discarded, and the only decision reached by the Constituent Assembly was that elections to the second chamber would be held on a regional basis.

Despite the fact that regionalism was enshrined in the Constitution, it was not until 1977, with Presidential Decree 616/1977, that powers were actually transferred to the regional governments. But it was a crisis in the political party system in the early 1990s that brought regional authority again to Italy. In particular, the party system encouraged the emergence of groups whose strength came from their close links to local situations (I am thinking here, for example, of Umberto Bossi's Northern League). This created the conditions for the 1999 Constitutional Law (1/1999) vesting full constitutional autonomy in the Ordinary Statute Regions and introducing the direct election of the regional presidents, giving them direct democratic legitimacy.

With the October 7, 2001, referendum, the Constitutional Bill enacting "amendments to Title V of the 2nd part of the Constitution" obtained final approval after the two chambers had already adopted it. This was the so-called "federalist" constitutional reform (even though that term is never actually used in the text). It introduced a series of substantial novelties: article 123 of the Constitution turned the institutional pyramid upside down by providing for the republic to be governed, in this order, by municipalities, provinces, metropolitan cities, regions, and the central government. The whole issue of regional legislative powers was then overhauled, sanctioning the existence of a "dual track" legislative system. The new article 117 listed the central government's powers, leaving all other matters not listed there subject to the legislative jurisdiction of the regional authorities.

In the earlier Constitution the regions had legislative powers over a limited, and detailed, list of subjects; but in the new text the traditional primacy of ordinary state legislation was abolished and replaced by the provision that "the legislative powers are exercised by central government and regional governments in compliance with the Constitution and with the limits deriving from Community law and international obligations." The new article 117 draws a distinction between the matters over which the central government has exclusive legislative powers, those governed by concurrent legislative powers (which are listed in detail in both cases), and the general and residual legislative powers of the regions. According to the third paragraph of the new article 117, the concurrent legislative powers concern not only "the regions' international relations, and relations with the European Union" but also issues of relevance to the EU: foreign trade, the protection of employment and safety at work; scientific and technological research to support innovation in the manufacturing sectors; health protection; food; transport and the national distribution of power/energy. The regions are also vested with "legislative powers governing all matters not expressly reserved for central government legislation" (article 117(4)). The body responsible for resolving conflicts between central and regional governments, or between different regional governments, is the Constitutional Court.

The Italian Regions and European Policy: Participation in the Ascending Phase of Community Law

One of the fundamental issues in relations between the central and regional governments in Italy is their relationship with the European Union, both in the ascending phase of Community law and in the descending phase.

With regard to the ascending phase—the framing of Community law—the system of consultation with the regions developed in different ways at different times. Initially the procedural system was preferred, with the result that the central government asked each region for its opinion on issues of relevance to them that were currently being debated in Brussels. Despite the drawbacks of this model, it was the only instrument possible in Italy, which had not yet fully implemented the system of regionalism.[7] It was after the implementation of ordinary autonomy in the 1970s that the first proposals began to emerge to install authorities specifically designed to represent substate entities, in the wake of which the Central-Regional Governments Conference was instituted in 1983. The introduction by the 1989 La Pergola Law (86/1989) of the Special Community Session of the Central-Regional Governments Conference raised many expectations, but with few results: for many years, the conference failed to meet with the intended regularity. Since the enactment of the La Pergola Law, however, the scenario has changed radically, and above all the sensitivity of the regional governments to the EU has changed.

In 1999 under the first D'Alema government (1998–2000), one of the first actions taken by the reinstituted Ministry for Community Policies was to convene a Special Community Session of the Central-Regional Governments Conference. Among the novelties introduced by the then minister for community policies, Enrico Letta, were the following of particular importance to the regional and local government authorities: more frequent meetings of the Community Session of the Central-Regional Governments Conference—which had previously sat only once a year—in order to involve the regional and local authorities in the sensitive phases of drafting Italian policy proposals on European Community issues; the possibility for regions to designate their own officials to represent Italy in dealings with the European Union; the institution of an annual session to debate the annual legislative program submitted by the European Commission by the central government departments, local government authorities, and the social partners.

> There were many reasons for these changes, all sharing a common feature: the conviction that in order to guarantee the success of Italy's work in Brussels it is necessary to facilitate and encourage the local authorities to play a more active and purposeful part in the crucial phase of preparing Italy's negotiating positions, . . . [considering that] it is appropriate for the local authorities to be given greater responsibility, and that access to information is a formidable weapon and a unique tool for promoting an effective linkage between different institutional tiers . . . conscious, moreover, that the isolation of a region or a local authority from their adjacent areas makes it impossible to achieve the critical mass needed to be visible in Brussels.[8]

Under the 2001 constitutional reform, the new article 117 "constitutionalized" the Community linkage with legislation, subjecting both the central government and the regional governments to it on an equal footing; it required the regions to participate in the phases of framing and implementing Community law. The article provides that "in the matters falling within their sphere of competence, the regions participate in decisions that relate to the framing of Community normative acts and are responsible for implementing international agreements and acts of the European Union consistently with the procedures enacted in central government law governing the ways the central government must act in the event of failure by the regional authorities to do so" (article 117). This therefore establishes that the regional governments have the right and duty to take part in the ascending phase of Community law. There still remain several areas of uncertainty, where the distinction between the two tiers of government (central and regional) is not clear-cut. Article 117 of the Constitution provides that central government has exclusive lawmaking powers in the matter of "foreign policy and the state's international relations, and relations between the state and the European Union," but the second part of the article provides that the matters falling within the competence of the regional governments include "concluding agreements with states and with local authorities within another state, in the cases and in the manner governed by state law." On the other hand, it says nothing whatsoever about the ways in which the regions shall participate, or what kinds of regional input are expected. Subsequent action was necessary to make the changes introduced by the constitutional reform more specific and "operational."

It was with Laws 131/2003 and 11/2005 that the involvement of the regions in the phase of determining Italy's positions was put into practice. Article 5 of Law 31/2003, also known in Italy as the La Loggia Law, provided for further participation by the regions in Community affairs. This provision introduced important supplementary rules following the revision of the Constitution. Whereas under article 117(5) of the Constitution the regional governments "participate," under the La Loggia Law, the regions "play a direct concurrent part" in the formation of Community acts; this direct concurrent role is performed by taking part in the work of the Community institutions—that is to say, the Council of Ministers of the European Community, and the Commission, "acting within the framework of central government delegated powers." However, the La Loggia Law still left a number of gray areas (for example, what, in practice, the regional representatives on the Italian delegations participating in the Council actually do, and how they do it), with the result that the Sardinia region and the autonomous province of Bolzano appealed that provision before the Constitutional Court. But in its judgment 239/2004 the Constitutional Court declared their appeal groundless and reiterated the importance of the principle that Italy must adopt a unitary position in its relations with the European Union.

Law 11/2005, also known as the Stucchi-Buttiglione Law, repealed the La Pergola Law by innovating in this area, placing greater emphasis on regional participation and strengthening previous instruments and adding others. As we saw in the chapter dedicated to the executive, the Stucchi-Buttiglione Law created an interdepartmental coordination organ, the Comitato Interministeriale per gli Affari Comunitari Europei (CIACE), in which the president of the Conference of Presidents of the Regions and Autonomous Provinces, or another president delegated to do so, can participate, on request, whenever the meeting deals with "issues that are also of relevance to the regions and the autonomous provinces." In addition to the CIACE, the Central-Regional Governments Conference, as the main instrument of interaction between the two tiers in the ascending phase, still may express an opinion in the course of the Community session "on general guidelines relating to the framing and implementation of Community Acts of relevance to regional competences." This law also retained the government's obligation provided by the earlier La Pergola Law to submit draft Community acts to the regional governments "officially and promptly" within twenty days of receipt, so that within twenty days thereafter the regional governments could submit their comments to the prime minister. The most important novelty introduced by this law was precisely this point, empowering the government to proceed, after that deadline, even without the regions' observations, but only when matters fall within the sphere of regional competence. Otherwise various other mechanisms are provided to protect the regions: first, provision was made that "whenever any one or more regions so request" the government must convene the Central-Regional Governments Conference within twenty days. After that deadline, or in the event of demonstrated urgency arising in the meantime, the government may proceed even without an agreement. This is one of the matters raised in the fact-finding survey performed by the Chamber of Deputies XIV Committee on Italy's participation in the formation of Community law by the regions—that Italian regions are unable to keep up with the fast pace of Community policymaking.[9] When there has been sufficient time, consultations have been successfully completed, as in the case of the drafting of the 2008 National Reform Plan on the Lisbon strategy.

The Italian Regional Governments and European Policies: Participation in the Descending Phase of Community Law

As mentioned in the previous chapters, for a long time Italy viewed European integration as a matter of international law. Consequently, initially the courts treated the domestic legal system and the Community legal system separately. It was constitutional case law that initially opened up this approach at the beginning of the 1970s, making this interpretation more flexible, but without breaking out of the separate treatment model. In judgment 142/1972 the Constitutional Court ruled, for the first time, that lower-tier authorities could also play a part in implementing Community law, and simultaneously declared that it was the responsibility of the central government to activate appropriate instruments to compensate for the inertia of the regional governments. A few years later, by Presidential Decree 616/1977, the regional governments were given the possibility of playing a part in implementing Community law while at the same time the central government was empowered to act in lieu of the regions in the event of their noncompliance. The possibility of directly implementing Community directives, although only in the case of the Special Statute Regions, was granted under Law 183/1987 (known as the Fabbri Law), which not only confirmed the general competence of the regions to implement directives by administrative means but also acknowledged that the Special Statute Regions were competent to immediately implement the directives also by enacting them, in matters falling to their exclusive competence. Later Law 86/1989 (the La Pergola Law) enabled the regions to implement directives in matters over which they had concurrent jurisdiction following the entry into force of the first "Community Law" enacted after notification of the directive to be implemented. Law 128/1998 later that made it possible for both the Special Statute Regions and the ordinary regions to proceed with the implementation of directives directly in matters falling within their jurisdiction.

Under the 2001 constitutional reform, new article 117 required the regional governments as well as the central government to comply "with the constraints imposed by Community law" and gave the regional governments the right and duty to participate in the implementation (or descending) phase of Community law, without prejudice to the right of the central government to act in lieu of them—pursuant to article 120 of the Constitution—in the event of inertia on the part of the regions. This confirmed the fact that the central government remains the sole legal personality in the eyes of the Community.

The Stucchi-Buttiglione Law (11/2005) also reiterated the fact, under article 8, that the regional governments, like the central government, were obliged to implement Community directives in matters falling within their legislative jurisdiction. In addition, the preliminary verification of the conformity of Community law with the Italian constitutional system was no longer the responsibility of the central government alone but was also the responsibility of the regional governments for matters falling within their jurisdiction. Last but not least, article 17 of the Stucchi-Buttiglione Law reiterated the importance of the Central-Regional Governments Conference as the main instrument in the Community law implementation phase (for example, when drafting the Annual Community Bill, discussed in chapter 5). However, as emerged in the course of the fact-finding survey conducted by the Chamber of Deputies XIV Committee in 2008–09, the local government authorities are often in default with regard to the implementation of Community law. According to figures submitted by the head of the Community Policies Department, Professor Roberto Adam, at a hearing held on November 19, 2008, before the XIV Committee, about 30 of the 160 noncompliance proceedings against Italy were cases for which the local authorities were directly liable. Most of these breaches related to environmental law (and the failure to reclaim landfills).[10]

The Long Path toward Opening the Italian Regional Offices in Brussels

The first European regions to set up an office in Brussels were the German Länder in 1985. At the beginning of 1994 there were 70 regional offices in Brussels, and five years later the number had already reached 179.[11] Today, virtually every European region is represented in one way or another in Brussels.

Compared with other countries, Italian regions were late, and, in more general terms, the central and northern regions acted earlier than the southern regions. The first Italian regions to open their Brussels offices (Tuscany, Lazio, Emilia-Romagna) did so in 1995. But until 1996 Italy's presence had to be mediated through other parties (chambers of commerce and agencies) because of legislative constraints. For example, Tuscany operated through "Fidi Toscana," Emilia-Romagna through ASTER (the Agency for the Technological Development of Emilia-Romagna), and the Lazio office operated through the BIC (Business Innovation Center).

Since the Italian legal system drew no distinction between the Community system and the international system and considered European policy to fall within the area of international policy, the possibility of having direct representation in Brussels was seen as an activity reserved exclusively for the central government, since the regions "could not perform any promotional activities abroad regarding matters falling within their jurisdiction except by agreement with the central government" (Presidential Decree 616/1977). Initially, the Constitutional Court upheld this approach, and in its judgment 170/1975 it stated that the regional authorities did not have the powers to conclude agreements with parties belonging to other legal systems that were vested solely in the central government, and quashed a number of regional resolutions approving international agreements concluded without the necessary central government assent. It was only later, with judgment 179/1987, that the court adopted a more flexible attitude, drawing a distinction between the regions' foreign promotional activities—which required the consent of the central government—and activities merely of an international character (such as exchanges of information or joint declarations of intent). At all events, the regions remained under an obligation to submit to the central government any agreements they had concluded with regional authorities in individual states. With the signing of the Maastricht Treaty and the repercussions this had for policies, international policy and European policy were finally separated. In 1994 the "1993 Community Law" (Law 146/1994) separated relations between the regional governments, and the Community institutions were no longer subject to the laws governing international policy, thereby removing the requirement that the central government approve regional promotional activities abroad. The 1993 Community Law and the following presidential decree of March 31, 1994, gave the regional and autonomous provincial governments ordinary jurisdiction over international affairs, drawing a distinction between the Community system and international legal system. The 1993 Community Law nevertheless provided that relations between the regional governments and autonomous provincial governments and the Community institutions had to be performed "in liaison with Italy's Permanent Representative to the European Union," for example, by sending a quota of regional representatives appointed by the Conference of Presidents of the Regions and Autonomous Provinces to "facilitate relations with Community bodies." Whether these relations had to pass through the central government representative or whether it was only necessary to coordinate the work with the regional authorities, leaving them with greater autonomy, was not specified in the text. Doubts therefore remained until 1996. With the "1994 Community Law" (Law 52/1996) the regions were finally permitted to open their own representative offices in Brussels. Basilicata, Sardinia (1996), Liguria (1997), Sicily, and the Valle D'Aosta then opened offices in Brussels. The 1994 Community law also raised the maximum number of experts to be sent to the Permanent Representative's Office from twenty-five to twenty-nine, and provided that these four additional experts could also be chosen from among regional officials appointed by the Conference of Presidents of the Regions and Autonomous Provinces.

Law 128/98 further broadened the sphere of action of the regional governments by giving them the right to set up offices jointly with regions or bodies belonging to other countries of the European Union under cross-border cooperation or international agreements. This therefore introduced innovations that had existed under previous laws (which made it possible to open joint offices only with other Italian regions and provinces) and under previous constitutional case law. For when the autonomous provinces of Trento and Bolzano had opened a joint office with the Austrian *Land* of Tyrol, in 1995, the Constitutional Court declared it null and void (Constitutional Court judgment 428/1997). Following these statutory changes, in 1999 Abruzzo, Calabria, Marche, and Umbria opened their own offices in Brussels. They were joined in 2000 by Molise and Puglia, in 2001 by Friuli, and in 2002 by Campania.[12] Today all of the Italian regions have their own offices in Brussels.

The Internal Organization of the Regions regarding EU Affairs and Links with the Central Government

The regions do not follow a standard organizational or operational model in their relations with the EU. The operational procedures are often based on specific contingent elements and not on best practices. The histories and traditions and individual regions also differ, as do the interests at stake and the interference of local political interests.

First, the offices of regional representatives can be either the direct extension of a region or represented in Brussels by a third party, such as an agency, a financial holding company, a chamber of commerce, or a foundation. This was the (inevitable) solution adopted by the regions when Italian law did not permit them to have representative offices abroad. Following the 1994 Community Law (Law 52/1996), and at different times, the regional governments that adopted this delegated form of representation, "regularized" their position by enacting specific regional laws. The first region to move was the Veneto (Regional Law 30/1996) followed by Lombardy (Regional Law 2/1997) and then Lazio; Emilia Romagna, Tuscany, and the two autonomous provinces waited until 1998, while Piedmont made its presence official only in April 2002. The other regions acted after 1996: Sardinia in that year, although the office was not opened until 1999, followed by Liguria and Sicily (1997) and then Abruzzo, Marche, Umbria, and Valle D'Aosta (1998), and finally Basilicata (1996) and Calabria (1999), which preferred to have noninstitutional representation under contractual agreements with Mondoimpresa and with BIC Calabria, respectively.

Some regions operate individually and others pool their efforts with other regional authorities. One successful pooling of effort is the central Italian "Common Home" group comprising five regions (Tuscany, Marche, Umbria, Abruzzo, Lazio) that share logistical and secretarial costs and organize their work jointly. This arrangement began in 1997 after a meeting in Orvieto at which the five central regions expressed dismay that they were hardly noticeable at the European level and intended to pool their resources. At a second meeting in Rome they agreed to set up the joint Brussels office in 1999. This undertaking saved each region both time and money, but also increased their "weight" with the European institutions: the one agency speaks on behalf of roughly 20 million citizens (rather than five individual regions). Like the EU institutions, the business community and the social partners also see the joint group as providing a solid benchmark, further strengthened by the partnership with Fidi Toscana, the financial holding company for the governing coalition of the region. Last but not least, the "Common Home" also helps to represent other parties such as banks, local organizations, trade associations, trade unions, and the chambers of commerce from the five regions. Tuscany has also tried to pursue an innovative approach with the enactment of a regional law (45/1997) proposing to incorporate a company under Belgian law, with not only the region as a member but also Fidi Toscana, Fidi Agricola, local entities, and other public agencies, trade associations, and trade unions. However, following the central government's referral of this law to the Constitutional Court the regional government of Tuscany withdrew its project, fearing that the judgment would not be in its favor. The soundness of the existing project, that is to say the pooling of the central Italian regions, has in any event been confirmed by the fact that other regions have sought to join it, including Molise and Liguria.

One notable experience is that of the autonomous provinces of Trento and Bolzano, which opened a joint office with the Austrian Land of Tyrol in 1995. After the Constitutional Court (judgment 428/1997) declared the office to be illegal, Trento opened its own liaison office in 1999 but maintained a common secretariat with Bolzano and Tyrol.

Some regional offices share space with other local associations and organizations. This is the case with, among others, the Veneto and Friuli-Venezia Giulia regions. Molise, Puglia, Friuli, and Campania decided to formally incorporate their Brussels offices into the regional organizational system.[13] The Italian regional offices are smaller than those of the German Länder and the Spanish autonomous communities. Staff numbers vary from one (Molise) to eleven (Lombardy); most common is an office with a manager and one or two officials, and sometimes a secretary. The best-equipped offices, in addition to Lombardy, are those of Veneto, Lazio, Tuscany, and Emilia-Romagna. To staff their offices in Brussels, the Italian regions can second officials or regional managers to run the office, or employ external consultants or even people from outside the regional government but with well-proven Community experience. Some regions have opted for the first solution (Campania, Friuli, Marche, Molise, Sardinia, Tuscany, Umbria, Veneto, and the two autonomous provinces), giving responsibility for the office to managers or officials already dealing with Community affairs for the region, together with a number of regional staff members seconded to Brussels.

In contrast, the Lombardy regional government has commissioned an agency to take care of its work in Brussels in order to recruit some of its own staff with past experience with European institutions: of the eleven employees, only one is a regional official. The same model has been adopted by Liguria and Valle D'Aosta, and partly by Calabria. Liguria is an interesting case because, with the changes in the government coalition in 2000, nothing short of a revolution took place in the staffing of the office, which was replaced in its entirety: until the year 2000, responsibility and management were vested in a regional director and an external consultant, together with a regional officer seconded to Brussels. But after the elections the organizational plan of the office changed completely, and now it is staffed entirely by people outside the regional government apparatus.

Other regions use a hybrid form of administration: Abruzzo and Puglia use external consultants and one regional official, while Sicily and Lazio employ regional staff to coordinate the office and use external experts for supporting activities (Sicily) or management duties (Lazio). Emilia-Romagna is a particular case: although the office manager is not formally a regional official, she has been the head of the office ever since it was opened, after managing

ASTER from 1994 to 1997; three external consultants and the two regional officials assist this manager.[14] Finally, responsibility for the Tuscany office has been given to three long-time officials of the regional government who have well-established and fiduciary relations with the political and administrative authorities in Florence, and are therefore able to implement the Tuscany regional government's strategies consistently. Tuscany's regional office therefore has a higher political profile than the other regions and is often entrusted directly with responsibility to negotiate with Commission officials.

With regard to the management of European policies in the regional capitals, in most cases the competences for international and European policies are vested in the regional presidents, and only in six of twenty-one cases does a member of the regional government (assessor) have specific delegated powers. This distinction is also reflected managerially and organizationally, except in Piedmont, where competence lies with the Community policies assessor and the administrative structures are in the presidency.[15]

Last, at the central government level, in order to support the regions but also to keep a certain degree of control over what they do, the Ministry of Foreign Affairs has proposed seconding its own diplomatic advisers to the regions (and sharing the costs) at the request of the Italian regional presidents. The diplomatic advisers are generally directly accountable to the president. In 2009 Lazio, Liguria, Campania, and Piedmont adopted this practice, which had previously also been used by Tuscany, Lombardy, and Sicily. Two structures have been instituted by the government to support the regions: in 2002 the general secretariat of the Ministry of Foreign Affairs established a "Regional Coordination Unit." In 2003 it was renamed "Regions Unit" and then changed again to "Unit for Major International Activities of the Regions and Other Italian Local Authorities," before it finally became the "Unit for the Country-System and Local Government Authorities," tasked with assisting the secretary general and the deputy secretaries general in their relations with Italian business and the regions and other local authorities in their work abroad. There is also a small office for international relations within the Department of Regional Affairs, which is located at the Presidency of the Council.

The Activities and Representative Offices of the Italian Regions in Brussels

While the organizational models differ, the objectives of the Italian regions in Brussels are the same: to engage in dialogue with the Community institutions to protect regional interests; to help their own regions understand the procedures and the mechanisms adopted by the Community; to forge relations with other regions; to take part in Community programs; to enhance their image and influence, and, in the case of some regions, to play a part in the lawmaking process. According to Alessandro Alfieri, the Italian regions essentially adopt two possible approaches in Brussels: either they focus on programs and Community Funds, or they adopt a broader strategy, coupling the management of Community programs with the creation of partnerships with other regions and participating in the ascending phase of Community law.[16] The second type of strategy will increase the regions' importance as well as their political and institutional weight and support for their regional development. But that strategy also requires a greater investment. Given that the regions have an average of only three staff members, the second strategy would be possible for only a few regions. Furthermore, like the central government, for the regions to be effective and efficient in Brussels they must first be efficient and effective at home.

According to Lorenza Badiello,[17] who served for a long time at the Emilia-Romagna Representative Office, the four main activities of the regional representatives in Brussels are:

—networking with the European institutions and the other European regions

—information gathering and monitoring

—representing regional interests

—providing technical assistance (Community projects)

Over time, the Italian regions have expanded their activities significantly, particularly with regard to their participation in European associations and in the partnership network for projects.

The institutional interlocutors of the regions in Brussels are the Committee of the Regions, the European Commission, the European Parliament, and the European Council. However, these institutions are not all equally open to the regional authorities.

The main forum for representing regional interests in Brussels is the Committee of the Regions. However, the Italian seats have not yet been assigned on the basis of one seat for each region and autonomous province, as one would expect them to be after the 2001 constitutional reform. Even though a Decree of the Presidency of the Council of Ministers (DPCM) on January 12, 2006, provided that there should be twelve Italian representatives of the regions and autonomous provinces, four representing the provinces and six representing municipalities, the full membership consists of thirteen regional presidents, three regional councilors, two provincial presidents, and one mayor.[18] It is even more difficult to understand the rationale for the appointment of alternate members: there are two councilors from small, remote villages, some areas that are overrepresented (for example, Friuli-Venezia Giulia), and others that are not represented at all. One gathers the impression that the representatives on the Committee of the Regions, particularly the alternate members, are appointed on the basis of patronage rather than representation, to defend the national interests. As a consequence, the representation, presence, and commitment, as well as the weight of the Italian member states, vary widely, and consequently the potential impact of the country-system on the Community institutions is reduced.

As for the other institutions, not all the regions have activated all the channels available to them with the same intensity. It is possible, though, to identify the main European policymaking activities developed and used by the Italian regions. According to Veronica Elena Bocci, the work of the Italian regions in the European Parliament consists of sending communications, taking part in the work of the committees that is relevant to their regions, and requesting individual MEPs to lobby on their behalf on these committees.[19] The same applies to their relations with the Commission, from which the representatives of the regions request advance notice of legislative proposals as well as information about draft legislation, and above all lobby in support of legislation that is under consideration. Conversely, relations with the Council are almost nonexistent and in any case are conducted through the Permanent Representative.

Some quite substantial differences exist between the regions' capacity to conduct their lobbying activities in Brussels. In a hearing before the Chamber of Deputies Committee XIV on March 26, 2009, Italy's Permanent Representative to the European Union, Ambassador Ferdinando Nelli Feroci, said that there is "a varied and complex presence of regions in Brussels, each one having its own Representative Office. There are no institutional representative offices. . . . They vary widely in terms of the number of persons present, their capabilities, and the will and enthusiasm of the individual regional representatives. Some of them are very good, demanding, and hands-on, while others are seen less frequently."[20]

According to Profeti, links exist between regional activity, political leadership, and Structural Funds.[21] If a regional government is seeking opportunities outside the national constraints, whether political or financial, it will tend primarily to use the Community channel. The degree of activity does not therefore depend on the socioeconomic state of a region or its institutional architecture, but rather on the capacity of the regional elites to exploit the opportunities offered by the Community, and even to turn the constraints they lay down to their own advantage. According to Bolgherini, the political and administrative regional elites determine whether a region is actively engaged and whether its activities are successful.[22] A region's level of activity and presence in the European forums is measured by its will and ability to create networks. Conversely, the regional elites become more European to the extent that they are incorporated into these networks and are capable of establishing and maintaining them. According to Bolgherini, Tuscany has a high level of activity in this sense, whereas Campania is less active.[23]

Broadly speaking, one can identify three groups of regions: (1) the ones with a high level of external projection, which are able to act promptly and with a high degree of commitment to all forms of participation (Tuscany, Lombardy, and Emilia-Romagna, and to a lesser degree Veneto); (2) those with low-level external projection, which act slowly and with a weak capacity to develop all the channels in Brussels (Molise, Basilicata, Lazio); and (3) an intermediate group comprising a range of different regional experiences.[24]

Tuscany, Emilia-Romagna, Lombardy, and Veneto are the most active regions in Brussels. According to the CIPI Report, there were 600 visits by officials of the Tuscany regional administration to Brussels, in addition to 1,200 visits by representatives of trade associations, local authorities and organizations, and NGOs.[25] The Tuscany region has a leadership role in the following organizations: AMRIE (Alliance of Maritime Regional Interests in Europe), AER (Assembly of European Regions), and AREPO (Quality Maritime Agriculture).

Among the successful lobbying efforts coordinated by the Tuscany region's representative office in Brussels was a move to change the Commission's position on genetically modified crops. This effort was undertaken in response to the region's environmental and agricultural strategy. Its success has enabled Tuscany to increase its rating as a "clean" region, and it has seen its market share in regional agrifood products rise. In addition, on the initiative of Tuscany and Oberösterreich (in Austria) a conference on GMOs was organized in Brussels in 2003, which adopted an important document supporting the coexistence of traditional, GM, and organic agriculture. This position was presented by the Tuscany region at a hearing before the European Parliament Agriculture Committee, which is engaged in preparing the EP's opinion on this subject. Follow-up conferences have been organized every year since. In 2005 a charter was signed by the participating regions in Florence, which was submitted in April 2005 to the European Commission. Austria has proposed a law against GMOs that the European Court of Justice declared unlawful because it contravened the rules of the common market. As a result, the GMO network has attracted publicity and gradually attracted new members and greater interest and involvement on the part of the Commission. Last, in October 2005 a group managed by the Brittany (France) region was established to promote agreements with politicians and companies in Brazil for the production of non-GMO seeds.[26]

In conclusion, the Italian regions have increased their presence in Brussels exponentially over the past fifteen years. The legal instruments for their participation in both the ascending and descending phases of Community law have also changed completely, and have opened up the regions considerably. However, this does not necessarily mean that the Italian regions have a major influence on Italy's position on European policies. Likewise, their physical presence in Brussels does not necessarily give them more influence. Evidence of this is the fact that since 2002 the Italian regions have never succeeded in spending all the Structural Funds allocated to them.[27] As the then president of the Tuscany region, Vannino Chiti, understood very clearly when he opened the first office in Brussels through Fidi Toscana, their presence in Brussels is above all preparatory in character; indeed, we might say that it is a pedagogical presence for the officials and for the elected representatives of the regions (and local authorities). But even though the Europeanization of the local and regional elites is moving forward slowly, there is still a widespread idea that "Europe" can also be the object of political patronage.

Furthermore, only a few regions have the necessary critical mass and political weight (and economic might) to have any direct impact on EU policies through the Community channel. These include Lombardy and the regions of central Italy led by Tuscany, Emilia-Romagna, and to a lesser degree Veneto, Piedmont, Liguria, and Puglia. The idea of a common home, as a kind of consortium of different regions, might therefore prove to be the most successful policy even for the southern Italian regions, whose presence in Brussels does not seem to have reached the necessary critical mass to enable them to make their voices heard, even though all the regions are represented there.

The Italian regions' ability to exert influence still depends on working through national channels, both institutional and otherwise. The evidence provided by the representatives of Italy's local and regional governments at the hearings before the Chamber of Deputies XIV Committee in 2008–09 were vague, and more a matter of "asking" rather than testifying. In other words, there is still a great deal more to be done.

The regions are still prevented from sending their own representatives to join Italian delegations attending the various Councils. This is a function which, in an extremely limited number of cases on a stable and permanent basis, applies only to the German Länder and the Belgian communities. Since 1986 the German Länder have been playing an institutionalized role in helping to draft Community legal acts at the national level through the *Bundesratsbeteiligungsverfahren*.[28] In order to control the work of the federal government, moreover, representatives of the Länder can also be delegated by the federal government to attend sessions of the Council at various levels.

However, any Länder wishing to send their representatives must also pay their expenses, which is the reason why only the rich Länder actually join the delegations attending the Council. The same would probably also have occurred in the case of the Italian regions if Italian law had been properly implemented. Until that happens, any continuous participation by the Italian regions at the European Councils would probably not make much sense.

Italian Organized Interests in Brussels

Italy is the EU's third-largest European economy, roughly on a par with the United Kingdom. There is a widespread conviction that the size and importance of the "underground economy" have been underestimated and are higher than in the rest of the EU. Italy is heavily dependent on energy and other strategic imports. Furthermore, a very large number of small and medium-size firms produce almost exclusively for export. Ninety-nine percent of Italian businesses have fewer than 100 employees. Big industry, however, through its association Confindustria, is extremely influential. Confindustria, along with the leading trade unions, is routinely consulted by the government on important decisions regarding economic and social issues. Italy used to have, and still does to a certain extent, one of the largest public sectors in the Western world, comprising not only the usual industries such as public transport, utilities, and telecommunications but also large manufacturing sectors (chemicals, oil and gas, steel, construction) and a financial sector (most major banks and one of the largest insurance companies). By the end of the 1980s, the three leading state-owned industrial groups—IRI, ENI, and EFIM[29]—accounted for over 10 percent of GNP, but were burdened by severe debt and inefficiency. Under the economic reform program initiated by Prime Minister Giuliano Amato in 1992 and the need to liberalize the economy to comply with European Community obligations, these state-owned groups were privatized and eventually dismantled (in the case of IRI and EFIM). Yet political interference and involvement in business (and vice versa) is hard to eradicate in Italy.

The affirmation of democracy, ethnic, cultural, and religious pluralism, modernization, and the resultant expansion of the role and duties of government all are factors in the rise of interest groups. At the European level, lobbying became a widespread practice following the Single European Act (SEA) in 1987. The first groups to react to it—attracted by the benefits they expected from the Single Market—were business groups. But as the SEA, initially, and the Maastricht Treaty later (in 1992) introduced new EU competences over such sectors as the environment and social policies, other kinds of groups also became established. As a consequence of the decision to act at the European level, most Eurogroups (meaning interest groups operating at the European level) decided to establish a permanent office in Brussels, for proximity to the EU institutions is vitally important in facilitating access to information and to making informal contacts with the EU decisionmakers.[30]

The Italian interest groups followed, and even in some cases anticipated, this trend. Indeed, the first firm to open a representative office in Brussels was the Italian Ferruzzi company. Over the years, all the large industrial groups followed its example.[31] According to the CIPI Report, there are some 199 Italian liaison and representative offices working with the European institutions, including 7 central government offices, 21 regional and provincial offices, at least 16 industrial federations and associations and confederated national sectoral entities, 13 sectoral associations, 14 belonging to industrial groups, 17 financial and insurance groups, together with legal offices, consultancies, "civil society" associations, and universities—all told, an estimated 4,000 people at a cost of 450 million euros a year.[32]

The largest industrial corporations, such as Fiat, Fininvest, Pirelli, and ENEL, have their own offices in Brussels. The task of an office in Brussels is threefold: to send information back to Italy, represent the group in Brussels, and lobby the EC institutions. In the past, Italian entrepreneurs were particularly noteworthy for their European activities, which took them to the leadership of European organizations. For example, EuroElectric was founded by the then vice president of ENEL, Alessandro Ortis, and Umberto Agnelli was one of the founders and vice presidents of the European Round Table.

But for the majority of Italy's (small and medium-size) firms, the cost of running their own representative office in Brussels is prohibitive. In most cases they opt to become members of trade or professional associations. These associations aim to speak with a "single voice" for a sector of composite and often heterogeneous activities. In addition to providing information to the public and to their own membership, these organizations act as a means of multiplying the efforts made by an individual company. The sectoral associations can often bring pressure to bear on broad issues more effectively than an individual company could on its own. In 2006 CIPI listed the following Italian sectoral associations with offices in Brussels: Anancam (lift construction and maintenance companies); Assonime (association of public companies); Assozucchero (sugar, alcohol, and yeast manufacturers); CIA (farms and agricultural enterprises); Confartigianato and CNA (for the craft industries and small and medium-size enterprises [SMEs]); CIA, Coldiretti, and Confagricoltura (in the agriculture sector); Confcommercio and Confesercenti (commercial firms, tourism, and services); Confcooperative (co-operative movement and social enterprises); FIT (resellers of monopoly goods, such as tobacco).

Certainly the most influential of all these professional associations is Confindustria. Confindustria seeks to bring Italian companies out of the "national syndrome" by organizing meetings between Italian entrepreneurs and the commissioners of other member states of the European Union and organizing "convergence" tables between Italian representatives around the leading confederation of economic and industrial interests. The exercise is of course complicated by their heterogeneous character.

But the greatest handicap for the trade and professional associations is that they often lack the support of Italian politicians and strategic and operational links with the work of Italy's Permanent Representative. At the February 2006 session of the European Parliament, for example, the European People's Party (EPP)—of which the Italian party "Freedom People" is a leading member—did not support the "country of origin principle" when voting on the services directive, which was backed by Confindustria.[33]

In some cases, the Italian organizations have succeeded in finding a common denominator and have acted together in their dealings with central government departments and agencies. This occurred, for example, with the 2005 sugar market reform. At the end of the negotiations in November 2005, the EU ministers of agriculture agreed to reform the sugar market, which for forty years had successfully held up any reform of the Common Agricultural Policy: it was agreed to cut the production of sugar by 36 percent over four years and to provide substantial accompanying and reconversion financial assistance. Advocates of the Italian cause included Minister of Agricultural Policies Gianni Alemanno, one of the most active negotiators of financial mechanisms to help countries like Italy whose sugar beet yields are low (only 6.05 tons per hectare compared with 10 in Belgium and 11.35 in France). Alemanno estimated that of Italy's nineteen sugar mills, only six or seven—almost entirely concentrated in the Po Valley—would be able to continue production and increase productivity. Sugar production will not therefore disappear from Italy, but, on the contrary, with the new scenario, about 50 percent of Italy's current sugar output should be preserved and remain competitive. The rest of the sugar industry received support of some 700 million euros over two years to restructure, and to help the farmers switch to different crops to avoid serious job losses or find alternative employment. The agreement reached in Brussels was made possible thanks to a group negotiating effort including Italian government officials, Coldiretti, Confagricoltura, and Confederazione Italiana Agricoltori (CIA).[34]

Another example of success by Italy's industrial representatives is Ferrovie dello Stato (the Italian state railway system), among the most active companies in Brussels. Its offices are closely integrated with the European railways federation (CER), of which it has held the presidency and the vice presidency;

it has also rallied support for projects related to the cross-border railway networks and has attracted the interest of MEPs from more than six countries. Ferrovie dello Stato is on the front line regarding regulations, promoting standard-setting initiatives and legal provisions to liberalize rail services. The Ferrovie dello Stato Brussels office has promoted and coordinated the informal "Brussels Group," which from time to time convenes meetings of the representatives of the national railway services companies.[35]

Despite these successes, the Italian lobbying record is not particularly brilliant and has sometimes operated contrary to Italian interests, as in the case of milk quotas. During negotiations on milk quotas (the amount of milk that an EU member state is allowed to produce in a year) in 1982–1984, in the absence of any concrete data on Italian milk production, Agriculture Minister Filippo Maria Pandolfi presented his EC counterparts with figures that underestimated Italy's milk production by a rather large amount. In response, on March 31, 1984, the Council agreed on the milk quotas for a period of five years.[36] When Calogero Antonio Mannino became minister of agriculture in 1988 he discovered the mistake but instructed UNALAT—the national association of milk producers—to keep it secret. UNALAT supported the minister's strategy, as its President Mr. Venino declared: "If the data were to be made public, Italy would be forced to pay for the extra production."[37] Consistent with Italy's tradition of politicizing economic issues, the prime minister at the time, Giulio Andreotti, wrote to Commission president Jacques Delors to plead Italy's case.[38] Although this failed to change the attitude of the Agriculture commissioner, Ray McSharry, or the other national ministers, and in particular the Dutch minister, negotiations were nevertheless reopened. At the Agriculture Council in May 1992, the new Italian agriculture minister, Giovanni Goria, was offered an extra quota of 850,000 tons, less than the 1.5 million tons that Italy had requested. After consultations with Andreotti, who raised the matter before the European Council in Lisbon, Goria turned the offer down. At Lisbon no decision was taken on the issue and a few days later the new minister of agriculture, Gianni Fontana, promised his EC counterparts to introduce a government bill to gradually scale down Italian milk production. As a consequence of misconduct Italy was obliged for many years to pay fines and engage in parallel renegotiations of the national milk quotas simply to be able to change the figures that Italy itself previously produced.

Italy's ability to lobby on its own behalf continues to be hampered by numerous structural problems at home, in particular the fragmentation and parochial nature of Italian interests, as well as underlying political and cultural conflicts. The very expression "to lobby" had negative connotations for many years in Italy, and even today, unlike in the English-speaking world and many other countries, lobbying is not regulated under Italian law. In other words, Italy is not particularly familiar with transparent lobbying—which requires access to massive technical data, among other things—and prefers a system dominated by political patronage.[39]

It is therefore hardly surprising that networking among Italians remains problematic. Some Italian entities, fully aware of the importance of having a presence in Brussels, are effectively using the networks there and are cooperating very effectively among themselves and with other European countries. Telecom Italia, Confindustria, the Tuscany regional government, the National Research Council (CNR), and Unioncamere are all good examples. Most Italian entities, however, are mainly active in informal Italian-only networks and make little use of the formal networks.[40]

They rely too heavily on the "goodwill" and the personal reputation of the representatives of the Italian pressure groups. But Italy, as a country, is not keeping pace with its European counterparts. According to the CIPI survey, Italian interests spend little effort even maintaining the positions they have already attained, often making quick compromises instead.[41] The perception that this behavior creates is that they are acting from a position of weakness rather than strength. Italian companies seem to have little understanding of the need to establish international alliances to create sufficient mass and "strike power" to influence Community competence in Brussels. With regard to the environment (negotiating and enforcing the Kyoto rules) or chemical products (the negotiations on the REACH directive), for example, while all the major countries mobilized their efforts three years in advance of the decisions, Italy's chemical industry was virtually absent. It is obvious that when matters are managed in this way the only thing left is to deal with infringement procedures.

The Italian companies represented in Brussels make little use of legal consultancy services to influence EU structures, with only a few exceptions (Poste Italiane, Telecom Italia, Banca Intesa). This is the approach adopted by virtually all the other countries. Italian companies seem also reluctant to use foreign or international legal firms for fear of revealing confidential information to competitors. They therefore opt, as a matter of priority, to use Italian lawyers, whom they consider to be more likely to protect their interests. Although there are some Italian technical consultancies in Brussels (working on European projects and programs and public funding), there are still very few lobbying consultancies.[42]

Finally, however surprising this may seem in the twenty-first century, Italians are still suffering from language difficulties. When one analyzes the rate of Italian responses to EU Commission consultations in comparison with those of the other EU member states, there is considerable variation depending upon whether the European Commission posts the questionnaire in Italian or not. Most of the consultations are conducted in English. According to a survey of the European institutions by the firm Burson-Marsteller, 85 percent of the people questioned at the European Parliament and at the Commission preferred to interact in English rather than in their national language (Italian accounted for less than 4 percent of the replies). [43] Italian companies and entities interact with and influence Italian MEPs and commissioners, partly for reasons of language. This problem exists at every level.

The consequence of this state of affairs, as the CIPI survey has shown, is that the European institutions view Italian lobbying as fragmented, dealing with private and particular cases.[44] Italy has a plethora of small, very weak influences in Brussels. Albeit with a few important exceptions, Italian lobbying is viewed as being badly prepared, vague, generic, and often slow. Italian lobbying is marred by a lack of persistence and method, poor technical preparation, and linguistic and cultural limitations. It is very rare to find Italian lobbyists acting on the basis of an agreed strategy with other non-Italian parties. Very frequently the Italian lobbyists express a need for, rather than an interest in, developing a strategy. In these cases the effectiveness of the lobbying work is thwarted by competing interests, which are expressed in clearer terms. Italian-only lobbying is increasingly less effective with regard to the Community processes, which have become more broadly multicultural. But even when it is possible to act through Italian political or other channels, it is Italy's lack of technical readiness and its lack of familiarity with the dossiers that hamper Italian lobbying. Maintaining good public relations, however cordial and constant, is not in itself enough to influence decisionmaking. What is essential are substantive knowledge and properly contextualized Italian communications. Without them, the Italian parties will continue to struggle in the competition with other countries and be ineffective in exploiting new opportunities.

8 | EU Constitutional Policies and High Politics

The EU is neither a classic international organization nor a federated state. It has been defined in umpteen ways. Alberta Sbragia, in 1992, called the European Community "unique in its institutional structure, it is neither a state nor an international organization."[1] According to Robert Keohane and Stanley Hoffmann: "If any traditional model were to be applied, it would be that of a confederation rather than a federation. . . . However, confederalism alone fails to capture the complexity of the interest-based bargaining that now prevails in the Community."[2] Elsewhere, the EC/EU has been defined as "a loose federation,"[3] "a multi-tiered system of governance,"[4] and "a multi-tier negotiating system."[5]

The EU produces three kinds of policies. Above all, the EU makes laws that have a binding effect on member states (and their citizens) and that take precedence over national legislation. In agreement with Stanley Hoffmann, here I call the negotiations over such legal provisions *low politics*.[6] Low politics in the EU are negotiated in a setting and in a way that can be better compared to domestic politics. As Simon Hix put it: "The EC is not inherently different to the practice of government in any democratic system. . . . To study the connection between political 'input' and 'output' on these issues, one would naturally use the discourse of 'comparative politics.'"[7] EU legislation and most EU policies are in fact negotiated by national officials (from desk officers to ministers, often assisted by diplomats) and by MEPs (elected at the national level). A pivotal role is also played by EU officials.

The EU also makes intergovernmental policies: these were called the II and III pillars under the pre-Lisbon version of the TEU. The negotiations that lead to these common policies—over foreign policy, security and defense policy, and home and justice affairs—are known as *high politics*. EU high politics come closer to classic international negotiations—that is, to "traditional" foreign policy. High politics are in fact typically negotiated by diplomats and ministers (mainly foreign ministers) in an intergovernmental setting. *Mutatis mutandis*, we are still in the era of the Congress of Vienna, the first case of modern multilateral negotiations. The influencing variables here are different from those in low politics.

Finally there are what Simon Bulmer, recalling Theodore Lowi, defined as *constitutive policies*: those affecting the overall architecture of the European Union (treaty reforms, the constitutional/legal order, the geographic parameters, and other broad reforms).[8] These too are closer to classic international negotiations than low politics; they too are negotiated by diplomats and ministers (mainly foreign ministers) in an intergovernmental setting.

Here and in the next chapter, I discuss Italy's behavior in each area of EU policy by looking at several specific cases—some successful, some not. I begin with three case studies of constitutive policies: negotiations that led to the Single European Act of 1985; negotiations that led to the Treaty of Maastricht in 1990; and negotiations for the European Constitution in 2003. Then I will look at two cases of high politics, affecting Home and Justice Affairs and the Common Foreign and Security Policy (CFSP). Chapter 9 looks at low politics.

Toward the Single European Act

Italy held the EEC presidency in the first semester of 1985. In presenting the key issues of the Italian presidency, Foreign Minister Giulio Andreotti declared to the European Parliament on January 16, 1985, that its main goal would be to convene an Intergovernmental Conference (IGC) to reform the EEC Treaty. The idea was consistent with proposals made by Jacques Delors's new European Commission to finally implement the common market—which had been foreseen in the original 1957 treaties but never happened. Great Britain, Denmark, and Greece strongly opposed the IGC, however, despite the fact that they had welcomed Delors's idea of working toward the completion of the Common Market. Italy supported Delors's ideas both about the common market and about the consequent need to reform the EEC treaties in order to make EEC decisionmaking procedures more effective. The United Kingdom was against an IGC, but favored intergovernmental cooperation in the field of foreign policy (called political cooperation).

The Italian presidency worked extensively on bilateral meetings before the European Council in Milan (June 28–29, 1985). In doing so, both Prime Minister Bettino Craxi (a Socialist) and Foreign Minister Giulio Andreotti (a Christian

Democrat) relied on extended personal and political networks. At that time, Conservatives and Christian Democrats held the majority of European governments, while the far-left anti-European parties (like the French Communists) were relatively weak. In addition, the Socialist parties in power (in France and Spain) had opted for a liberal market policy while the European economic elite lobbied their governments for further economic and market integration (the only way for them to succeed in competing with the United States and Japan). The European industrialists—both through the European Round Table (ERT) and the Union of European National Industry Confederations (UNICE)—lobbied in favor of a common market and institutional reforms.[9]

Keith Middlemas believes that the British prime minister, Margaret Thatcher, seemed "not to have been aware until too late that [German chancellor Helmut] Kohl had . . . concerted his tactics before the Summit with fellow Christian Democrats in Rome."[10] In her own words: "It is also possible that some kind of secret agreement had been reached on this before the Council began. Certainly when I had a bilateral meeting with Craxi early on Friday morning he could not have been more sweetly reasonable. . . . I came away thinking how easy it had been to get my points across."[11]

Hence, during the European Council, the United Kingdom, Greece, and Denmark continued to oppose convening the IGC. According to Thatcher: "Matters were not helped by the chairmanship of the Italian prime minister, Bettino Craxi. Craxi, a socialist, and his foreign minister, the Christian Democrat Andreotti, were political rivals, but they shared a joint determination to call an Intergovernmental Conference."[12] After a tense debate, the Italian presidency decided to take an unprecedented step: when Andreotti made his official proposal to call an IGC, Craxi asked to take a formal vote on the question. In an institutional setting, where consensus is the way of doing things, it was a very strong political step. While Great Britain, Greece, and Denmark voted against it, all the other member states voted in favor. A majority of seven votes was thus reached in favor of convening the IGC, which began its work on September 9, 1985.

The Danish prime minister, Poul Holmskov Schlüter, stated that it was a "violence," and the Greek leader, Andreas Papandreou, spoke of a "coup d'état."[13] And Thatcher was furious:

> It was Craxi himself as president who suggested at the Council that we should have an IGC. Battle lines were quickly drawn. . . . But it was to no avail. Having come to Milan in order to argue for closer cooperation I found myself being bulldozed by a majority which included a highly partisan chairman. I was not alone: Greece and Denmark joined me in

opposing an IGC. . . . To my astonishment and anger Craxi suddenly called a vote and by a majority the Council resolved to establish an IGC. My time—not just at the Council but all of those days of work which preceded it—had been wasted. I would have to return to the House of Commons and explain why all of the high hopes which had been held of Milan had been dashed. And I had not even had an opportunity while there to go to the opera.[14]

Italy's influence also reached the IGC negotiations. During the second semester of 1985, the EEC foreign ministers met four times in addition to a two-day conclave before the Council in Luxembourg. The European Parliament was "associated" with this process by holding three *échanges de vues* between the two people in charge of the negotiations, European Parliament president Pierre Pflimlin and Italian MEP and former commissioner Altiero Spinelli. Documents were presented to the IGC by Italy, France, Germany, and the Commission, which was represented by its president, Jacques Delors, and Secretary General Emil Noel. Although difficulties emerged—especially relative to the harmonization of legislation—the pragmatic approach proposed by the Commission made it possible to reach a consensus. Given that a number of responsibilities were taken away from the national parliaments, the European Parliament needed a guaranteed role in the decisionmaking process. In other words, the institutional questions were not dealt with separately, apart from the concrete problems: this had an important consequence in that, given their interest in a common market, Great Britain and Denmark could not oppose the reforms that were proposed. The final agreement was reached at the European Council in Luxembourg (December 2–3, 1985), where the Single European Act was adopted.

Preparing for the Treaty on the European Union

The fall of the Berlin Wall in 1989 inspired hope, but also fear among European leaders. On October 25, 1989, in a speech to the European Parliament, French president François Mitterrand declared that the only answer to events in Eastern Europe was to create a political Europe, in the belief that a stronger Europe would better deal with a stronger Germany. Thus on November 18 he invited the other EEC heads of state and government to have dinner at the French presidential palace. On November 28, Helmut Kohl presented the Bundestag with a program of ten steps that would lead to a reunited Germany. On December 8–9, 1989, the European Council in Strasbourg decided to call two IGCs, on political union and on European Monetary Union (EMU).

The president of the EEC Commission, Jacques Delors, had meanwhile presented, at the European Council of Madrid (June 26–27, 1989), a report on monetary union. The report proposed the creation of a European currency to replace the national currencies and the creation of a European central bank. On the issue of political union, the European Parliament approved the "Martin Report" on institutional reforms on March 14, 1990.[15] On March 20, Belgium circulated a memorandum, and on April 18 Mitterrand and Kohl proposed, in a letter addressed to their European counterparts, to complete European monetary union (EMU) with a political union. Such a union would be aimed at ensuring democratic legitimacy, institutional efficiency, and the EEC's unity and coherence in the economic, monetary, and political sectors. It would also establish a common foreign and security policy.

At the first European Council in Dublin (April 28, 1990), Mitterrand and Kohl's proposals were discussed and a general agreement was reached on the need to move toward a political union, with dissenting opinions from the United Kingdom and Portugal. In May, the Spanish leader, Felipe Gonzales, proposed to add the issue of European citizenship to the agenda of the Intergovernmental Conference. At the second European Council in Dublin (June 18–19, 1990), it was thus decided to summon two IGCs before the end of the year: one to work on European monetary union and the other to deal with political union. The opinions regarding this latter issue were, however, far apart.

On July 1, 1990—the day that marked the beginning of the monetary union between the two German republics—Italy again assumed the EEC presidency. Shortly after that, Giulio Andreotti was elected prime minister. In setting its priorities, the Italian presidency considered the preparation of the IGC on EMU to be more pivotal than that on political union and channeled its efforts accordingly. Andreotti proposed to hold a special informal European Council in Rome (October 27–28, 1990). There, despite the United Kingdom's opposition, the "Carli Report" on EMU was approved.[16] During Italy's six-month presidency, Thatcher made little secret of her disdain for Andreotti's chairmanship, and on at least one occasion gave him a trademark "hand-bagging." At a meeting with Thatcher at Chequers, the British prime minister's country residence, the tone of the gathering deteriorated rapidly. In the helicopter ride back to London, Andreotti acknowledged that he and his British counterpart had agreed on absolutely nothing. Diplomatic humiliation for Britain arrived at a late-night press conference in Rome, when the presidency read a long list of items agreed by eleven countries, noting that only "one nation" was not in accord. The following week, Thatcher, in reporting about the summit at the House of Commons, made her famous outburst: "No, no, no!" in replying to a question about further EU integration. This stance, however, sparked the resignation of Britain's foreign secretary, Sir Geoffrey Howe, and within weeks Thatcher was prime minister no longer. The Italian version is that there was no conspiracy. British officials, however, saw it as a ruthless act of revenge for Thatcher's rudeness and intransigence. Thatcher herself called it a "Florentine trap"—a clear reference to Machiavellian politics.[17]

Despite Thatcher's departure and her replacement with John Major (November 28, 1990), Giulio Andreotti was still worried that an overloaded agenda could spoil the chances of success of the second European Council in Rome (December 14–15, 1990) and thus resolved to negotiate as much as possible beforehand. The Italian presidency thus engaged deeply in both bilateral and multilateral meetings, with Andreotti focusing his efforts in particular on fellow Christian Democrat leaders around Europe. At the time, six of the twelve European leaders were Christian Democrats: Giulio Andreotti (Italy), Ruud Lubbers (the Netherlands), Jacques Santer (Luxembourg), Wilfred Martens (Belgium), Constantine Mitsotakis (Greece), and Helmut Kohl (Germany). Traditionally, Christian Democrat leaders gathered before each European Council session in order to discuss their actions and their positions, creating what the *Financial Times* once described as "the most influential cabal of the EC."[18] Indeed, according to the British daily, the summit of Christian Democrats set the phases of EMU.

In addition to the Christian Democrat network, Andreotti had an excellent personal relationship with the two Socialist leaders of the time: French president Mitterrand and Spanish prime minister Gonzales. According to Keith Middlemas, only Andreotti's capabilities and skills as president could make the convening of two parallel IGCs possible.[19] In fact, the European Council in Rome (December 14–15, 1990) officially called for the opening of the two IGCs, which were to last for all of 1991 and resulted in the Treaty on the European Union—also known as the Maastricht Treaty. In particular, the work of the Italian presidency allowed the IGC on EMU to run smoothly and successfully.

The Failure of the Constitutional Treaty

The story of the Constitutional Treaty, on the contrary, is not a success story. Recall that Prime Minister Silvio Berlusconi's selection of his deputy Gianfranco Fini to be his representative in the European Convention proved a successful move, in terms of both domestic and external politics. Other Italians at the convention that first drafted the so-called EU Constitution were Professor Giuliano Amato, vice president of the convention; Italian parliament member

Marco Follini, a Christian Democrat representing the majority in government; and Senator Lamberto Dini representing the opposition. The substitutes were Francesco Speroni, a Northern League MEP (and, at the time, also chief of cabinet for the minister of institutional reforms, Umberto Bossi); Valdo Spini (Democrats of the Left); and Senator Filadelfio Basile (Alleanza Nazionale, or National Alliance). Other Italians who took part in the convention included three MEPs—Antonio Tajani (Forza Italia), Cristiana Muscardini (National Alliance), and Elena Paciotti (as a substitute for Democrats of the Left); Claudio Martini, president of the Tuscan region, on behalf of the Committee of the Regions; and Emilio Gabaglio on behalf of the European Trade Unions (he was secretary general). In general terms, even apart from the enhanced role of Amato, the Italian members of the convention were very active, in contrast to Italy's tradition of absenteeism in the European Parliament.

On July 18, 2003, in Rome, the chairman of the European Convention, Valéry Giscard d'Estaing, presented the "Draft Treaty Establishing a Constitution for Europe" to the Italian EU presidency. In order to complete the EU reform process, it was now necessary to formally open a conference of representatives of the governments of the member states—another IGC—according to the procedure laid down by article 48 of the Maastricht Treaty. There were divergent opinions among member states, however, about how to proceed. Seeking to gain from the positive impetus provided by the convention, the European Council asked the Italian presidency to launch the IGC. Berlusconi also wanted the new treaty to be agreed upon in Rome, before the end of the Italian semester, so he put considerable pressure on the IGC negotiations.

On July 1, 2003, therefore, the Italian presidency made a formal request to the Council to convene the IGC. As recommended at the Thessaloniki European Council, the presidency also pointed out that it intended to conclude negotiations by December 2003, so that the new treaty could be signed after May 1, 2004 (the date of enlargement to include ten new member states), but before the European elections of June 2004.

On July 21–22, Foreign Minister Franco Frattini reported to his EU counterparts on the steps taken to convene the IGC. Throughout August, bilateral contacts continued, with a view to preparing for the IGC. The informal Foreign Ministries Council met in Riva del Garda on September 5, 2003, to establish the working method and agenda for the IGC. However, negotiations were already becoming difficult. First, at a summit in Prague on September 1, Austria, Greece, Sweden, Denmark, Portugal, Ireland, and Finland—together with countries preparing for EU accession, Poland, Hungary, the Czech Republic, Slovenia, Slovakia, and the three Baltic states—affirmed their opposition to ending the rotating presidency as stated by the "Constitution."[20]

On September 17, 2003, the Commission formally presented its opinion regarding the opening of the IGC—also including some suggestions about the size and composition of the Commission, the extension of the scope to which qualified majority voting should apply, and simplification of the procedure for amending the Constitution in the future.[21] On September 24 the European Parliament also adopted a resolution constituting its formal opinion before convening the IGC. This resolution acknowledged the effectiveness of the method of amending the treaties through the convention and called on the IGC to approve the draft without altering the basic balance of the convention's proposal.[22] The General Affairs Council then gave the official go-ahead for the IGC at its meeting on September 29, 2003. The date of the first meeting was scheduled for October 4, 2003, in Rome. It was also decided at that meeting that the European Parliament would be involved in the work.[23]

The work of this IGC was organized differently than in the past. Given the length of the preparatory work carried out by the convention, this IGC was held only at the highest policy levels, that is, among the heads of state and government, assisted by their ministers of foreign affairs. In contrast to previous IGCs, no meetings of government representatives or civil servants were planned initially. At the ministerial level, two representatives of the Commission were also included: Commissioner Michel Barnier, and then, following Barnier's departure from the Commission, his colleague António Vitorino. The European Parliament was involved in the work through its two representatives: MEPs Klaus Hänsch and Iñigo Méndez de Vigo (replaced by his colleague Elmar Brok in November). At the head of state or government level, the Commission was represented by the president of the Commission himself, Romano Prodi, and the European Parliament by its president, Pat Cox. The acceding countries participated fully in the negotiations, the Treaty of Accession having been signed well before the launch of the IGC, while Romania, Turkey, and Bulgaria acted as observers.

The Italian presidency sought to underscore the continuity between the convention and the IGC. All the documents were made available on the Internet, the European Parliament was fully involved in all stages of the discussions, and the proceeding were conducted solely at the political level, thus avoiding any rediscussion of the technical issues agreed upon during the convention. However, during the summer, member states that had examined the convention's proposals carefully pointed out several problematic points that demanded renegotiation by the IGC.

In order to facilitate work and channel the flow of information, each member state appointed a civil servant to act as a contact person—a "focal point"; he or she was to play a primarily administrative role. This decision proved vital to the smooth running of the negotiations. The Italian focal point was Ambassador Rocco Cangelosi, director general of European integration at the Italian Foreign Ministry. He was supported by Minister Vincenzo Grassi.

The presidency sent a series of questionnaires to the delegations before the official opening of the IGC, summarizing the convention's proposals and setting out the wishes of each national delegation.[24] Throughout the negotiations, the presidency remained in close contact with the delegations and organized virtually nonstop bilateral meetings. At the policy level, the president of the European Council, Silvio Berlusconi, and the president of the General Affairs Council (CAGRE), Franco Frattini, met their European counterparts outside official meetings, notably during a tour of capitals. In addition, the Italian presidency asked a group of legal and linguistic experts to check the draft treaty being prepared by the convention. The group, chaired by Jean-Claude Piris, director general of the Council Legal Service, comprised representatives of the member states, the Commission and Parliament, and observers from the three candidate countries, in a "1+1 format" (one person at the table and one behind him or her). The Italian members were Roberto Adam and Nicola Verola. The scope of the mandate of the Working Party of Legal Experts was further expanded on November 4, 2003, to speed up the work.[25] At the end of November, the experts presented their results.[26] This contained an examination of the purely editorial and legal aspects of the draft treaty. It served as a basis for the IGC negotiations. "Addendum 1" was produced after examining the protocols and annexes to existing treaties and the protocols drawn up by the convention.

The heads of state and government met in Rome on October 4, 2003, for the official opening of the IGC. The foreign minister had had intensive bilateral meetings to prepare for it, and even the Italian president of the republic, Carlo Azeglio Ciampi, had contributed by writing to the German president and inviting the guests to dinner at Castel Porziano. The final procedural matters relating to the IGC were adopted, and a general policy discussion and exchange of views on the negotiations took place. In a statement entitled the "Declaration of Rome," the heads of state and government reaffirmed the importance of the process of integration and the need to adopt a constitutional text. They claimed the text represented a vital step in a process aimed at "making Europe more cohesive, more transparent and more democratic, more efficient and closer to its citizens."[27] Still, the debate revealed significant differences of opinion among the member states, especially a widening gap between France and Germany on one side and Spain and Poland on the other.

The first ministerial meeting also took place on October 4, 2003. The Italian presidency had produced a document containing replies from the delegations to questionnaires on the proposed Legislative Council about its formations and its presidency: these served as a basis for discussion.[28] On the issue of the Council's legislative function, the responses to the questionnaires showed overwhelming support for separating the Council's public legislative function within each formation rather than concentrating it in one single "legislative" formation. In other words, the member states rapidly agreed to take away one of the most significant innovations introduced by the convention—a "Legislative Council" whose meetings would be public. After the meeting, the Italian presidency then circulated a revised version of article I-23, according to which the Council would still legislate in public. To that effect, the agenda of each Council was to be divided into a legislative and a nonlegislative part. For the presidency of the Council, Italy had suggested moving toward a two-year "team presidency system" of four or five member states.[29]

The second ministerial meeting took place on October 14, 2003. Before it, the Italian presidency had sent delegations a new questionnaire concerning the Commission and the future European minister of foreign affairs.[30] Some member states wished to amend the convention's proposals on these issues, and the Italian presidency attempted to evaluate how to reach a compromise by addressing a series of very specific questions to the delegations (for instance, about the question of the "double-hat" to be worn by the European foreign minister). In order to prepare for the European Council of October 16–17, in Brussels, the foreign ministers also dealt with sticky institutional questions and issues related to defense—in particular structured cooperation and the solidarity clause.

The October meeting of the European Council was divided into two parts: the first dealt with the IGC, the second with European Council dossiers. During the first afternoon, the heads of state and government discussed institutional questions prepared by the foreign ministers at their previous meeting. They thus focused on the composition of the European Parliament, the role of the European Council and its president, the calculation of a qualified majority, and defense issues. The purpose of the meeting was not to obtain specific solutions to the points discussed, but to establish broad guidelines for continuing negotiations at the ministerial level.[31] The Italian presidency, at this stage, had intended to continue the bilateral consultation phase, without making its specific proposals public.

Indeed, the presidency had prepared three separate documents for this meeting. One dealt with unresolved noninstitutional issues: the Preamble, the values and objectives of the Union, the Charter of Fundamental Rights, finance and budgetary procedures, economic and financial policy, justice and home affairs, external relations, amendment of the treaties, and numerous other points relating to EU policies. The second document dealt with the scope of qualified majority voting (QMV). The last document launched a new proposal for the Council presidency and its various configurations. These documents included subjects that demanded further debate by the delegations. Overall, the presidency counted ninety-one points raised by one or more delegations.

The economic and finance ministers (Ecofin Council) had challenged some of the convention's proposals at an informal meeting in Stresa in September. The changes requested by the Ecofin Council related in particular to the European Parliament's powers in the adoption of financial perspectives and financial regulations and those of the Commission in implementing the excessive deficit procedure.

With regard to the scope of QMV, the presidency pointed out that some delegations wished to maintain the balance obtained by the convention, while others wished to extend QMV to other areas or even return to unanimity in sensitive areas.[32] Some delegations were also opposed to "bridging clauses." (Bridging clauses were among the most innovative convention proposals, allowing the Council to decide, unanimously, to apply QMV and/or the ordinary legislative procedure—co-decision—in a given area.) The presidency also submitted a new proposal concerning the Council presidency and Council formations, reaffirming the principle of the "team presidency" despite resistance from some small countries.[33]

Last but not least, there was an objection to the reference in the Preamble to the Christian heritage of Europe, supported by Italy. Spain, Ireland, Malta, Poland, Portugal, Slovakia, Lithuania, and the Czech Republic wished to enlarge this to refer to ancient Greek philosophy, Roman law, Jewish and Christian roots, and rationalism; Turkey and Cyprus were opposed.[34]

For the fourth ministerial meeting (November 18, 2003) the presidency prepared two documents relating to the future European minister of foreign affairs and the procedures for amending the future Constitutional Treaty. The proposed amendments included the independence of the future minister, procedures in the eventuality of his/her resignation, and the question of coherence between the Common Foreign and Security Policy and external relations. During the meeting, the positions of the delegates on the status of the minister of foreign affairs drew closer; indeed, a substantial portion of the delegations supported the presidency's proposals. With regard to treaty revision, the discussion focused mainly on bridging clauses, which some of the member states opposed. As for the general revision clause of the treaty, which many judged too cumbersome, with 27 member states, and others wanted to keep rigid, the presidency proposed a *nihil obstat* procedure (authorization if no national parliaments object) that seemed a step in the right direction. Agreement would still be by common accord, but national parliaments would in effect retain a veto over any proposed revisions.[35]

In preparation for the ministerial discussions at the Naples "conclave" at the end of November, the presidency published a document containing its thoughts on the matters under discussion. It provided, in effect, a sort of interim review of the situation. In its proposal, the presidency wished to remain faithful to the convention's draft Constitutional Treaty and to retain the main balance of the text. The presidency proposed basing all discussions on the text issued by the convention, as finalized by the group of legal experts. It did not issue a proposal on the issues of Christian roots or QMV, being of the opinion that it was necessary to continue reflecting on those issues. The conclave had in fact devoted a whole dinner to the question of voting in the Council. Wherever possible the presidency drew conclusions; where it was not yet possible to do so, the presidency described the situation and outlined a possible solution. For instance, the presidency noted "that a large majority of member states are opposed to the creation of a Legislative Council, but recalled that this could be done subsequently by means of a decision of the European Council."[36] After an initial round of discussions, the presidency thought that the member states' reaction was largely positive. Following the trilateral meeting of Germany, France, and the United Kingdom on the eve of the conclave, the three countries presented new proposals on methods of structured cooperation. An agreement was reached in principle, in particular on structured cooperation and the mutual defense clause.

The meeting held on the morning of November 29 dealt mainly with institutional questions. According to the presidency, the conference had made progress with regard to the Commission and the European minister of foreign affairs. The most contentious issue remained the question of double majority voting in the Council. Together with defining QMV for decisionmaking in the Council, institutional questions remained the most difficult questions to resolve throughout the negotiations. Certain states opposed the solution proposed by the convention, especially Poland and Spain. From the start of the negotiations, these two countries took a strong position in favor of weighting votes by country, as defined in Nice in 2000. Neither country wished to give up the advantages it had obtained at that time (twenty-seven votes, as opposed to twenty-nine for the most populous countries). The presidency did not make any specific proposals. Finally, with regard to the sensitive issue of the Preamble, the presidency restricted itself at this stage to gathering ideas, leaving it to the European Council to reach decisions. After the meeting, Minister Frattini commented that "great steps forward" had been achieved. Yet

German foreign minister Joschka Fischer, on his way back to Germany, claimed to be worried about the lack of pro-European enthusiasm.[37]

During a meeting of European and national parliamentary members of the European Convention on December 5, 2003, in Brussels, the chairman, Giscard d'Estaing, made an appeal to the IGC. He said: "We would rather do without a Constitution than have a bad one."[38] Also at that meeting, the Council president, Franco Frattini, affirmed that the presidency would not accept a low-quality compromise but would continue to defend the draft proposed by the convention. On December 4, the European Parliament also supported the draft proposed by the convention, adopting a resolution on the IGC's work. It called on the heads of state and government to continue their efforts to overcome their differences in order to arrive at a balanced and positive result on December 13. On the occasion of a hearing in front of the Italian parliament before the European Council in Brussels, Frattini also admitted, for the first time, that in the long run it would be better not to have an agreement than to have a bad one.[39]

On the agenda of the sixth ministerial meeting (December 9, 2003) there were only two items: defense and budget. Following the agreement reached at the Naples conclave, the presidency had presented a new document on defense, giving detail to that agreement in the form of draft articles. The presidency did not, however, propose a compromise for budgetary questions, wishing to retain the solution proposed by the convention, which had increased the powers of the European Parliament in the annual budgetary procedure. Yet, during the meeting, the ministers for foreign affairs were unable to reach a compromise on defense and budgetary questions. The wording of articles on mutual defense was still problematic, in particular for neutral countries, which wished to avoid any automatic response. Likewise, with regard to the budgetary procedure, the positions of the various parties were still irreconcilable.

On the eve of the European Council, President of the Republic Ciampi published an article advocating the need to create a political union in the EU.[40] Three days before the European Council, the presidency made public its proposals in a document accompanied by two addenda. Addendum 1 addressed those issues on which the discussions, in particular the Naples ministerial conclave, had given the presidency sufficient guidance to be able to put forward concrete proposals. These proposals took the form of draft treaty texts. In all, it comprised forty-four issues, including the formations of the Council of Ministers, the draft decision of the European Council on the exercise of the presidency of the Council of Ministers, the European minister for foreign affairs, the European External Action Service, the budget procedure, and the multiyear financial framework, etc.[41] The presidency believed that since it had taken into account the different views of delegations, the document constituted a balanced package. Addendum 2,[42] released on the eve of the European Council, dealt with matters that were still unresolved. Indeed, it included only four questions: the Preamble (in particular the question of whether to include a reference to Europe's Christian roots); the composition of the Commission; qualified majority voting and its eventual extension ("The presidency notes that a very large number of delegations continue to support the convention text on the definition of QMV, in particular because it meets the overall objective of decisionmaking procedures which are simple, efficient and transparent. Nevertheless the presidency is aware that, for a few delegations, the Convention proposal is not acceptable as it currently stands"); and the minimum number of seats in the European Parliament. The document did not contain any specific proposals, but suggested routes to explore in order to reach a final compromise. Where an issue was not covered in either document, nor subsequently raised by any delegation, the presidency considered that the text of the draft Constitutional Treaty, as reviewed by the group of legal experts,[43] remained unchanged.

The Intergovernmental Conference was to be preceded by the customary quarterly meeting of the European Council. Meticulously prepared by the Farnesina, that part of the meeting did not last beyond the morning of December 12. Then it was time to move to the IGC. The presidency recognized that the only real problem remaining was QMV, due in particular to the opposition of both Spain and Poland (the latter not yet an EU member state). Its strategy was therefore to reach a compromise on this point above all, in the hope that it would then be possible to quickly resolve the other outstanding problems.

The first meeting of the Intergovernmental Conference began in the evening, with an initial round of discussions. The meeting was closed shortly afterwards to enable the presidency to meet the delegations separately, in "confessional" meetings. These meetings, which were strictly confidential, were to help the presidency find possible compromises. The bilateral meetings began during the afternoon and continued late into the night, with the presidency meeting certain member states several times. The confessional meetings were also held during the morning of Friday, December 13. It became clear over lunch that the delegations' positions on the issue of voting in the Council remained irreconcilable. Some delegations wished to retain the convention's proposal, while others (namely Spain and Poland) were in favor of the system established in the Treaty of Nice. Similarly, the informal proposals for possible changes to the thresholds for a qualified majority were not acceptable to everyone. Overnight, the presidency perceived that Poland would be willing to negotiate but that Spain would be harder to convince, despite the personal friendship between Berlusconi and Spanish prime minister José María Aznar. Aznar, in fact, had told Berlusconi at the beginning of the meeting that the margin for negotiation was very slim. According to one participant in the meetings who wishes to remain anonymous, Aznar said, "I came to Brussels in a 100 horsepower car and I cannot leave with less than that; I would, however, be willing to accept a different car, say an Alfa Romeo instead of an Audi, if the horsepower is the same." In concrete terms, in Nice, Spain had been given a power that was greater than what it could ever hope for, and it wanted to hold on to the '2 big + 2 small' power block within the Council.

During the December negotiations and bilateral meetings, the presidency perceived that there was possibly space for a "95 horsepower car," but then opposition came from French president Jacques Chirac and German chancellor Gerhard Schroeder who, during the bilateral meetings, had gone to eat sushi in a Brussels restaurant with Chirac and Guy Verhofstadt (the Belgian prime minister) and came back only to tell Berlusconi that they felt the meeting was over. So it was. The presidency had prepared three possible compromises: keep the Nice voting system, while giving Germany more votes; adopt the convention proposal, but raise the threshold to 55 percent of the member states and to 65 percent of the population; introduce the convention proposal in 2014. None of these compromises was accepted by all member states, despite the incentives offered by the presidency (increasing the number of MEPs, commissioners, etc.).[44]

The presidency still wished to avoid abandoning the proposal of the convention and hoped rather to amend it. At a first meeting, the German chancellor affirmed that he might eventually accept a compromise to save the treaty. However, at a second meeting later in the evening, Schroeder came back with a much less conciliatory position. At their sushi dinner, Schroeder, Chirac, and Verhofstadt had in fact agreed that it was better not to make demands during the negotiations; they also agreed on a possible Commission presidency for Verhofstadt. The French attitude was not particularly helpful either: since his arrival at the European Council, Chirac had in fact made it clear to the Italian presidency that he had booked his presidential plane for Saturday after lunch—a way of saying that there wasn't much time to come up with a compromise.

Faced with this deadlock, the Italian presidency found itself unable to make a balanced proposal that was acceptable to everyone. All that remained, therefore, was for the presidency to state that it was impossible to reach an overall agreement. The Intergovernmental Conference accordingly issued a statement declaring that negotiations had failed and asking the Irish presidency to continue consultations. The conclusions of the European Council did not set a deadline or a specific goal for the future of the "Constitutional Treaty," saying only that "the European Council noted that it was not possible for the IGC to reach overall agreement on a draft treaty at this stage. The Irish presidency was requested on the basis of consultations to make an assessment of the prospects for progress and to report to the European Council in March." This would have resulted in a postponement *sine die*, had it not been for the terrorist train bombings in Madrid on March 11, 2004, and the subsequent election of José Luis Rodriguez Zapatero as Spain's new prime minister.

Despite the positive results of the convention and a brilliant beginning to a difficult IGC, the final result was failure to agree on a new treaty. Deadlock over voting regulations for the Council, with Spain and Poland on one side and Germany and France on the other, doomed the negotiations to failure. Yet the main negative factor at the European Council of Brussels on December 12–13, 2004, was that the Italian presidency lacked the support of both France and Germany. The support of those two countries had been fundamental to the success of the 1984 and 1990 Italian presidencies, when Italy had been forced to square the circle.

Justice and Home Affairs—The Case of the European Arrest Warrant

The second pillar of the Treaty of the European Union is Justice and Home Affairs (JHA). It has an intergovernmental character, though its provisions have been progressively "communitarized"; that is, it has moved into what under the Maastricht Treaty was called the first pillar (of EC policies), thanks to the "bridging clause." There has been only one case in which Italy fought for its own interests, and that is the case of the European Arrest Warrant. The issue occupied a high place on Italy's European agenda both in 2001 and in 2004, under the Berlusconi II and III governments.

In 2001 the EU member states were negotiating the European Arrest Warrant. Under the proposed new warrant, the European Union member states' judiciaries would no longer be able to exercise a formal extradition procedure to forcibly transfer a person from one member state to another for criminal prosecution or to execute a custodial sentence or detention order. Italy opposed the change, together with Ireland, expressing concern over two key aspects of the document: the list of offenses the arrest warrant would cover and the length of sentences for terrorism and other serious crimes.[45] However, some suggested that the real reason the Italian government opposed the measure was Prime Minister Silvio Berlusconi's concern that it could be used against him. For instance, *Der Tagesspiegel* wrote: "Suddenly it is back again, the ugly face of Silvio Berlusconi," claiming that Berlusconi was trying to protect his own financial empire and his managers. The newspaper went so far as to call on the other fourteen EU member states to "give Berlusconi hell" at the forthcoming European Council in Laeken, where the issue was to be discussed. Another German newspaper, the *Süddeutsche Zeitung*, suggested, on the other hand, that the Italian prime minister's action was less an attempt to protect criminals than it was a clever bargaining ploy ahead of the summit. "Berlusconi's move could be part of an attempt to link the arrest warrant to unrelated issues at Laeken, notably the seat of the new food agency," it suggested. This newspaper too called for EU nations to take the toughest action against Italy, if Berlusconi resorted to playing games with security in the future.[46]

However, in a spectacular 180-degree reversal, at the European Council in Laeken (December 6–7, 2001), the Italian government decided to support the European Arrest Warrant. The government's handling of the warrant issue had been the main topic in the Italian press for some days. In an interview with the daily newspaper *La Stampa*, Finance Minister Giulio Tremonti had expressed the government's concern about the wide scope of the arrest warrant. "There has been a breach of the democratic process, which has its own timeframes, involves discussions and rational prospects." Tremonti continued: "There is no EU appeal, no EU police, and no EU constitution; furthermore, in most countries, there are government-dependent public prosecutors." On the contrary, in an interview with *Il Corriere della Sera*, the European Commission president Romano Prodi stressed the need for an agreement, attaching to this issue "huge importance." His role and that of Belgian prime minister Guy Verhofstadt, who met with Silvio Berlusconi before the European Council, is thought to have been critical in persuading the Italian premier to withdraw his objections, on condition that the warrant would be introduced in Italy only after constitutional changes.[47] Still, the real question remains what Berlusconi got out of the deal. Italian justice minister Roberto Castelli is said to have commented on the decision thus: "I did not approve of the European Arrest Warrant. . . . I can't say why Berlusconi did. He will only know that himself." One possibility, suggested by some, in private, is that Berlusconi agreed to give up his opposition to the European Arrest Warrant in exchange for a promise of support for locating the food agency in Parma. The battle over the food agency was a long one, fought between Italy (supporting Parma) and Finland (supporting Helsinki). The starting point was the same European Council of Laeken, where Berlusconi strongly defended Parma as the only logical choice. Negotiations were concluded at the European Council in Brussels (December 2003) where Parma was selected.[48]

In any event, in 2004 Italy was the last of the EU countries to adopt the directive creating the EU Arrest Warrant—a sign that the government was still not enthusiastic about it. The already established fifteen EU member states had until December 31, 2003, to introduce the warrant, while the ten new members were given until June 2004.[49] Italy's reluctance to implement the directive as national law was eventually overcome by introducing an exception to the application of the warrant: according to this exception, Italy does not have to transfer the suspect to another country if the victim has given his or her consent to remain in Italy; if the suspect is pregnant or the mother of a child under the age of three; if the suspect is Italian and did not know the conduct was prohibited; or if the crime is political.

Facing the Albanian Crisis

The case of Albania is particularly interesting. Albania represents a long-standing strategic interest for Italy. After the demise of the Communist regime in Albania (1989–90), diplomatic ties between the two Mediterranean countries intensified, with Italy trying to sustain Albania through a severe economic crisis. In August 1991, Italy launched Operazione Pelicano, which sent 700 Italian soldiers to Albania on a humanitarian mission until December 1993.[50] Unfortunately, after only a few years, the situation deteriorated again, ultimately leading to a follow-up expedition, Operazione Alba.

Operation Alba may be considered one of the most important instances in which Italy has acted as a regional power, taking the lead in executing a technically and politically coherent and determined strategy. Although it was not specifically an EU operation (because, as we will see, that option became impossible), it nevertheless merits inclusion as an example of high politics.

Operation Alba was mounted in response to the Albanian crisis that broke at the beginning of February 1997. This crisis, which exploded in a surge of mass violence, was the result of simultaneous economic and political causes. Underlying the former was the collapse of the pyramid investment schemes that had wiped out the savings of one in every two Albanians.[51] This was compounded by the loss of support for the democratic leader Sali Berisha who, after putting himself forward as the right man to manage the democratic transition—after many years of living under an obscurantist regime—had concealed the dramatic level of national underdevelopment and, indeed, had made it worse by tolerating continuing financial instability, of which he was the prime cause.[52] This led to the collapse of the authority of the state and the rise of what were essentially local revolutionary committees all over the country, leaving plenty of leeway for criminal organizations to exploit the chaotic situation.

The alarm sounded by the Italian ambassador to Albania, Paolo Foresti, was taken up as a matter of urgency by Prime Minister Prodi, because of both Italy's considerable economic interests in Albania and the two countries' historical and cultural ties. He also wished to demonstrate to the many skeptics that Italy was a country ready to take direct responsibility in addressing emergency situations on Europe's periphery.

Italy's strategy, summarized by the undersecretary of state for foreign affairs, Piero Fassino, at the joint session of the Chamber of Deputies and Senate Foreign Affairs committees on March 15, 1997, was to achieve four objectives. The first objective was to encourage the political dialectic between the government and the opposition; the second was to establish relations with the representatives of the towns in which autonomous political committees had been established; the third was to safeguard the large Italian community living in Albania; and the fourth was to establish preventive and precautionary measures for taking in refugees.[53]

While the Italian armed forces handled the operations to evacuate foreign nationals from Albania on March 3, 1997, and while measures were taken to host Albanian refugees, the first steps adopted by the Italian diplomatic machine aimed to encourage dialogue between the Albanian government and the opposition. Prime Minister Prodi himself facilitated the agreement in a long telephone call with President Berisha on March 2, 1997: he suggested that both sides recognize each other and engage in peaceful debate, and he offered Italy's full support to this end.[54]

That same day, Foreign Minister Lamberto Dini asked the Dutch presidency of the European Union to organize a meeting of the political directors as soon as possible to take stock of the crisis in Albania. Meanwhile, Italian diplomacy had succeeded in persuading Berisha to declare a forty-eight-hour truce, during which two delegations visited Tirana—one from the Council of Europe and one from the EU (the latter headed by the Dutch minister of foreign affairs, Hans Van Mierlo). But they failed to persuade the stubborn president to open up in any way to the opposition.[55]

However, where European mediation failed, Italy's succeeded. On March 9, 1997, in the course of a lightning-quick visit to Tirana, Foreign Minister Dini met President Berisha and the leaders of the opposition; after intense negotiations, he succeeded in securing an agreement between the two sides, sanctioning the beginning of the constitution of a "government of national reconciliation" headed by Albania's prime minister, Bashkim Fino, with Italy standing as guarantor.

After the signing of the agreement in Tirana, however, the violence continued unabated. If anything, it increased, driving Berisha to call for military intervention from NATO, the European Union, and the United Nations and to ask the Office of Security and Cooperation in Europe (OSCE) to provide humanitarian support.

Italy spoke for the Albanian authorities by requesting an ambassadorial-level meeting of the NATO Atlantic Council, and attended a meeting of the representatives of the Western European Union (WEU) (both held on March 13, 1997), where it requested that the Albanian question be put on the agenda of the European Union foreign ministers' meeting at Apeldoorn in the Netherlands (March 15–16, 1997).

The NATO option was quickly rejected by Italian diplomats because of the United States' refusal to become involved in a new mission on European soil after the intervention in Bosnia. The U.S. military apparatus felt that there was only a very remote possibility of violence spreading throughout the whole Balkan area.

Having ruled out the NATO option, Italy turned to the European Union. France immediately expressed its readiness to undertake military operations in the area. Spain, the Netherlands, Greece (which, like Italy, was involved in the crisis as a neighbor), Portugal, Austria, and Denmark also expressed their support. But there were two hurdles to overcome. The first came from outside, in the form of pressure from Russia and the United States to ensure that the crisis would be addressed exclusively within the OSCE. Russia adopted contradictory positions with regard to the Albanian question. In the OSCE, Russian representatives offered to send armed forces to the Albanian government if such action was deemed useful, but the very next day the Duma opposed any deployment of Russian or international forces in Albania.[56] The second problem was within the European Union itself, connected to the refusal by the United Kingdom to accept any operation—especially a military one—that smacked in any way of a "European foreign policy." Then there was the German veto, probably caused by Germany's lack of interest in defending the area, and perhaps also by the fact that any successful mission headed by Italy would make it all the more difficult to later rule Italy out of the running as a permanent member of the United Nations Security Council, on which Germany had also set its sights. In view of the opposition from London and Berlin, the EU option was also shelved. Curiously, in this connection, the Italian defense minister, Beniamino Andreatta, commented at the time that "relations between the WEU and the European Union are more complicated than relations between the European Union and NATO."[57] Indeed, in this case, British and German opposition to a WEU mission had made it inconceivable that a mission might be deployed from within the European Union itself.

As an immediate response to the worsening Albanian crisis, the only card that Italy had left to play was with the OSCE. Italy therefore worked politically and diplomatically, as well as logistically, to plan an OSCE mission to guarantee the regular flow of humanitarian assistance, underpin dialogue between the political authorities and the insurgents, identify ways for militants to surrender weapons, and reestablish respect for human rights.[58] On March 27, the OSCE Permanent Council finally decided to set up the organization in Albania, sending as its local representative a former Austrian chancellor, Franz Vranitsky. The remit of the OSCE mission was to provide Albania with consultancy services and assistance with the democratization process by establishing independent media and protecting human rights, and to prepare and monitor the elections.[59]

As the popular uprising worsened and thousands of refugees turned up on the southern Italian coast, Italy had to act with extreme urgency to put in place a coalition of "willing and able" European countries that, de facto, would make it possible to deploy the OSCE mission. The Italian government agreed to lead an OSCE support mission to Albania, and also insisted on obtaining the necessary multilateral legitimation from the United Nations. Thanks to the diplomatic commitment of Italy's permanent representative to the United Nations, Ambassador Francesco Paolo Fulci, the UN Security Council voted unanimously in the record time of only eleven hours—with China alone abstaining—to adopt resolution 1101, establishing a multilateral intervention force to protect the OSCE's humanitarian workers in Albania.[60]

That resolution expressly provided that the mission would be neutral and impartial, although there were a number of reservations initially, considering Italy's substantial interests in the region. These reservations were overcome in consideration of the military and political success of Italy's earlier humanitarian "Operation Pelicano" from 1991 to 1993.

Whereas the foreign ministers of the fifteen member states had merely made timid declarations at the meeting on March 24, 1997, in Brussels (welcoming "the efforts of certain member states to put together a multinational protection force to create a secure framework for international assistance"),[61] Italy succeeded in getting a mission put in place under the OSCE, with the blessing of the United Nations. This mission, the first to be headed by Italy since World War II, and the first European-level mission without the direct support of NATO (and therefore without the leadership and participation of the United States), was made up as follows: Italy 3,800 units; France 950; Greece 800; Turkey 760; Romania 400; Spain 350; Denmark 110; Austria 60; Slovenia 20; and Belgium 15. Despite this multinational effort, the Prodi government was obliged to put the question of sending a military contingent to

Albania to a vote of confidence in the parliament: it was carried with 503 votes in favor (the center-right Polo delle Libertà and center-left Ulivo both voted in favor), 85 against (including Rifondazione Comunista and the Green Party), and 7 abstentions.[62] The first Italian troops landed on March 15, 1997, and the mission came to a successful conclusion on August 12 that same year.

As Prodi has recalled on many occasions, the purpose of the Italian mission was purely humanitarian; it had been studied to ensure that it was quick, efficient, and peaceful.[63] Italian policy was focused exclusively on providing support, distributing humanitarian aid, and guaranteeing transparent and trauma-free elections in June.[64] The whole international community considered these elections to be crucial to putting an end to the violence and reaffirming the will of the Albanian people.

To make it clear to the local leadership that it was vital to keep the national coalition government together until the elections, Defense Minister Andreatta had to threaten to recall the peace contingent several times should the March agreement (concluded in Tirana between the opposition and the government) be breached. Eventually, a date for the elections was agreed, and they duly took place on June 29, 1997: Berisha was defeated, and the socialist party secretary, Rexhep Qemal Meidani, was proclaimed the new president of the Albanian Republic.

The Italian mission was deemed essential in overcoming the Albanian crisis both by the outgoing president, Berisha, and by the incoming government, as the new Albanian prime minister, Fatos Nano, himself declared.[65] The Italian-led mission, therefore, had achieved its goals; it could rightly claim that it had fulfilled the Security Council's mandate, guaranteeing logistical support and necessary protection to the OSCE mission. Italy made an essential contribution to resolving Albania's emergency, enabling the new government to lay the foundations for a fresh period of reconciliation and development.

9

Negotiating Low Politics

Italy and the Economic and Monetary Union

The first case examined in this chapter is Italy's membership in the Economic and Monetary Union (EMU). This analysis focuses on two historical periods: 1989–91, in which the Maastricht Treaty (1992) negotiations were concentrated; and the period immediately before Italy's accession to the EMU, from the beginning of 1996 to the end of 1997. I lay out the strategy adopted by Italy in the Economic and Monetary Union negotiations and analyze whether Italy's efforts matched Italian interests.

The Economic and Monetary Union was intended to be a means of enabling the European Community to achieve the free movement of capital, coordinate economic policies, establish a fixed parity between the national currencies, and ultimately to institute a single currency. On June 27–28, 1988, the Hanover European Council established the Committee of Wise Men to examine all aspects of the establishment of an EMU. This committee, made up of the governors of the central banks (with Italy represented by Lamberto Dini and Tommaso Padoa Schioppa, as the governor and deputy director of the Bank of Italy at the time) and chaired by Commission president Jacques Delors, submitted its report to the Madrid European Council on June 23–24, 1989. It looked ahead to the establishment of an Economic and Monetary Union in three phases. The aim of the first phase would be to coordinate economic policies and monetary cooperation by incorporating all the currencies into the European Monetary System (EMS). The second phase would institute a European System of Central Banks and a European Central Bank to manage monetary policy within the EMU. In the third and final phase, fixed exchange rates against the single currency would be set for each of the participating currencies, and the single currency would then be brought into circulation.[1]

At the European Council in Strasbourg (December 8–9, 1989) it was decided to convene an Intergovernmental Conference (IGC) in 1991 to amend the treaties. The year 1990 was therefore to be the preparatory year. The inaugural session of the IGC was convened in Rome on December 15, 1990, followed by several meetings in 1991. The main issue proved to be the question of the conditions for entry to the third and final phase of EMU. While the German government argued in favor of compliance with specific "convergence indicators" as the means of indicating the capacity of the individual member states to accede to the Union, the Italian government supported the idea that the mere tendency of policies to achieve economic recovery, rather than the attainment of a fixed numerical parameter, should enable a country to enter the third phase of the Union.[2] Ultimately it was the German and Dutch positions that won the day, with strict numerical criteria required for admission to phase three. In the final sessions of the IGC the Italian treasury minister, Guido Carli, nevertheless succeeded in securing acceptance of the idea of a "dynamic" rather than a "static" assessment of these numerical convergence parameters.[3] The draft treaty was approved by the Maastricht European Council on December 9–10, 1991, and the final version of the treaty was signed by the heads of state and government of the twelve member states on February 7, 1992. As far as the EMU was concerned, the treaty required compliance with several criteria for access to the third phase of monetary union (known as the Maastricht criteria): (1) the public deficit should not exceed 3 percent of GDP; (2) the public debt should not exceed 60 percent of GDP; (3) the interest rate should not be greater than 1.5 percent above the average of the three member states with the lowest levels of inflation; (4) the average interest rate paid on government debt should be below the average of the same three countries, plus 2 percent; and (5) the candidate country must have been a member of the European Monetary System, the EMS, for at least two years without any unilateral devaluations.[4] Only if a country met these criteria would it be able to participate in the third and final phase of the Economic and Monetary Union, from January 1, 1997, or January 1, 1999, at the latest.

These rules were prohibitive for Italy. As Foreign Minister Gianni de Michelis said at the time, Italy would have a stock of debt in excess of 60 percent of GDP for at least another twenty years.[5] The only chance of success was therefore to apply the criterion in a more flexible way (that is, as a "tendency" toward achieving the targets), agreement to which the government had partially managed to secure from its allies in the final phase of the negotiations. Over the years, continuing greater Italian expenditures had occurred because the country was governed by coalitions. Government instability and the fragmentation of the political parties ruled out any agreement on unpopular restrictive economic measures (cutting public expenditures and/or increasing taxation). And coalition government also contributed to higher expenditures by demanding budget increases for individual ministries. Christian Democrat–led government coalitions preferred to avoid raising taxes, and the left-wing parties demanded that the government keep welfare expenditures high. It was therefore de facto impossible to keep public finances under control.[6]

The Maastricht Treaty therefore offered Italy only two possibilities. Having failed in its strategy to make the parameters flexible, Italy had to decide between seeking entry to the EMU and acting in consequence, or being relegated to the tail end of the Union. The changed conditions at home made it possible to exploit the opportunity provided by Maastricht (they are known as "external constraints") to revive the economy.[7] Italy's exclusion from the EMU would have been a political defeat and would have done incalculable damage to the Italian economy resulting from Italy's loss of credibility on the financial markets.[8] The first person to understand how the EMU constituted a great opportunity for change was the treasury minister at the time, Guido Carli, who, relying on the "Europe effect," was committed to balancing central government accounts at the beginning of the 1990s. To reduce the size of the primary deficit and tackle an extremely high level of public debt, a number of structural reforms were in fact necessary.[9] Such prestigious economists as Carlo Azeglio Ciampi, Mario Monti, and Luigi Spaventa also noted the possible scope for change opened up by the European linkage and wrote and spoke repeatedly in the main media about the need for Italy to pull more closely into line with economic and fiscal models compatible with Maastricht.

The first consequence of the obligations imposed by the process of establishing the EMU was a greater separation between the Bank of Italy and the executive, to adjust the Italian monetary system to the mechanism for the operation of the future European Central Bank (which would be independent of the individual governments). After the beginning of 1992, the governor of the Bank of Italy (then Carlo Azeglio Ciampi) was thus given sole responsibility for setting the official discount rate (an instrument that was often used in Italy, together with the devaluation of the lira) and was no longer required to share this privilege with the treasury minister.[10] This made it impossible for the government to steer monetary policy to meet its own budgetary requirements. It obliged the government to act on the public expenditure side, which was the only area in which it had any room for maneuver to rebalance public accounts and honor its Maastricht commitments.

It was in this period that what became known as "bribesville" threw Italy's postwar political framework into turmoil. For the first time, the prime minister of the day, Giuliano Amato (June 1992–April 1993), found himself in an ideal situation to decouple the executive from party dictates, which he exploited immediately by implementing a number of measures to revive the Italian economy once and for all. The governments that followed between 1992 and 1996 (Giuliano Amato, June 1992–April 1993; Carlo Azeglio Ciampi, April 1993–April 1994; Silvio Berlusconi, May 1994–December 1994; Lamberto Dini, January 1995–January 1996) were therefore able to begin redressing Italy's public finances, more or less radically, with the ultimate purpose of reassuring Italy's partners that Italy intended to focus on the objectives to which it had subscribed at Maastricht.

In April 1996, Prime Minister Romano Prodi came to power after an election campaign in which he had stressed the need for Italy to join the Economic and Monetary Union despite the fact that Italian public finances had not met the requirements for accession.[11] Over that period Italy seemed destined to be left out of the EMU. But as Andrea Monorchio wrote: "It is precisely in the most sensitive and important moments that Italy manages to find the strength and capacity to overcome difficulties and to attain objectives deemed to be impossible."[12] In the end it was the genuine motivation and resolute action of the government rather than fortuitous circumstances that made it possible for Prodi to succeed.

One of the first actions taken by the Prodi government to redress public finances was the decision to merge the Ministries of the Treasury, Budget, and Economic Planning into one umbrella Economics Ministry (Legislative Decree 430 of December 5, 1997). The new minister for the economy, former Bank of Italy governor Carlo Azeglio Ciampi, thus acquired greater powers and more weight in the cabinet. He was also equipped with a computer system capable of monitoring public expenditure flows both centrally and locally. The Budget Law was also redesigned to be governed by the economic principles of efficiency and effectiveness (Law 94/1997). Taken together, all this made it possible for the minister to rebalance the public accounts more effectively.

But the first real challenge facing the Prodi government was the 1997 Budget Law. In order to pacify the extreme left of the government coalition (Rifondazione Comunista), the objectives set out in the June 1996 DPEF (Economic and Financial Planning Document) were identical to those planned a year earlier by the Dini government, which had not been completed in time to qualify Italy for inclusion in the Economic and Monetary Union.[13] A further reduction in the deficit was contemplated as a mid-year adjustment, but only if economic conditions made it possible.[14] At a hearing before a joint session of the Senate and Chamber of Deputies, the governor of the Bank of Italy, Antonio Fazio, said that any more severe adjustments to the public accounts would have negative repercussions for national growth.[15] The rather unambitious Budget Law was seen as a partial betrayal of Prodi's election campaign commitment. And at the end of the summer of 1996, Prodi too realized that it would be impossible for Italy to successfully pass scrutiny for EMU membership.[16]

Since it was impossible to achieve the planned results by "tampering with the budget," because of the constant opposition encountered from the government coalition partner, Rifondazione Comunista, the Prodi government began to look for a "political" solution to the problem. First, Economy Minister Ciampi tried to argue with Italy's European partners that the Maastricht criteria only had numerical value and it was more important to appraise them in political terms.[17] Germany flatly rejected this interpretation: Chancellor Helmut Kohl said that any negotiations to postpone the Maastricht deadlines would weaken the efforts of the member states to reduce public expenditure and debt: "If more time is given to someone to do something, they will take longer to do it."[18] As the German finance minister, Theo Waigel, said emphatically, in reference to the public debt limit: "Three percent means *dreikommanull* [three point zero]."[19] It was therefore obvious that the more "virtuous" countries would not think twice about justifying Italy's exclusion on objective and macroeconomic grounds.

Italy then considered establishing an alliance to create a blocking minority.[20] Spain was the natural candidate for this, considering that its budget deficit was similar to Italy's. At a bilateral meeting in Valencia on September 17, 1996, Romano Prodi suggested to Spain's prime minister, José María Aznar, that they create an alliance promoting the postponement of the start of the Economic and Monetary Union. The Spanish prime minister not only rejected Italy's proposal but, rather undiplomatically and with scant respect for the confidentiality of their bilateral discussions, then gave an interview to the *Financial Times* in which he revealed Prodi's request, adding that "[Prodi] wanted Spain and Italy to walk together holding hands toward Maastricht. . . . I'm not interested in holding hands. I told him we'd better be there right from the start." [21] Although the Italian government did not deny that the Valencia meeting included a discussion of the EMU accession criteria and deadlines, there is no doubt that the meeting bolstered Italy's determination to be among the initial EMU core group.[22] If Spain succeeded in meeting the Maastricht criteria in time for EMU entry and Italy did not, the lira would have been dragged into a disastrous spiral of devaluations, not to mention the costs related to Italy's marginalization within the Union, as one of the founding countries of the European Community. Prodi therefore decided to keep faith with the promises made during his election campaign, regardless of the domestic costs.

Only a few days after the Spanish episode the Italian government introduced a number of supplementary measures worth 62,500 billion lire, sending a clear signal to the markets that the Italian government intended to meet the Maastricht criteria.[23] One of the principal measures adopted was the introduction of what was called the "Eurotax," a one-time fee levied on the Italian population to make it possible to reduce the deficit by 0.6 percent in one year.[24] The already financially burdened Italian population accepted this tax in the hope that the EMU would lead to economic and financial stability in Italy.[25]

Finally, Romano Prodi pledged to resign if Italy were not admitted to the EMU.[26] Three days later, on November 24, 1996, the lira rejoined the European Monetary System, meeting the first of the Maastricht criteria. Rejoining the EMS was an event worth analyzing in its own right. Negotiations on the central parity of the lira against the other EMS currencies were initially conducted by a monetary committee whose members included, for Italy, Mario Draghi and Pierluigi Ciocca (representing, respectively, the Ministry of the Treasury and the Bank of Italy). Their position was to defend a lira-mark parity of 1,010–1,020, but their efforts were blocked by the hardline demand of the French delegation for an exchange rate of 950 lire to one mark. This exchange rate would have severely penalized Italy's exports.[27] The final decision was referred to the Ecofin Council meeting on November 24, 1996. At that meeting Ciampi's main aim was to secure a parity of 1,000 lire to the mark, rather than the 950–970 lire laid down initially by the Council of Economy Ministers. Minister Ciampi, accompanied by the governor of the Bank of Italy, Antonio Fazio, successfully struck a compromise with his colleagues during the night of November 25, 1996, for a fixed parity of 990 lire to the mark, which was very close to their original aim.[28] Another negotiating success achieved by Minister Ciampi was the generous construction placed in article 109j of the Maastricht Treaty, which stipulated that a country could be admitted to the EMU only if the currency had been a stable member of the EMS for at least two years. Italy succeeded in obtaining a six-month "discount" on the rigorous application of this criterion, without which EMU entry would not have been possible before January 1, 1999.[29]

The last word was then up to the financial markets. Three factors helped to convince Europe that Italy's promises to meet the Maastricht criteria would be honored: (a) the promise that Prime Minister Prodi would resign in the event of Italy's failure to gain admission to the EMU; (b) the readmission of the lira into the EMS; and (c) the gradual reduction in inflation. The confidence of the market also helped to rapidly lower interest rates, to the point of reducing the gap between Italian government bonds and German bonds to zero. Thanks to this confidence, which was achieved at the end of 1997, Italy succeeded in cutting the deficit even more than the Maastricht Treaty demanded, to 2.7 percent, and reducing inflation to 1.7 percent.[30]

The final hurdle was therefore the adoption of the Convergence Report drafted by the governors of the central banks (Frankfurt, March 24, 1998), on which a country's exclusion or participation in the EMU would depend. But the governors' report spoke of "serious concerns" about the Italian situation. Meanwhile the German Constitutional Court had to rule on whether the merger of the mark with "weaker" currencies was constitutional. If the court ruled against it, it might have thrown into doubt the birth of the single currency or led to the exclusion of Italy in order to save the euro. The fact remains that the news was leaked, and fortunately it reached Ciampi's ears. The night before the text was printed for publication the economy minister phoned his former central bank colleagues (Hans Tietmeyer, Alexandre Lamfalussy, and Wim Duisenberg) and succeeded in having the wording "serious concerns" changed to "ongoing concerns" so that Italy (and other countries) could continue their progress toward the euro.[31] Having overcome the obstacle of compliance with the Maastricht criteria and the scrutiny of the governors of the central banks, Italy became one of the countries given the green light to join the founding core group of the EMU by the European Council meeting in Brussels on May 2, 1998.

The 20-20-20 Climate-Energy Package

A first Europe-wide strategy for combating climate change—an issue that has been hotly debated since the 1990s—has been set forth in the "Climate-Energy Package," also known as the "20-20-20 Plan." This package, which has become a benchmark model for all the countries wishing to embark on a similar path, is an attempt to provide a coherent approach to the problem of global warming, as part of a broader energy policy framework. It is also an interesting case for analyzing what Italy has been doing on the European political scene.

The nominal targets set in the 20-20-20 package are a reduction of CO_2 emissions to 20 percent below 1990 levels, a 20 percent increase in energy efficiency (energy savings), and a 20 percent increase in the share of renewables in the energy mix by 2020, taking 2005 as the benchmark year (for it was only in 2005 that sensitive data on all twenty-seven European Union member countries became available).

The package was launched under the German presidency of the European Union at the European Council on March 8–9, 2007, when the twenty-seven heads of state and government approved guidelines for an integrated environmental policy. The purpose of this policy was to hold the increase in the average temperature of the Earth's surface to less than 2°C above preindustrial levels.

An initial draft of the Climate-Energy Package was submitted to the European Parliament on January 23, 2008, by Commission president José Manuel Barroso. The Commission had set in motion what was initially a diplomatic, and subsequently a political, process to accommodate the package primarily in the interests of the European Union states. The Climate-Energy Package was adopted on first reading by the European Parliament using the codecision procedure, after being discussed at the European Council on December 11 and 12, 2009, under the French presidency. The Council gave its final approval to the Climate-Energy Package on April 6, 2009, after adopting, with a qualified majority vote, all the amendments made by the European Parliament on December 17, 2008.[32]

There were five measures in the package: a proposal for a directive revising the greenhouse gas emission quotas trading system, known as the Emissions Trading System (ETS), which applied to large-scale plants; a proposal for a decision regarding national targets to reduce the emissions of pollutants by 10 percent in the non-ETS sectors (low energy-intensive manufacturing, transport, and construction); a proposal for a directive on renewable energy sources setting binding national targets on every member state for energy quotas produced from renewable sources; a proposal for a directive to encourage the spread of carbon capture and storage (CCS) technologies; and last, a proposal for a regulation to reduce the CO_2 emissions from motor-powered passenger vehicles.[33]

The original version of the package required Italy to increase its share of energy produced from renewable sources to 17 percent of final consumption by 2020 (from 5.2 percent in 2005), and to reduce CO_2 emissions from the ETS sector by 21 percent and from the non-ETS sector by 13 percent below 2005 levels, by 2020.[34]

The cost-benefit rationale defining CO_2 emissions reduction targets for each state was "mitigated" by the principle of solidarity among the member states, such that the less wealthy countries would have a large quantity of emission permits available—giving them the possibility to grow in the more polluting sectors—while requesting the wealthier countries to balance this by offsetting total emissions, reducing theirs proportionally.

For the sectors included in the European Emissions Trading System, Italy's energy-intensive companies, like those of the other European countries, would no longer be required to honor a particular quota or "national" cap but to comply with the single European maximum quota. After 2013, emission rights would be sold directly to large corporations, creating an internal European quota market. These quotas would be gradually reduced to reach the lowest possible level by 2020.

Italy's reactions to the package were somewhat pessimistic, and the director general of the Environmental Research and Development Directorate General at the Ministry of the Environment, Corrado Clini, spoke about the "risk" it posed to Italy and to the Italian production system. The head of the Technical Secretariat of the Energy Directorate at the Ministry of Economic Development, Luciano Barra, was of the same opinion, saying that the renewables target would demand "immense effort" on the part of Italy.[35] According to them, the European Commission had merely set a cap on emissions reductions and then split the quotas among the different member states, without, however, devoting adequate concern to the instruments identified by Brussels for focusing the targets. According to these two senior civil servants, this was a bureaucratic and administrative approach that had to be corrected in the course of the negotiations.

At the political level, the reactions may be summed up by the position adopted by the minister of European policies at the time, Emma Bonino, and the minister for economic development, Pier Luigi Bersani (cautious), and by the minister of the environment, Alfonso Pecoraro Scanio (favorable).

The day after the package was officially announced, Minister Bonino said that it contained various positive aspects, but that the 17 percent target for renewables assigned to Italy was too burdensome. According to Minister Bonino this was because "the Commission had decided not to take account of the peculiarities of the different member states, starting with their natural features, but had only worked on the basis of their relative wealth . . . the approach did not consider the repercussions in terms of systemic costs and corporate competitiveness."[36] Minister Pier Luigi Bersani held the same view; after reiterating the excessively burdensome nature of the target for renewables, he noted that "the emissions reduction target for Italy [–13 percent for the non-ETS sectors against the European average of –10 percent] was severe for Italy, as was the commitment to biofuels, which would mainly have to be complied with through imports." According to Minister Bersani, the debate had to be taken further "within the Community, partly to evaluate costs of the measures to be adopted in order to achieve these targets, and of their repercussions on the industrial system and the competitiveness of European businesses."[37]

Conversely, the minister for the environment, Alfonso Pecoraro Scanio, was wholly in favor of the package, declaring that the targets provided "an important opportunity which the country cannot and must not fail to exploit."[38]

The pro-environment view of the minister for the environment nevertheless ignored the costs to the Italian system in order to comply with the targets to which Italy had committed, while Bonino and Bersani took these into account. These different approaches made it difficult for the ministries to coordinate their efforts, and impossible, in the time remaining to the Prodi government (until May 2008), to adopt a single position and a consistent Italian stance.

After the collapse of the Prodi government, the negotiations were taken over by the new ministers of the fourth Berlusconi government (beginning in 2008).

However, the coherence of the Italian strategy in the defense of national interests in the passage from one administration to the next was in any event guaranteed by the Permanent Technical Committee of CIACE (the Interministerial Committee for European Community Affairs). CIACE had been dealing with the climate-energy file since January 2007 and had resolved to set up a dedicated "Energy-Climate Working Group" to establish the Italian position on the package of initiatives within the Community.[39]

From the outset, the policy approach followed by the new government was to ensure that the package would strike a balance between achieving environmental goals and defending European economic competitiveness (particularly in the European manufacturing sector). Consequently, the fourth Berlusconi government requested a revision of the effort required of Italy and in particular the Italian production system. At the beginning of July 2008, Minister for the Environment Stefania Prestigiacomo and Minister for Economic Development Claudio Scajola submitted a report to the European Commission setting out Italy's position regarding the main problems raised by the package, and its proposals for overcoming them.

The government was unhappy about both the renewables directive and the CO_2 emissions reduction directive. On renewables, it felt that the criteria were too restrictive, as it allowed the count to include imports of renewables from non-European countries. On the second directive (reducing carbon emissions) Italy asked to change the criteria for burden sharing by the member states in the non-ETS sector (construction, transport, and manufacturing), as they were based only on per capita GDP.[40] Furthermore, at the end of July 2008, the minister for European policies, Andrea Ronchi, wrote to the prime minister to draw his attention to the current situation in view of the imminent European-level meetings.[41]

The sensitivity of the Italian government to the whole issue was based on its assessment of the impact that the package would have on the domestic economy. The European Commission's cost-benefit analysis (*Impact Assessment*) of January 23, 2003, said that the annual cost to Italy for the implementation of the Climate-Energy Package would be about 13 billion euros. However, a Ministry for Economic Development analysis of September 8, 2008, using data provided by the Bologna-based Società per le Ricerche Industriali Energetiche (RIE), stated that the real cost of the package to Italy would be at least double that figure, 23–27 billion euros annually.[42]

Drawing on these figures, the minister for the environment, Stefania Prestigiacomo, asked the environment commissioner, Stavros Dimas, to produce a clearer and more precise cost-benefit analysis of the package, which he delivered in September 2008.

According to the comparative assessment, entitled "Model-Based Analysis of the 2008 EU Policy Package on Climate Change and Renewables," the total cost to the Italian energy system would be around 181.5 billion euros (about 18.2 billion euros annually). This figure referred to the case if "scenario no. 2" of the analysis were implemented. This analysis examined seven possible scenarios; the one considered by Minister Stefania Prestigiacomo provided the worst-case scenario in which Italy would find itself if it failed to take advantage of any of the flexible measures introduced by the climate package (massive recourse to renewables, green certificates, the sustainable development mechanism, reducing hydrocarbons dependency).

However, this new result confirmed the Italian government's doubts and led it to alert the other European partners to review the efforts demanded by the directives set out in the package. According to the new scenario analyzed, Italy would be able to reach the target for renewables, but would fall short of the target for reducing greenhouse gas emissions: according to the more realistic scenario, Italy would only manage to reduce emissions to 15 percent below 2005 levels, while the directive demanded a target of −13 percent in the non-ETS sector and −21 percent in the ETS sector. And further CO_2 emissions reductions would only be covered by buying emissions quotas from third countries, giving rise to yet further costs.

Italy's negotiating priorities for the 20-20-20 package were laid out at a policy summit on September 17, 2008, at Palazzo Chigi, attended by all the relevant ministries (Economic Development, Environment, Economy, and Foreign Affairs), headed by the Ministry of Community Policies. Environment Minister Stefania Prestigiacomo's presentation drew the attention of the other member states to Italy's concerns. She proposed bilateral meetings with the other European partners before the European Council on October 15 and 16, 2008, in Brussels, not to overturn the whole package but only to improve the clarity and transparency of the targets. Her second aim was to obtain a degree of flexibility in the targets under a safeguard clause for reviewing the agreement in the event that the political and economic conditions made this advisable.[43]

Italy's efforts to sensitize the twenty-seven member states to the potentially damaging effects of the package began with France, which held the presidency of the European Union. At their meeting at Palazzo Chigi on September 19, 2008, Prime Minister Silvio Berlusconi told the French prime minister, François Fillon, about the concerns of Italian industry regarding the European Commission's package of proposals. At the same time, on a visit to Nice to hold conversations with her French opposite number, Jean Louis Borloo, Minister Prestigiacomo stressed that the intermediate targets should not be binding and that the power plants built by Italian companies in the Balkans Energy Community and in the Mediterranean region should be taken into account when calculating renewable energy sources.[44]

Another essential phase in this Italian diplomatic process involved Germany, under whose EU presidency the Climate-Energy Package had originally been designed and the first essential agreements approved. At his meeting in Berlin, the minister for European policies, Andrea Ronchi, said he had found that "Germany greatly shared Italy's concerns about the consequences that the Climate-Energy Package might have on the national industrial system."[45]

The purpose of sending members of the Italian government to the European capitals was to broaden the group of countries that were not in favor of the package; these included Poland and the other eight eastern European countries (Hungary, Romania, Bulgaria, the Czech Republic, Slovakia, Estonia, Latvia, and Lithuania.[46] What worried the eastern bloc countries the most was the choice of 2005 as the benchmark year for reducing CO_2 emissions, because lower economic growth and stagnating output had resulted in lower pollution emissions in that year, and it would be much harder to reduce them further. The nine eastern European countries therefore asked that 1990 be taken as the benchmark year, when their emissions had been very high, although Italy's had been comparatively low, such that their reasoning differed from Italy's.

Italy's shared concerns with Germany, with which it is most comparable in terms of production structure, eventually proved crucial for reiterating the Italian government's position at the European Council on October 15 and 16, 2008. The problem most commonly raised by Italy, Germany, and the eastern European countries had to do with the risk of "carbon leakage," that is to say, the danger that given the strict conditions established within the EU for such crucial industrial sectors as pulp and paper, aluminum, steel, and a number of chemicals industries, these companies might choose to relocate to less heavily regulated countries, causing serious losses to the national economy.

Unlike on other occasions, Italy refused to budge on its request for four changes to the directives: (1) the abolition of the intermediate targets; (2) the abolition of the commitment to cut CO_2 levels by 30 percent resulting from an international agreement within the IPCC (the Intergovernmental Panel on Climate Change); (3) easing the commitments required of Italy's vehicle industries; (4) exempting the largest energy-intensive industries from the ETS capping system. These four points were set out by the Italian foreign minister, Franco Frattini, on the margins of the European Council on October 15–16[47] and were reiterated by Environment Minister Prestigiacomo at the Luxembourg Environment Council on October 20, 2008.[48]

What emerged from the European Council was a formal commitment by all the countries to reach an agreement by the end of the year, while the French presidency deployed all its efforts to guarantee a unanimous vote, even though this matter was subject to co-decision with a qualified majority vote on the Council. Conversely, the "rebel" countries succeeded in obtaining the right of companies most exposed to the risk of relocation to freely pollute 100 percent after 2012.

Instead of blocking or delaying the package, Italy therefore succeeded in ensuring that in the short time that remained until the next European Council in December 2008, the dialogue could be reopened and the aspects that would have severely affected Italian industry could be reframed.

The climate issue therefore remained at the top of the Italian political agenda throughout the period. The government's position was broadly endorsed by Italian industry.[49]

At the end of the Luxembourg Environment Council on October 20, 2008, Environment Minister Prestigiacomo managed to secure the establishment of a technical working group between the European Commission and the Italian authorities (representatives of the Ministry for Economic Development, the Ministry for the Environment, the Ministry for Community Policies, and the Ministry for Foreign Affairs) to set the costs of implementing the package and, on the Italian side, to try to "improve it" by securing a few further concessions.

With regard to the measures requested by the government on individual aspects of the package, for the directive regarding the non-ETS sectors, Italy requested a different distribution of the targets in the EU countries to be calculated on the basis of per capita emissions, and not per capita GDP.[50]

For the directive revising the ETS system, Italy requested that greater attention be given to energy-intensive plants (pulp and paper, glass, ceramics, electric furnace steel producers), assigning free or partially free rights to the industrial plants most exposed to the problem of industrial relocation and exempting small plants making insignificant contributions to global emissions from the ETS system.

For the renewables directive the focus was on leaving more room for physical and virtual imports from the Energy Community countries (Albania, Bosnia and Herzegovina, Croatia, the former Yugoslav Republic of Macedonia, Montenegro, Serbia, and the United Nations Interim Administration Mission in Kosovo), nonbinding intermediate targets and greater use of the instruments provided by the Kyoto Protocol (articles 6 and 12), namely the Clean Development Mechanism (CDM) and Joint Implementation (JI), including the use of the credits obtained from the reduction of emissions in third countries (developed for the CDM, and in the developing countries for JI).

Italy also insisted that there should be no automatic transition from the 20 percent to the 30 percent reduction in emissions if an international agreement were to be reached, and that under the climate package there should be a discussion of the regulation for the further reduction of car emissions, requesting the introduction of a maximum penalty of 15 euros per gram on producers remaining within 3 grams of the target, and the abolition of any penalties for cars falling below the average European target of 130 grams per kilometer or the specific producer target.

Finally, Italy asked to be allocated, if possible, one of the twelve carbon capture and storage (CCS) demonstration plants.[51]

Before the December European Council, work became so intense on the CIACE that sometimes two meetings were held on the same day. The first result of the technical-level negotiations related precisely to the final crucial point as far as Italy was concerned, namely, defining automobile emission limits. As Italy suggested, according to the "polluter pays" principle of environmental responsibility in the EU, which was laid down in Directive 2004/35/CE of April 21, 2004, the compromise provided for small fines to be levied for minor breaches of the pollution limits (the average CO_2 emissions from new automobiles sold in Europe should not exceed 130 grams/kilometer, and Fiat must not exceed 122 grams/km) with increasingly severe fines on producers whose products are more than 4 grams over the target.[52]

On the eve of the European Council, Minister Claudio Scajola succeeded in obtaining a mid-term revision clause (that is, to take effect in 2014) on renewables. The Italian share of renewables in the European mix would always remain at 17 percent (with no discount on the target to be achieved), but in 2014, if individual countries were behind in complying with their targets, Italy would be able to discuss ways of achieving that 17 percent target.[53] On the question of renewables, Italy also succeeded in obtaining a reduction in the specifications limiting the physical imports of renewables only to the non-European countries whose legal systems were compatible with those within the European Union.

Despite this, however, just before the EU Foreign Affairs Council in December 2008, Foreign Minister Franco Frattini felt it appropriate to reiterate the steps forward and the three "red lines" beyond which the Italian government would not give way: "carbon leakage"; the need to include in the accounting of the renewable energy national target the energy produced from green sources in non-EU Mediterranean countries; the cause for revising the targets in 2014.[54]

On the eve of the European Council two points on which Italy had threatened to place a veto had been accepted: renewables and car emissions. This left in abeyance the question of a clause for the general revision of the package and the reservation linked to defending the interests of the industrial sectors that were most concerned about the costs of the new antipollution rules, namely, the small and medium-size enterprises that make up the bulk of the Italian industrial system. On this latter request, Italy said that it would never accept a compromise and threatened to use its veto if the agreement failed to take account of Italian interests.

Thanks to this steadfast determination, and also thanks to France's desire to reach an agreement before the end of the French presidency, the third demand of the Italian government was also granted: "permissions to pollute" would be distributed free of charge to the pulp and paper, glass, ceramics, and steel rod industries; authorization was also given to streamline the procedures for small businesses that contribute only marginally to emissions[55] and the clause for a general revision of the package in 2010 in view of the results achieved at the Copenhagen summit, making it possible to review the binding constraints if other polluting countries failed to follow the "European example."[56]

Last, Italy succeeded in obtaining permission to build one of the twelve planned demonstration plants to promote the application of carbon capture and sequestration (CCS) technology within the European Union, which will be financed from part of the revenues from selling emission allowances.

This was an important agreement for the French presidency and a victory for Italy. After an initial phase of disorientation followed by concerted coordination among government departments, and after placing intense pressure on its partners, Italy's diplomats succeeded in bringing home a compromise solution that fully reflected their country's national interests.

10

Conclusion: The Long Road to Brussels

A survey conducted in the second half of the 1990s to compare the management of European affairs by Italy and Portugal showed that "small" Portugal was more capable of promoting and defending its national interests in the decisionmaking processes of the European Union than "big" Italy.[1] Italy's difficulties had to do with four main variables: the instability of its governments; the lack of government cohesion; the government's inability to implement a learning process; and above all the country's political culture. More specifically, government instability, reflected in the high turnover among political players and in working groups, penalized Italy by undermining the government's credibility. The lack of government cohesion made the process of adapting the country's institutions more difficult for both the government and parliament; interparty rivalry within the coalition governments also prevented effective coordination both within and between ministries. The political and administrative leadership appeared to be incapable of analyzing and learning from the solutions adopted in the other member states. Finally, whereas one aspect of Italy's political culture, namely the politicians' widespread positive perception of European integration, helped Italy to defend its position in the high politics negotiations, other aspects of Italy's political culture hampered Italian action within the Union. One example was the provincial attitude of Italian policymakers. Their lack of interest in national issues and in promoting them at the European level hindered Italy's work in Community decisionmaking, and in particular in the matter of low politics.

This book shows that in the first ten years of the twenty-first century the situation improved notably. And since the 1990s, Italy has made great strides in the way it addresses European issues, resulting in greater success in asserting its interests in both low politics and high politics. Despite this progress, Italy's image as described in the specialized media and academic literature has not essentially changed. Are these assessments correct? Or has Italy's handling of European relations changed *sufficiently* to be able to say that the country has turned the corner? Last but not least, has the level of Europeanization displayed by Italy increased since the 1990s? These are the questions explored in this final chapter.

Improvements and Setbacks

The Italian institution demonstrating the longest level of Europeanization is definitely the parliament. Any independent observer looking at the Italian parliament's role in EU affairs should be impressed by the improvements of the past ten years or so. In a short span of time, the Italian parliament has successfully addressed many issues that had remained unresolved for years, thereby greatly narrowing the gap between its own performance and that of the national parliaments that were best organized to scrutinize EU affairs. While maintaining its traditional model of "paper-based scrutiny," the Italian parliament now has in place a well-developed scrutiny system in which the Standing Committees specializing in EU affairs play the leading role. It has expanded the scope of its scrutiny of EU policies, is kept regularly informed of developments in EU affairs, and has developed specific procedures for scrutiny and fact-finding; it has even protected its prerogatives by introducing a scrutiny reserve system. In addition, the executive branch has created an interdepartmental EU affairs coordination body: the Interdepartmental Committee for Community and European Affairs (CIACE).

In addition, legislative changes signal a significant evolution in the way relations between Europe and the parliament are perceived. In the 1980s, scrutiny of EU legislation was considered a matter for the European Parliament. The national parliaments were then called to review, or scrutinize, proposed EU policies to compensate for the democratic deficit at the European level. The focus of the Italian parliament's action in the matter of EU affairs was therefore largely the implementation of EU directives. In the wave of reforms that followed the signing of the Amsterdam Treaty, the Italian parliament's role in EU affairs moved away from primarily implementing EU directives, toward a more positive and proactive role in shaping the national position on draft EU legislation. This change reflects the idea that the EU and the Italian political systems are no longer "two separate legal systems," but rather two closely interconnected systems of governance. Consequently, the national parliament's participation in EU decisionmaking is also essential for ensuring the quality of domestic legislation, since parliament has to factor in EU policy priorities when legislating. Conversely, parliamentary input can be instrumental in assessing the likely impact of EU draft legislation on the domestic system, thereby contributing to the preparation of a more robust and better argued national posture in negotiations on the European Council. The Italian government and parliament have therefore become allies—not rivals—in formulating national positions on EU policy.

Despite this positive picture and the positive developments, there remain a few things that need to be improved: the pace of parliamentary business needs to be stepped up; parliamentary opinions must become less generic and more targeted; and there is a need to improve the implementation of EU law and its compatibility with domestic law. Although parliament now has a new system of "scrutiny reserve" (which allows government representatives in the Council not to take an official position on an issue until the national parliament has examined it), it has been used infrequently. For this instrument to be useful, both the parliament and the government must be willing to employ it, and even more important, parliament must be able to complete the scrutiny quickly. It is also important to note that change took so long because the improvements were piecemeal rather than part of an overall root-and-branch reform.

The Italian executive's long resistance to the process of Europeanization has finally been reversed. The creation of CIACE, the interdepartmental coordinating body for EU affairs, was a fundamental step forward. The specialized literature emphasizes the role of the national executives to define and foster national interests in the European Union, and in particular the importance of interdepartmental coordination. David Spence, for example, considers interdepartmental coordination key to enabling governments to properly defend their interests in EU negotiations.[2] However, coordination is not easy, and the very nature of the Union's decisionmaking processes, in addition to domestic variables (the importance of Europe as an issue in the national debate, the party system, the stance adopted by the head of government and the ministers, the capacity of the administrator to produce a set of coherent policy proposals, the level of integration and the centralism of the civil service and the internal divisions within the bureaucratic machinery) are all factors that make coordination difficult to implement. The introduction of CIACE has proven that it is capable of working properly, and in some cases—the 20-20-20 energy directive, for example—it plays a leadership role both at home and within Europe. The introduction and operation of CIACE was made possible—and this is also a sign of improvement—partly thanks to the willingness of government coalitions to continue in this direction, and to a compromise reached between the two main institutions involved, namely, the Ministry of Foreign Affairs (which since its creation has led it with one of its top diplomats, Minister Massimo Gaiani) and the Prime Minister's Office (which hosts it).

Still, CIACE has a number of weaknesses. First and foremost, the establishment of an interdepartmental coordination body does not necessarily coincide with the introduction of corresponding facilities in each ministry. The coordination work performed by CIACE is not yet being adequately supported by the individual units it is intended to coordinate. Second, CIACE is understaffed, and it therefore manages to coordinate its work in the ascending phase of Community law in only a limited number of cases, leaving many negotiating areas completely uncovered. Third, the involvement of the regional governments in the coordination effort is still fraught with difficulties, even though the regional governments have gradually seen their powers and prerogatives in the matter of foreign affairs, and particularly Community affairs, being broadened. Last, CIACE does not always succeed in framing its positions quickly enough to keep pace with the European decisionmaking process.

One of the weaknesses mentioned above—the continuing absence of some of the Italian regional governments from the work of the CIACE—reminds us that the quality of the regional governments' presence in Brussels has nevertheless improved enormously since the late 1990s. This change can be seen as an additional element of Europeanization of the Italian system. The laws governing the regions' participation in both the ascending and descending phases of Community law have also become more inclusive. However, the physical presence of the regions in Brussels has not necessarily led to their greater influence in European policymaking. Since 2002, for example, the Italian regions have never succeeded in spending all of the Structural Funds allocated to them. And only a few regions have the necessary critical mass and political weight (and economic might) to have any direct impact on EU policies through the Community channel. These include Lombardy and the regions of central Italy led by Tuscany, Emilia-Romagna, and, to a lesser degree, Veneto, Piedmont, Liguria, and Puglia. But the story is different with regard to the southern Italian regions, whose presence in Brussels has not reached the necessary critical mass to enable them to make their voices heard consistently.

This analysis thus shows a marked difference in the way the Italian regions organize and even conceptualize their role in European affairs. The Italian regions' ability to exert influence still requires working through national channels, both institutional and otherwise. Yet the channels established by law are not particularly effective. Although the law allows the regions to send their own representatives to join the national Italian delegations attending the European Council, many still do not do so.

THE SAME SCENARIO of enlightened forward movement and provincial attitudes also emerges when we examine the work of the Italian pressure groups in Brussels. The analysis in chapter 7 describes a number of structural problems in Italy that are reflected in the lobbying work in Brussels. First, Italian lobbying in Brussels reflects the fragmentation and the parochial nature of Italian interests. Moreover, Italy's delay in joining the European lobbying scene was also due to a political and cultural problem: for many years, the expression "lobbying" had negative connotations and even today, unlike many other countries, Italy still has no form of regulating it. In other words, Italy has little familiarity with the practice of transparent lobbying, which, for example, presupposes wide access to technical data, but prefers a system in which political patronage reigns supreme, demonstrating that the paradigm that the political patronage culture prevails in Italy still applies to this day.[3]

Some Italian entities, realizing the importance of being present in Brussels, effectively use the networks that they find there, and cooperate effectively, transmitting information and widely communicating among themselves. Telecom Italia, Confindustria, the Tuscany regional government, the National Research Council (CNR), and Unioncamere are particularly active in developing networks, also with non-Italian organizations. But most Italian entities operate primarily through informal and purely Italian networks. Too often, action is left to the "goodwill" of the representatives of Italy's pressure groups. The representatives of Italian corporations act largely on the basis of the personal trust vested in their representative, but Italy, as a system, is absent and fails to follow them. It is therefore natural that Italian lobbying is perceived by the European institutions as piecemeal and fragmented, addressing narrow and parochial cases, situations, needs, and expectations, some of which are even in conflict with each other. There is a mass of small, weak lobbying entities, and despite a few important exceptions, Italian lobbying is viewed as lacking in preparation and specialization, and often even as irrelevant to the context and the timing of the system in which takes place. The effectiveness of Italian lobbying is hampered by a lack of insistence and method, by poor technical preparation, and by language and cultural limitations. It is very rare to find an Italian lobbyist acting on the basis of a strategy agreed to with non-Italian parties who share the same interests.

Frequently, Italian lobbyists express a *need for something* rather than an *interest in developing a strategy* to acquire it. In such cases the effectiveness of their work is often thwarted by competing lobbyists who promote their interests more clearly. Italian lobbying, conducted in isolation, is always less effective than multicultural efforts in influencing Community processes. Maintaining good public relations, however constant the effort, is not in itself sufficient to have an impact on decisionmaking. Conversely, what is essential are the substance and the capacity to communicate, tailored to suit the context. Italy's shortcomings in these areas make it less competitive with other nationals, particularly the British and the Germans, substantially reducing the effectiveness and the operational relevance of Italian lobbying.

THIS BOOK EXAMINES examples of both high politics and low politics in which Italy has been involved. According to Andrew Moravcsik, European high politics are determined by the convergence of domestic policy preferences in the largest member states: the United Kingdom, Germany, and France.[4] Italy is therefore excluded from the group of the leading countries that count. There are a number of "practical" reasons for this exclusion, not least of which is the difficulty of accessing sources and, for foreign observers, the difficulty of dealing with Italy's domestic decisionmaking processes. Nevertheless, there have been important cases of high politics in which Italy has played a crucial part: two good examples are the Single European Act (1985) and the Maastricht Treaty (1991–92). But the case of the 2003 Intergovernmental Conference showed that although the Italian presidency had prepared the working papers and dossiers very thoroughly, a lack of German and French support eventually caused the negotiations to fail, highlighting an important variable to which we shall be returning below: the lack of a stable network of European alliances.[5]

The case of "Operation Alba," Italy's effort to help an Albania in crisis, is open to various interpretations. For while the operation itself demonstrated Italy's leadership capability, the fact remains that Italy failed to convince its Community partners to create "reinforced cooperation" for that initiative. For the record, I must add that Italy learned its lesson and in recent years has succeeded in creating a coalition with the Mediterranean countries to put immigration at the top of the Union agenda.

The European Arrest Warrant is also a case in point, where the sudden change in the government's stance made it possible to restart the stalled negotiations and enabled the agreement to go through. But did Italy simply realize that its political veto was unsustainable, or was it a classic case of Community quid pro quo, in which Italy changed its position in exchange for having the new Food Quality Agency located in Parma?

CHAPTER 8, ON *low politics*, discussed two extremely interesting cases. Both cover a long period of time, offering a comprehensive picture of Italy's negotiating strategies and particular Italian features. In both cases the European measures were too stringent for Italy to implement properly, with the result that Italy began by using delaying tactics, stressing the "peculiarity" of the Italian case. In particular, the government first tried Italy's classic tactic: work for a postponement of the requirements. When that approach failed, Italy changed strategies.

After it became clear that root-and-branch economic and financial adjustments would be necessary if Italy were to meet the Maastricht criteria, an elite group that recognized Italy's historic opportunity to join the EMU acted in unison to ensure that the needed domestic reforms would be implemented; at the same time, they invested all their personal credibility into making it possible to introduce a number of adjustments to the criteria to enable Italy to at least attempt entry.[6]

The more recent case of the "20-20-20 directive" to reduce carbon emissions and increase energy efficiency is perhaps the most interesting of all those discussed here because it marked the start of a new Italian negotiating strategy after the general election and the creation of a new government coalition. With the new government, the perception of Italy's priority interests was reversed; whereas the Prodi government had two groupings holding opposite views, the greater cohesion of the following government made it possible to adopt a single stance that it effectively defended within the Union. The 20-20-20 directive was also a test for the new CIACE, which succeeded in defining and coordinating a complex and highly technical negotiating position.

It must be noted, however, that in both cases Italy's change of direction on the fly can also be interpreted, by its European partners, as an example of inconsistency and "typically" Italian unreliability. And while both these cases show that when Italy wants something it has the resources and the capacity to act, its successes were largely due to the work and persistence of a few individuals rather than the Italian system as a whole.

Another problem made evident by this analysis is that Italy has not always accurately or clearly defined its goals, particularly when the government coalition is divided on important issues. This problem is exacerbated by the high turnover among Italian policymakers and Italian governmental instability, compounded by the fact that most ministers are generalists rather than specialists.[7] At the EU level, generalist ministers may also have difficulty, particularly at informal meetings where they do not have the direct support of experts to back them.

These issues lead to a consideration of Italy's negotiating alliances and strategies in the European Union.

Italy's Past and Future Alliances

Italy is on the same footing as the United Kingdom, France, and Germany with regard to voting on the Council, inasmuch as they are all "big" countries. So, on paper at least, Rome carries the same weight as Berlin or Paris. However, a country's ability to pool its votes with those of other countries obviously enhances its ability to enforce its positions; in a multilateral environment it is important to act in conjunction with others, to work within a framework of alliances. Ultimately, a country's ability to move on the complex multilateral chessboard depends on the professional skills of the players.

Negotiating methods used on the Council are akin to those of traditional multilateral diplomacy, despite the profoundly innovative nature of the European Union initiative. Today, although the number of members has risen, their working and negotiating methods have remained practically unchanged. Traditional international negotiation procedures remain in effect, and the drafting of dossiers still follows a process that moves from working groups to high-level committees, then to the Committee of the Permanent Representatives (COREPER), the Council, and of course the European Parliament. This multilayered and lengthy process often makes decisions difficult to reach. For the Council members to reach agreement, it is sometimes necessary to adopt procedural ploys: sometimes, for example, "very select" meetings are convened, from which all the aides are barred. Alternatively, work can be momentarily suspended so as to allow the so-called "confessional" to take place—a two-person conversation between the current EU president and an individual national minister. Another technique often used is the "package deal," or the inclusion, in a single proposal, of solutions to different problems, in order to hammer out a compromise deal acceptable to all the parties. It is interesting in this connection to look at what has now become the focal point of the Council of Ministers' meeting: namely, the "working lunch." It has become customary to debate the most controversial issues on the agenda at lunchtime, possibly in the presence solely of the ministers. It is possible at such a small, select meeting to turn discussion of the more controversial issues from a technical discussion into a political debate: an expert chair can find it easier to win the support of the member states for a decision that would have been hard to reach in plenary session. However, when ministers are not particularly familiar with the issue under discussion—and that is the risk with "nonspecialist" ministers, as is often the case with the Italians—they may find themselves endorsing decisions that they cannot deliver on subsequently.[8]

Two additional factors need to be taken into consideration: the degree of flexibility in negotiations and a country's use of its veto. While the Council has hitherto worked behind closed doors, and individual member states' positions are never (at least never officially) disclosed, it is also the case that the member states' flexibility in negotiations varies. Italy's representatives, for example, usually enjoy a higher degree of flexibility than Danish and Swedish representatives, who often have no option but to go along with the position approved by their parliaments.[9] In such cases, a country either rejects outright any position that differs from its own, or it resorts to the ploy of pegging acceptance to subsequent parliamentary scrutiny, with the result that the national representative cannot tell his partners how his country will vote until consultations have (yet again) been held with the national parliament. Even countries such as France, the United Kingdom, and to some extent Germany occasionally resort to this ploy. As we saw in chapter 5, under Law 11/2005, Italy's representatives on the Council now have the theoretical option of resorting to the parliamentary scrutiny tactic. Nevertheless, parliamentary scrutiny is not something the Italian parliament fully appreciates; as far as we know, it has only been used once.

The other factor is a country's use of its veto power. While qualified majority voting is the official method of reaching (most) decisions in the Council, in practice almost all decisions are reached by consensus, without being put to a vote. Only if one member state or a minority group of states (but not enough to constitute a "minority bloc") insists on vetoing a proposal might the chair decide to order a formal vote to "unfreeze" the situation. But such cases are very rare. The member states that tend to use their veto power include the United Kingdom, the Scandinavian countries, Germany, France, and, since the recent enlargement, Poland. Italy, on the other hand, tends not to: even when some parties were calling for it during the Treaty of Lisbon negotiations, Italy did not use its veto.

Finally, there is the "cross-table bargaining" technique of combining several different issues, even if they are negotiated on different Councils. For example, one member state may help another with an issue that the second state considers of vital importance in return for the second state's assistance on another issue. But this technique requires member states to prove their ability to remain in control of the situation at every negotiating table (in other words, they need a strong degree of domestic coordination); in addition, they must be prepared to invest heavily in bilateral diplomatic relations. Former prime (and foreign) minister Giulio Andreotti, for instance, was well known for forging ties with the "small" and "medium-size" countries, so that by the time the Council meeting was held, he could rely on those countries to vote with Italy. In Italy's case, for a long time the past lack of coordination had made it difficult to adopt a cross-table bargaining strategy. But there is also an "ethical" aspect that needs to be highlighted, which has carried some weight, in the past at least. This is Italy's desire to emphasize the difference between the EU and other international organizations of a more traditional kind (such as the United Nations); in these other forums, which are solely in the Foreign Ministry's hands, Italy often succeeds with cross-table bargaining. As for using the veto, Italy's negotiators are reluctant to do so when issues that are truly crucial to the national interest are at stake, although they would have been prepared to use it, for instance, in the event the country had been barred from the EMU's "core group." One alternative to these negotiating techniques is to establish alliances on an issue-by-issue basis.

The enlargement of the Union to twenty-seven states has increased the tendency of subgroups of member states to attempt to establish stable alliances with one another. At the European level, cooperation entails weekly meetings for the Permanent Representatives, as well as ongoing discussions ahead of Council meetings (at every level) and ahead of the European Council meetings. The Scandinavian countries have a long tradition of harmonization forged on the Nordic Council. Coordination also exists among the Benelux countries, and between Germany and Austria. Since the 1990s, even Spain and Portugal—whose bilateral ties only began with EEC membership in 1987—have coordinated before European Council meetings, and often before specific Council meetings. They discuss the agenda items and decide what course of action to pursue on the basis of three potential scenarios: where their interests coincide, they forge a single bloc; where only one of the two countries has a specific interest and the other has no conflicting interests, the latter backs the former's position; and where their interests diverge, it is "every man for himself." Nevertheless, they continue to support each other in general.

Italy does not appear to be part of any stable alliance. Although the six larger member states (the United Kingdom, Germany, France, Italy, Poland, and Spain) have regular consultations, they cannot be considered to have a stable alliance. Jan Beyers and Guido Dierick studied the negotiating patterns of a representative sample of working groups within the Council, showing the importance of two particular variables in the choice of allies by the member states' representatives.[10] The first variable is a player's credibility: the round of informal negotiations and contacts varies according to the players' nationality and the perception of their credibility. Southern countries—with the partial exception of Spain—are defined as "peripheral": they are less sought-after as allies. Countries deemed to be the most desirable as allies are the ones holding the rotating presidency and the "major" countries, except Italy. If a country is seeking allies in southern Europe it will most likely prefer Spain's representatives over Italy's. The authors argue that the reason for this lies in the "lack of consistency" in Italian policymaking: Italy's representatives are not perceived as reliable, and neither are they considered to be strategic allies. This would also explain, for instance, Andrew Moravcsik's decision not to include Italy in his analysis of the work of the Union's "major member states."[11]

Curiously, it appears that sociogeographic homogeneity is more highly valued by the northern European member states than by the southern states. According to J. Beyers and G. Dierick, the representatives of the northern countries (Germany, Denmark, Benelux, the United Kingdom, and Ireland) tend to communicate mainly among themselves rather than with representatives of the southern countries. The southern countries' representatives also interact mainly with each other, but their interaction (unlike that of the Scandinavian countries) tends not to constitute a full-fledged network. There is no stable cooperation among the countries of southern Europe, despite the fact that the closeness of their interests often leads to their substantial convergence on sectoral issues. Various explanations have been suggested for this absence of continuing cooperation. Enrico Letta, for instance, has argued that "Italy cannot consider its geographic position superficially, and must envisage ways of enhancing its role in the Mediterranean. This aim must be pursued . . . through relations with France, Spain, Portugal and Greece, . . . [but] there is a big difference between that, and imagining that it is possible to forge some kind of ongoing and comprehensive alliance among the member countries of a hypothetical Mediterranean constituency."[12] Lucio Caracciolo has said, "The constraint of the convergence criteria imposed by Maastricht . . . has an eminently geopolitical significance: it split the stable and reliable countries in the Deutsche Mark area from us 'Mediterraneans'—cleverly dubbed 'Club Med' by some, or even 'Pigs,' from the initials of Portugal, Italy, Greece and Spain." But he immediately adds that "an imaginary Latin axis embracing Italy, France and Spain is not credible. Naturally, there is a common interest in preventing Germany from lording it over the EU too much, but when push comes to shove, the Italians, the Spanish and the French each play their own game. Disputes among the Latins are also more virulent than those in which we are pitted against the northern countries."[13]

Other objections to the establishment of a priority network among the countries of southern Europe revolve around the fact that the southern countries do not constitute a majority bloc on the Council, or around the fact that France has no interest in being considered part of the "South." Nevertheless, even in a Europe with twenty-seven members, the southern countries have a large enough share of votes to constitute a minority bloc on the Council. In practice, the southern countries often find that their interests coincide, and they therefore end up cooperating anyway. But without an established program of ongoing consultations, this cooperation does not have such an effective impact.

The "Olive Group," the (weak) network of Mediterranean countries, is nevertheless viewed complacently by Italian diplomats, and it will eventually die, even though Italy could choose to take charge and convert it into a stable alliance within the Union. This observation is a reflection of the main contradiction in Italy's European (and foreign) policy: on occasion, the fact that Italy considers itself to be a leading country without actually being one has hampered its ability to forge strategic alliances. As Carlo Maria Santoro has put it: a "middle-size power" (as he calls Italy) cannot act as though it were a "great power"; it does not look credible. What it can do, however, is acquire added value when it becomes a member of, or even the leader of, a cohesive group of countries.[14]

Yet Italy started losing its traditional framework of alliances in the mid-1990s. During the "First Republic" Italy was part of a stable framework of alliances under Christian Democratic (DC) leadership, comprising the Benelux countries and Germany. The collapse of the DC and changes in the political scenario revolutionized that framework. Italy frequently found itself excluded from the core group of countries that carry weight and exert influence. And Italy is still trying (sincerely, but so far unsuccessfully) to get back into a group. Examples include the Italy-Spain Forum and regular consultations with Poland, but these are by no means stable alliances. The lack of stable alliances has proven to be extremely costly to Italy.

As discussed in chapters 2 and 3, the first Berlusconi government (1994–95) was a spectacular example of this. That government, which comprised not only the party that Berlusconi himself had founded (Forza Italia) but also the Northern League and the post-fascist National Alliance, found itself up against a wall of obstructionist resistance from its Community partners. And that was not all. When his European counterparts met their respective European political families before the European Council (and on other occasions), Silvio Berlusconi was totally isolated. Indeed, it is no coincidence that Berlusconi's first priority, once he became the leader of the opposition (1996–2001), was to get Forza Italia into the European People's Party (EPP), thus pegging it to a framework of stable European alliances. His second priority, which he achieved on his return to government (2001–2006), was to "enfranchise" the National Alliance within the Community. He did this by appointing the deputy prime minister, Gianfranco Fini, as the Italian government's representative at the European Convention. After initially arousing the overt hostility of the Belgian government and others, as a result of his commitment and efforts at the convention, Fini eventually succeeded in being viewed as a credible European leader rather than merely as the chairman of a post-fascist party.

Nevertheless, and despite the fact that Forza Italia has become an important player in the EPP (thanks, among other things, to the unconditional surrender of its main rival, the People's Party), Italy has not managed to win back the same importance and credibility the country enjoyed in the days of the Christian Democrats.

On the other hand, Italy's traditional European allies—namely the Benelux countries and Germany—have changed considerably over the past twenty years. Germany, in particular, began to adopt a different vision for its foreign policy and geopolitical position under the government of Gerhard Schröder. In the cold war days, Germany and Italy both labored under the burden of their pasts (and reacted to that by playing the role of European honest broker and becoming champions of pro-Europeanism), but post–cold war Germany is pursuing a far more aggressive European policy today. That policy is only partly mitigated by the tone and performance of Chancellor Angela Merkel; indeed, it is no coincidence that Helmut Kohl personally chose her as his successor.

For Italy, it has proven more difficult to rethink and implement a new role in Europe and in the world; progress has been stop-and-go rather than gradual and smooth. A 2006 Italian Foreign Ministry paper entitled "Italy 2020" is possibly the only coherent and comprehensive attempt to reflect on Italy's changed role in Europe and in the world.[15] It is a pity that it was soon discarded by the new Berlusconi government in 2008.

The Need for Strategy, Consistency, and Credibility in European Negotiations

A member state is successful in European negotiations if it has properly defined goals and credible players, and if it uses them to formulate and pursue consistent strategies. Properly defining one's goals demands efficient underlying coordination. For the many years until the CIACE was set up, Italy's major weakness was a lack of interdepartmental coordination. In its absence, Italy's negotiating positions were often defined by the Permanent Representative on the eve of the Council meetings. Italian diplomats have experienced this situation as both a source of frustration and an opportunity.

While the absence of a properly defined national position enabled Italy to enjoy a broader negotiating spectrum and to better respond to other countries' demands, in the long run this situation has undermined Italy's credibility in the EU arena, and it will take a long time before trust can be fully restored. A credible player is one who, regardless of rank, role, or position, is well known around the negotiating table for his or her authoritative standing at home or in the institution that he or she represents at the Community level. In some cases these individuals manage to stave off difficulties thanks to their own personal credibility. But in other cases, the lack of continuity in the representatives sent to Brussels by different departments can cause serious damage. Once again, this situation has frustrated Italian diplomats, who are an elite corps within the Italian civil service, but it has also provided an opportunity for them to play a far greater role in EU negotiations than their European colleagues. But like a snake that bites its tail, so long as diplomats play a paramount part in EU negotiations, the prevailing idea will be that the EU policies form part of Italian "foreign" policy but are not "domestic" policy because of the peculiar nature of European Union law.

Unfortunately, this parochial standpoint typifies the Italian political classes at all levels and allows them to avoid addressing European issues. By "parochialism," I mean Italian politicians' tendency to give priority to local over national issues and, even more detrimentally, over European and international issues. As a famous Italian politician, who shall naturally remain anonymous, once said, "Why should I bother going to Strasbourg [to the plenary session of the European Parliament] if no one even takes any notice of me?" Incidentally, the fact that it was possible until not so long ago for Italian politicians to hold several offices simultaneously at various levels led to high absenteeism in the European Parliament. Likewise, Italy's ministers and undersecretaries tend to delegate their attendance at Council meetings to their underlings to a far greater extent than their European counterparts. The result of this practice is that the person attending ministerial level meetings is often the Permanent Representative, which means that Italy has a far weaker negotiating capacity.

One prime example of Italians not paying sufficient attention to European decisions was the Council's attempt to reduce the number of Italian MEPs. The "wrong" done to Italy by the so-called Lamassoure Report (albeit subsequently remedied in part) had been approved in the course of the European Council meeting held in Brussels on June 21–23, 2007—a meeting attended by the Italian prime minister and the foreign minister. Didn't they realize what was happening? Had they left the room, as several authoritative sources claim, to resolve some domestic political problem? Or were they aware of what was happening, but hoped that it would pass unnoticed back home? Even worse, despite the noise and objections from the Italian government and the Italian media over the issue, when the vote was actually taken on the Lamassoure Report on the European Parliament's Constitutional Affairs Committee, there was only one Italian present in the room.

So while other countries put the promotion of their national interests *before* political loyalties, in Italy the reverse is the case. Such short-sighted party-related considerations include the now legendary clashes between the left- and right-wing members of the Italian DC at the European People's Party (EPP) meetings following the collapse of the Christian Democratic Party in the 1990s. As we saw in chapter 4, the breakup of the Christian Democratic Party reduced the bargaining power of the Italian delegation as a whole, particularly the former DC parties that joined the European People's Party (EPP). For years, the new Italian parties in the EPP, split between the center-right and the center-left, were known for their high level of infighting, until the 2009 European elections finally did away with a whole range of minor parties. Infighting between the Italian members of the Socialist Party was less intense but certainly not to be ignored. These internal divisions made it more difficult to appoint Italian MEPs to strategic posts. Also, traditionally Italians tend to prefer "status" posts over "authoritative" positions: therefore there have been few Italian rapporteurs on matters of national interest. Indeed "armchair politics" has been one of the axioms of the Italian diplomatic tradition and political culture.

These considerations lead to the question of international posts. When the opportunity arises to appoint Italians to fill international posts of responsibility, Italy's governments often choose undistinguished candidates from their own parties over qualified and competent candidates from the other side of the political divide. One example of this was the appointment of the international community's High Representative for Bosnia back in 1997: Italy, alone among the other fourteen European governments and the United States, (pointlessly) put forward the candidacy of internationally unknown Giangiacomo Migone against that of the respected Spanish diplomat Carlos Westendorp, a former European affairs minister and later foreign minister.[16] Antonio Tajani's appointment to replace Franco Frattini on the European Commission also triggered international reservations for his elusive track record.[17] Then there was what was the virtual self-candidacy of Massimo D'Alema, former Italian foreign minister, to occupy the post of the EU's High Representative for Foreign Policy. D'Alema, a member of the European socialist family, had been working quietly in the wings on his own candidacy, which he made public in the autumn of 2009. Officially supported by the European Socialist party, D'Alema's candidacy attracted great attention from the Italian media and was supported by the fourth Berlusconi government (center-right), not least for national and local domestic policy reasons on the eve of the spring 2010 regional elections. But the opposition of the eastern European countries because of D'Alema's past as a Communist Party leader (supposedly he speaks better Russian than English), as well as American (and Israeli) reservations about his position on the Middle East and Russia, gave his candidacy very little chance of succeeding. So when the crunch came—that is to say, when the Socialist heads of government met before the European Council to make the new appointments (November 18, 2009)—the new leader of the Italian Democratic Party, Pier Luigi Bersani, did not feel the need to attend. In this meeting the Socialist leaders did not hesitate to torpedo the Italian candidate in favor of the British nominee, Lady Catherine Ashton, thereby guaranteeing Italy a gratuitous defeat of which it was its own architect.

In other European countries we see the opposite approach being adopted: as a rule, when it comes to international appointments, governments search for their best national candidate for a post, regardless of political affiliation. Two examples of this have been the appointments of Javier Solana (a Socialist) to the post of "Mr. CFSP" (Common Foreign and Security Policy) by a government headed at the time by José Maria Aznar (a member of the People's Party), and the appointment of Pascal Lamy (a Socialist) by the French president, Jacques Chirac (a Conservative), as director general of the World Trade Organization (WTO).

This practice of Italian politicians—namely, their failure to consider the national interest and to properly promote that interest at the European level—is part and parcel of an approach to politics that hampers Italy's participation in the EU decisionmaking process. As chapter 3 discussed, the way the different Italian parties rallied around pro-European values in the late 1970s did not result in a more proactive Italian European policy, but gradually set in motion a "depoliticization" of Italian European policy. Gradually, the EC became a nonissue in the Italian political arena. Two notable exceptions were the making of the Single European Act (1985) and the Maastricht Treaty (1990), but Italy's successes there were more the result of individual action on the part of a few leaders than of a concrete policy underwritten by the Italian parties. It is the Italian, rather than the European, dimension that appeals to Italy's politicians. All too often—following a pure party-based rationale—they view "Euro-jobs" as (well-paid) sinecures or interim posts to tide them over until they can get back into the national political arena.

Conclusion: A Long Way to Go . . .

Without doubt, since the year 2000 a process of Europeanization has been developed in the main Italian institutions: the parliament, the government, and the regions. Yet its influence has not been strong enough to Europeanize the mindset or actions of the most relevant Italian actors and policymakers. There have been positive changes, as well as examples of Italian excellence, but why have these not led to better perceptions of Italy by the specialized press and in the leading literature? First, Italy's image as an unreliable country is proving hard to bury. It is not because of a plot against Italy, but it is a prejudice based on past events. There are both historical and more recent grounds for this attitude. On a continent where history weighs heavily, Italy is still the country that changed sides in both the First World War and the Second. This is a historical burden, often underestimated in Italy, that no political class in Italy has ever managed to throw off, however excellent its work. This historical perception of Italy is further strengthened in the suspicious eyes of European partners when they see Italy's wavering positions, for example, in the matter of alliances. Many other Europeans have networks of alliances that remain stable over time, with homogeneous geographic and socioeconomic interests. But for twenty years Italy has played the game of shifting alliances. Furthermore, Italy seems to be wavering today between its past as a European honest broker and giving way to temptations of power, with the result that its conduct is increasingly perceived as unpredictable.

Italy's image as an unreliable country within the European Union will take more than a few years to change. The last issue to be dealt with here is therefore to try to understand why the change has been incomplete and what prospects lie ahead.

As noted earlier, until the mid-1990s Italy's difficulties were largely attributable to its unstable governments, lack of government cohesion, inability to implement a learning process, and political culture.[18] Italy's greater political stability since 1996 has made it possible for the country to embark on a *learning process* and to institute a series of reforms encompassing the executive and the legislature, as well as the regional governments, and these changes have enabled Italy to make major strides forward. There remains, however, a lack of *government cohesion* and a problematic *political culture*, which are closely linked to each other, like a snake biting its tail. Taken together, they are preventing Italy from achieving the prominent position that it might otherwise occupy in European relations.

Since 1996, center-right coalitions have alternated with center-left coalitions in government. What is new is that all the parliaments except one completed their natural terms, with a de facto total of six governments headed by four different prime ministers. For Italy, this is an extraordinarily stable record. But there remains a high level of infighting between the individual parties and their leaders within the government coalitions. Without a widespread external perception of stability, there cannot be any beneficial fallout from the political and administrative system, particularly with regard to the complex management of European affairs.

In contemporary democracies, it is the responsibility of the members of the executive to promote and direct public policies. This is possible, first and foremost, if the executive is capable of taking a policy stance in concert with the parliamentary majority so that these policies can be embodied in normative instruments. But there are two other phases of equal importance in the policymaking process: drafting the normative proposals, and subsequently, after their adoption by parliament, implementing the policies. It is crucial in this phase for the members of the executive to be able to rely on all of the ministries and government departments for which they are responsible, and therefore the relations they establish with leading civil servants are vitally important.[19] The generally accepted position today is that civil servants are an integral part of political and administrative decisionmaking.[20]

This raises the whole issue of relations between politicians and civil servants. According to the literature, politicians have essentially four resources: legitimacy; portfolio control (which limits the availability of funding to managers); control over the decisionmaking autonomy of the organization; and popular representation. The six typical instruments in the hands of civil servants are: their expertise and monopoly of the sources of information; better and more effective decisionmaking; stable links with pressure groups and the social sectors influenced by the work of the civil servants; the nonpolitical character of the bureaucracy; the bureaucratic ideology (for example, the idea that the bureaucracy is more technically skilled); and time: the life of a politician at the head of an organization is unlikely to exceed that of his civil servants. But in a climate of instability, the importance of this latter variable is much greater than when there is stability. When instability becomes chronic (or is perceived as such) it becomes the most important variable.

The creed of the civil service in Italy is the principle that politicians come and go while civil servants remain. This situation helps to underpin resistance to change and reform, including improved relations between the country and the European Union. For example, it helps to explain why the institution of an interdepartmental coordination body such as CIACE has not triggered a series of reforms within the ministries and government departments. As Herbert Simon wrote, a distinction has to be drawn between cooperation and coordination.[21] *Cooperation* is the activity in which the participants share a common goal, while *coordination* is the process that enables each participant to know what the others are doing. Administrative organizations are systems of cooperative conduct. Members of the organization must direct their conduct to achieve certain objectives, which are taken on as "objectives of the organization." In other words, they must figure out how to coordinate their conduct, keeping everyone informed about what the others are doing, as the basis for making their own decisions. In cooperative systems, even if all the participants agree on the goals to be attained, as a general rule they are not allowed to choose the strategies used to achieve that goal, given that the choice of a sound strategy requires that each party be aware of the strategies of all the others. The management of European affairs in Italy reminds us that cooperation is possible, but only if there is coordination.

In some respects Italy appears to be stuck in the age of the Guelphs and the Ghibellines, in which the victory of one faction over another is what counts, and the fact that this may be damaging to the country matters little. For the Italian political class the old thesis of Gabriel Almond and Sidney Verba still seems to hold, according to which Italy is characterized by the limited spread and acceptance of the idea that civic duty plays a part in politics, little interest in and poor information about politics, and a widespread sense of impotence on the part of individuals to influence national and local political decisionmaking.[22]

This attitude pervades the political and administrative system and is also fueled by the media, whose style is very different from the investigative journalism practiced by their English-speaking colleagues. True coordination on European (and other) questions is not yet possible in Italy because of the divisions between the parties, within the parties, and outside them, and between stable and transient power groups. Resistance to cooperation is so firmly entrenched because people are afraid that if they share information and activities their "neighbors" will become more powerful, forgetting that in Europe unity is strength.

But these issues date back too far for any of the improvements introduced since the late 1990s to radically change the situation. The cases presented in this book demonstrate that Italy's political successes in Europe can usually be attributed to specific talented and motivated individuals, rather than to an effective strategy or system. The 20-20-20 directive is the exception that proves the rule. Only when consistent action within a stable system becomes the rule will it be possible to say that Italy has truly turned the corner.

Notes

Chapter Two

1. W. Wallace, *The Dynamics of European Integration* (London: Pinter, 1990), pp. 276–330.

2. D. Rometsch and W. Wessels, eds., *The European Union and Member States: Towards Institutional Fusion?* (Manchester University Press, 1996).

3. S. Bulmer and C. Lequesne, eds., *The Member States of the European Union* (Oxford University Press, 2005), p. 390.

4. K. H. Goetz and S. Hix, eds., *Europeanised Politics? European Integration and National Political Systems* (London: Frank Cass, 2001), p. 10.

5. V. Wright, "The National Coordination of European Policy Making: Negotiating the Quagmire," in *European Union: Power and Policy-Making*, edited by J. Richarson (London: Routledge, 1996).

6. H. Kassim, G. B. Peters, and V. Wright, eds., *The National Coordination of EU Policy: The Domestic Level* (Oxford University Press, 2000).

7. P. Norton, "National Parliaments and the European Union," *Journal of Legislative Studies* 1, no. 3, Special Issue (1995); P. Norton, *National Parliaments and the European Union* (London: Frank Cass, 1996); A. Maurer and W. Wessels, "National Parliaments after Amsterdam: From Slow Adapters to National Players?" in *National Parliaments on Their Ways to Europe: Losers or Latecomers*, edited by A. Maurer and W. Wessels (Baden Baden: Nomos Verlagsgesellschaft, 2001).

8. Y. Meny, P. Muller, J.-L. Quermonne, *Adjusting to Europe: The Impact of European Integration on National Institutions and Policies* (London: Routledge, 1996).

9. A. Guyomarch, H. Machin, E. Ritchie, *France in the European Union* (London: Macmillan, 1998); C. Closa and P. M. Heywood, *Spain and the European Union* (New York: Palgrave, 2004); B. Laffan and J. O'Mahony, *Ireland and the European Union* (Basingstoke, UK: Palgrave Macmillan, 2008).

10. J. Monnet, *Mémoires* (Paris: Fayard, 1976), p. 427.

11. E. Haas, *The Uniting of Europe: Political, Social and Economic Forces, 1950–1957* (London: Stevens & Sons, 1958), pp. 5–7, 58–59.

12. J. Monnet, "A Ferment of Change," *Journal of Common Market Studies* 1, no. 12 (1963): 203–11.

13. A. Spinelli, *Il Manifesto di Ventotene* (Bologna: Il Mulino, 1991), pp. 37–57.

14. R. O. Keohane and J. S. Nye, "Interdependence and Integration," in *Handbook of Political Science*, edited by F. I. Greenstein and N. W. Polsby (London: Addison-Wesley, 1975), vol. 8, pp. 363–414; S. Hoffmann, "Obstinate or Obsolete? The Fate of the Nation-State and the Case of Western Europe," *Daedalus* 95 (1966): 862–915.

15. W. Sandholtz and J. Zysman, "1992: Recasting the European Bargain," *World Politics* 42 (1989): 95–128.

16. W. Wallace, *Policy-Making in the European Community* (New York: Wiley, 1983).

17. H. Wallace and W. Wallace, eds., *Policy-Making in the European Union* (Oxford University Press, 1996), pp. 452–53.

18. R. Keohane and S. Hoffmann, "Conclusions: Community Politics and Institutional Change," in *The Dynamics of European Integration*, edited by W. Wallace (London: Pinter, 1990), pp. 276–300.

19. See G. Marks, F. W. Scharpf, P. C. Schmitter, and W. Streeck, *Governance in the European Union* (London: Sage, 1996); F. W. Scharpf, *Community and Autonomy: Multilevel Policy-making in the European Union* (Florence: European University Institute, 1994); S. Bulmer, "Institutions, Governance Regimes and the Single European Market: Analyzing the Governance of the European Union," paper presented at the ECPR Joint Working Session, Madrid, April 17–22, 1994; J. Peterson, *Europe and America: The Prospects for Partnership*, 2d ed. (London: Routledge, 1996); and B. Kohler-Koch, *Europäische Integration* (Opladen: Leske + Budrich, 1996).

20. Wallace and Wallace, eds., *Policy-Making in the European Union*, p. 445.

21. A. S. Milward, F. M. B. Lynch, F. Romero, R. Ranieri, and V. Sorenson, *The Frontier of National Sovereignty: History and Theory* (London: Routledge, 1993), pp. 3–4.

22. Ibid., pp. 20–21.

23. A. Milward, *The European Rescue of the Nation-State* (London: Routledge, 1992), p. 44.

24. A. Moravcsik, *The Choice for Europe: Social Purpose and State Power from Messina to Maastricht* (Cornell University Press, 1998).

25. A. Moravcsik, "Negotiating the Single European Act," in *The New European Community: Decisionmaking and Institutional Change*, edited by R. Keohane and S. Hoffmann (Oxford: Westview Press, 1991), pp. 67–68.

26. Milward, *The European Rescue of the Nation-State*.

27. Moravcsik, "Negotiating the Single European Act," p. 47.

28. Ibid., p. 42.

29. Ibid., pp. 67–68.

30. H. Wallace, W. Wallace, and C. Webb, eds., *Policy-Making in the European Community*, 2d ed. (New York: Wiley, 1983), pp. 27–30.

31. Ibid., pp. 28–30.

32. A. Moravcsik, "Introduction," in *Double-Edged Diplomacy: International Bargaining and Domestic Politics,* edited by P. Evans, H. Jacobson, and R. Putnam (University of California Press, 1993).

33. T. Risse-Kappen, ed., *Bringing Transnational Relations Back In: Non-state Actors, Domestic Structures, and International Institutions* (Cambridge University Press, 1995), p. 63.

34. Wallace, Wallace, and Webb, eds., *Policy-Making in the European Community.*

35. W. Wallace, *The Dynamics of European Integration* (London: Pinter, 1990), p. 215.

36. S. George, *Politics and Policy in the European Union,* 3d ed. (Oxford University Press, 1996).

37. S. Bulmer and C. Lequesne, "New Perspectives on EU–Member State Relationships," paper prepared for the ECSA Biennial Conference, May 31–June2, 2001, Madison, Wisconsin.

38. Bulmer and Lequesne, eds., *The Member States of the European Union.*

39. K. Middlemas, *Orchestrating Europe: The Informal Politics of the European Union* (London: Fontana Press, 1995).

40. E. Zeff and E. Pirro, *The European Union and the Member States: Cooperation, Coordination, and Compromise* (Boulder, Colo.: Lynne Rienner, 2001).

41. Rometsch and Wessels, eds., *The European Union and Member States.*

42. Ibid., pp. 328–29.

43. Ibid., pp. 353–54.

44. Ibid.

45. Ibid., p. 358.

46. Kassim, Peters, and Wright, eds., *The National Coordination of EU Policy,* p. 235.

47. S. Andersen and K. Eliassen, *Making Policy in Europe: The Europeification of National Policy-Making* (London: Sage, 1993).

48. Meny, Muller, and Quermonne, *Adjusting to Europe.*

49. Goetz and Hix, eds., *Europeanised Politics?*

50. T. Raunio and S. Hix, "Backbenchers Learn to Fight Back: European Integration and Parliamentary Government, in *Europeanised Politics?*" edited by Goetz andHix.

51. K. H. Goetz, "European Integration and National Executives," in *Europeanised Politics?* edited by Goetz and Hix.

52. Raunio and Hix, "Backbenchers Learn to Fight Back."

53. Goetz, "European Integration and National Executives," p. 220.

54. M. Green Cowles, J. Caporaso, and T. Risse, eds., *Transforming Europe: Europeanization and Domestic Change* (Cornell University Press, 2001).

55. H. Wallace, *National Governments and the European Communities* (London: Political and Economic Planning, 1973).

56. Wright, "The National Coordination of European Policy Making," pp. 162–63.

57. See F. Laursen and S. A. Pappas, eds. *The Changing Role of Parliaments in the European Union* (Maastricht: European Institute of Public Administration, 1995);

J. Schwartze, I. Govaere, F. Helin, and P. Van den Bossche, *The 1992 Challenge at National Level* (Baden-Baden: Nomos Verlagsgesellschaft, 1990); H. Siedentopf and J. Ziller, *Making European Policies Work: Comparative Syntheses* (London: Sage, 1998); A. Lenschow and C. Knill, *Change as "Appropriate Adaptation": Administrative Adjustment to European Environmental Policy in Britain and Germany* (Vienna: ECSA-Austria, 1998).

58. A. M. Slaughter, A. Stone Sweet, and J. H. H. Weiler, eds., *European Courts and National Courts: Doctrine and Jurisprudence* (Oxford: Hart, 1998).

59. D. Spence, "The Co-Ordination of European Policy by Member States," in *The Council of the European Union*, edited by M. Westlake (London: Cartemill, 1995), pp. 353–72.

60. F. Hayes-Renshaw and H. Wallace, "The Council of Ministers," in *Policy-Making in the European Union*, edited by Wallace and Wallace.

61. Wright, "The National Coordination of European Policy Making."

62. Kassim, Peters, and Wright, eds., *The National Coordination of EU Policy.*

63. Ibid.

64. Ibid., p. 253.

65. Ibid., p. 254.

66. Goetz, "European Integration and National Executives," p. 220.

67. Ibid., p. 225.

68. V. Herman and R. Van Schendelen, eds., *The European Parliament and the national Parliaments* (Farnborough, UK: Saxon House, 1979).

69. Maurer and Wessels, "National Parliaments after Amsterdam," p. 429.

70. Ibid., p. 28.

71. Raunio and Hix, "Backbenchers Learn to Fight Back," p. 152.

72. Norton, "National Parliaments and the European Union."

73. G. Laprat, "Parliamentary Scrutiny of Community Legislation: An Evolving Idea," in *The Changing Role of Parliaments in the European Union*, edited by Laursen and Pappas, p. 1.

74. Raunio and Hix, "Backbenchers Learn to Fight Back."

75. Maurer and Wessels, "National Parliaments after Amsterdam."

76. Raunio and Hix, "Backbenchers Learn to Fight Back."

77. Laprat, "Parliamentary Scrutiny of Community Legislation," pp. 4–9.

78. See Maurer and Wessels, "National Parliaments after Amsterdam."

79. See Laprat, "Parliamentary Scrutiny of Community Legislation."

80. Norton, "National Parliaments and the European Union"; and Norton, *National Parliaments and the European Union.*

81. T. Bergman, "National Parliaments and EU Affairs Committees: Notes on Empirical Variation and Competing Explanations," *Journal of European Public Policy* 4 (September 1997): 373–87.

82. Maurer and Wessels, "National Parliaments after Amsterdam."

83. Raunio and Hix, "Backbenchers Learn to Fight Back."

84. Maurer and Wessels, "National Parliaments after Amsterdam."

85. C. C. Schweitzer and D. Karsten, eds., *The Federal Republic of Germany and EC Membership Evaluated* (London: Pinter, 1990); P. Keating, ed., *Ireland and EC Membership Evaluated* (London: Pinter, 1991); S. Bulmer, S. George, and A. Scott, eds., *The United Kingdom and EC Membership Evaluated* (London: Pinter, 1992); L. Lyck, ed., *Denmark and EC Membership Evaluated* (London: Pinter, 1992); M. A. G. Meerhaeghe, ed., *Belgium and EC Membership Evaluated* (London: Pinter, 1992); M. A. Almarcha Barbado, ed., *Spain and EC Membership Evaluated* (London: Pinter, 1993); F.-G. Dreyfus, J. Morizet, and M. Peyrard, eds., *France and EC Membership Evaluated* (London: Pinter, 1993); P. Kazakos and P. C. Ioakimidis, eds., *Greece and EC Membership Evaluated* (London: Pinter, 1994); F. Francioni, ed., *Italy and EC Membership Evaluated* (London: Pinter, 1992); M. Walters and P. Coffey, eds., *The Netherlands and EC Membership Evaluated* (London: Pinter, 1990); J. Da Silva Lopes, ed., *Portugal and EC Membership Evaluated* (London: Pinter, 1994).

86. Guyomarch, Machin, and Ritchie, *France in the European Union*.

87. C. Closa and P. M. Heywood, *Spain and the European Union* (New York: Palgrave, 2004); B. Laffan and J. O'Mahony, *Ireland and the European Union* (Basingstoke, UK: Palgrave Macmillan, 2008).

88. See C. Lequesne, *Paris-Bruxelles, comment se fait la politique européenne de la France* (Paris: Presses de la Fondation National des Sciences Politiques, 1993).

89. C. Lequesne and Y. Doutriaux, *Les Institutions de l'Union Européenne*, 2d ed. (Paris: La Documentation Française, 1998).

90. M. Clamen, *Bruxelles au jour le jour: Petit guide des négociations communautaire* (Paris: La Documentation Française, 1996).

91. Francioni, ed., *Italy and EC Membership Evaluated*.

92. A. Albonetti, *L'Italia, la politica estera e l'unità dell'Europa* (Rome: Edizioni Lavoro, 2005).

93. M. Cartabia and J. H. H. Weiler, eds., *L'Italia in Europa: profili istituzionali e costituzionali* (Bologna: Il Mulino, 2000).

94. S. Fabbrini, *L'europeizzazione dell'Italia: l'impatto dell'Unione Europea sulle istituzioni e le politiche italiane* (Rome: GLF Editori Laterza, 2003).

95. G. Di Palma, S. Fabbrini, and G. Freddi, eds., *Condannata al successo? L'Italia nell'Europa integrata* (Bologna: Il Mulino, 2003).

96. S. Fabbrini and S. Piattoni, eds., *Italy in the European Union: Redefining National Interest in a Compound Polity* (Lanham, Md.: Rowman & Littlefield, 2008), p. 251.

Chapter Three

1. T. Salmon and W. Nicoll, eds., *Building the European Union: A Documentary History and Analysis* (Manchester University Press, 1997), pp. 26–28.

2. A. Spinelli, *Il Manifesto di Ventotene* (Bologna: Il Mulino, 1991), p. 37.

3. P. Gerbet, *La Construction de l'Europe* (Paris: Imprimerie Nationale, 1983), p. 57.

4. P. Gerbet, *Le Relèvement, 1944–49* (Paris: Imprimerie Nationale, 1991), p. 371.

5. A. Varsori, *L'Italia nelle relazioni internazionali dal 1943 al 1992* (Rome: Laterza, 1998), p. 52.

6. Gerbet, *La Construction de l'Europe*, pp. 85–86.

7. G. Scirocco, "Il PSI dell'antiatlantismo alla riscoperta dell'Europa (1948–1957)," in *Atlantismo e Europeismo*, edited by P. Craveri and G. Quagliarello (Soveria-Mannelli: Rubettino, 2003), p. 158.

8. V. Capperucci, "La sinistra democristiana e la difficile integrazione tra Europa e America (1945–1958)," in *Atlantismo e Europeismo*, edited by Craveri and Quagliarello, pp. 71–93.

9. Varsori, *L'Italia nelle relazioni internazionali*, p. 74.

10. J. Monnet, *Mémoires* (Paris: Fayard, 1976), pp. 319–20, 427.

11. M. Telò, "L'Italia nel processo di costruzione europea," in *Storia del l'Italia Repubblicana*, vol. 3 (Turin: Einaudi, 1996), pp. 144–49.

12. A. Albonetti, *Preistoria degli Stati Uniti d'Europa* (Milan: Giuffrè, 1960), p. 133.

13. E. Roussel, *Jean Monnet* (Paris: Fayard, 1996), p. 562.

14. Scirocco, "Il PSI dell'antiatlantismo," p. 179.

15. Ibid., pp. 144, 179.

16. L. Guiso and T. J. M. Haliassos, *Stockholding: A European Comparison* (London: Macmillan, 2003), pp. 207, 219.

17. Telò, "L'Italia nel processo di costruzione europea," pp. 194–95.

18. S. Pistone, *L'Italia e L'Unita' Europea* (Turin: Loescher, 1982), p. 153.

19. R. Marjolin, *Architect of European Unity: Memoirs, 1911–1986* (London: Weidenfeld & Nicolson, 1989), p. 287.

20. Scirocco, "Il PSI dell'antiatlantismo."

21. Before 1954, Algeria was an integral part of France. The region was composed of departments, like those of the mainland, with over 1 million white French living there (the so-called *pieds-noirs*). However, demands of Algerian nationalism became unmistakable immediately after the end of the war in Europe. By 1954, terrorist violence and French reprisals had become an established pattern in Algeria. A French general in Algeria expressed the mood of the moment, and the apparent best hope for the *pieds-noirs*, when he declared: "We appeal to General de Gaulle to take the leadership of a Government of Public Safety." Charles de Gaulle, the war hero, waiting in retirement for his country's call, affirmed that he would resume the leadership of the nation only if he were given unrestricted powers for a period of six months and the authority to draft a new constitution for a fifth French republic. On June 2, 1958, the National Assembly accepted his terms.

22. L. V. Ferraris, *Manuale di politica estera italiana (1947–1993)* (Bari: Laterza, 1996), pp. 155–57.

23. Every six months—hence the term "semester"—each member state assumes the presidency of the Union. The presidency is a position in the Union's service. It plays a neutral role and cannot be exploited to pursue national interests. Although in the beginning its role was quite formal and almost honorary, from the 1970s onward it assumed

an increasingly substantial and "institutional" role. With the TEU and the definition of new sectors for the Union's activities (Common Foreign and Security Policy [CFSP] and judicial and legal cooperation in penal matters), the member states decided to provide the presidency with a number of responsibilities that, in the community system, should have been given to the Commission. Along with the traditional responsibilities of representing the Community on an international level (including any possible official declarations and negotiations) and of determining the working program (in collaboration with the Commission), the agenda of the sessions, and the priorities for the semester, the presidency is also responsible for implementing common actions and expressing the Union's position in organizations and international conferences. The Treaty of Amsterdam increased its role even further by allowing the Council to put the presidency in charge of negotiating international agreements for the Union and providing it with the same responsibilities in the JHA sector that it has in the CFSP sector. The presidency is thus the "political motor" of the Council. In fact, the presidency exercises its influence at all levels, from the European Council to the workgroups. In addition, the presidency suggests compromises, confirming, for example, bilateral contacts with the delegations outside the reunions, as well as with the representatives of the Commission and the European Parliament. See F. Bindi, *Il Futuro dell'Europa* (Milan: Franco Angeli, 2005).

24. The Council has three possible voting procedures: unanimity, qualified majority, or simple majority. Which to use in any given case is laid down in the treaties. *Unanimity* was the most widely used procedure throughout the first two transitional phases (1958, end of 1965); it is still used in a limited number of cases, such as for treaty amendments. Simple majority is used only for procedural matters. Today the *qualified majority vote* (QMV) is the norm. A *qualified majority* is reached if the two following conditions are satisfied: (a) the majority of the member states approve (in certain cases a two-thirds majority is required); (b) a minimum of 232 votes must be in favor of the proposal, that is, 72.3 percent of the total.

25. Ferraris, *Manuale di politica estera italiana*, p. 163.

26. The "monetary snake" or "snake in the tunnel" was the first attempt at European monetary cooperation in the 1970s. Its aim was to limit fluctuations between European currencies. It was an attempt at creating a single currency band, essentially pegging all the EEC currencies to one another.

27. R. Perrisich, *L' Unione europea: una storia non ufficiale* (Milan: Longanesi, 2008), p. 175.

28. Ferraris, *Manuale di politica estera italiana*, p. 224.

29. Ibid., p. 220.

30. Ibid., p. 120.

31. Ibid.

32. Ibid., pp. 231–32.

33. Ibid., p. 233; A. Spinelli, *La mia battaglia per un'Europa diversa* (Manduria: Lacaita, 1979), p. 831.

34. Ferraris, *Manuale di politica estera italiana*, pp. 323–24.

35. Ibid., p. 325.

36. Ibid., pp. 341–42.

37. Ibid., pp. 243–45.

38. E. Di Nolfo, *Storia delle relazioni internazionali (1918–1999)* (Bari: Laterza 2002), p. 1342.

39. *The Economist*, December 7–13, 1991.

40. *La Stampa* and *Il Sole 24 Ore*, December 8, 1995.

41. *Il Sole 24 Ore,* May 24, 1994.

42. *Il Sole 24 Ore*, May 17, 1994.

43. *Il Sole 24 Ore*, July 16, 1994.

44. *Il Sole 24 Ore*, July 17 and August 31, 1994.

45. *Il Sole 24 Ore*, September 3, 1994.

46. S. Romano, *L' Italia scappata di mano. Cause ed effetti della crisi nazionale nella lucida analisi di uno storico* (Milan: Longanesi, 1993), p. 109.

47. *Il Sole 24 Ore*, June 4, 1998.

48. *European Voice*, July 3, 2003.

49. *La Repubblica*, June 3, 2006.

50. Romano Prodi, speech to the Italian parliament, May 18, 2006 (www.camera.it).

51. Ministry of Foreign Affairs, *Rapporto 2020: Le scelte di politica estera* (Rome, 2008), p. 15.

52. Silvio Berlusconi, speech to the Italian parliament, May 13, 2008 (www. governo. it/Presidente/Interventi/dettaglio.asp?d=39036).

Chapter Four

1. J. Di Palma, *Surviving without Governing: The Italian Parties in Parliament* (University of California Press, 1977); J. La Palombara, *Interest Groups in Italian Politics* (Princeton University Press, 1964).

2. L. Morlino, *Democracy between Consolidation and Crises: Parties, Groups, and Citizens in Southern Europe* (Oxford University Press, 1998), p. 250.

3. Ibid., p. 181.

4. G. Sartori, *Una occasione mancata* (Rome: Laterza, 1998), pp. 61–62.

5. J. P. Frognier, "Elite Circulation in Cabinet Government," in *The Profession of Government Minister in Western Europe*, edited by J. Blondel and J. L. Thiebault, eds. (London: Macmillan, 1991), pp. 77–85, 92–93.

6. Di Palma, *Surviving without Governing.*

7. C. De Micheli and L. Verzichelli, *Il Parlamento* (Bologna: Il Mulino, 2004), p. 95.

8. S. Gundle and S. Parker, eds., *The New Italian Republic: From the Fall of the Berlin Wall to Berlusconi* (London: Routledge, 1996).

9. L. Bardi and G. Pasquino, *Euroministri: il governo dell'Europa (*Milan: Il Saggiatore, 1994), p. 12.

10. Ibid., p. 1.

11. *La Stampa*, December 8, 1995.

12. G. Guzzetta and F. S. Marini, *Diritto Pubblico Italiano e Europeo* (Turin: G. Giappichelli Editore, 2006), pp. 235–37.

13. *Eurobarometer 72* (Fall 2009), http://ec.europa.eu/public_opinion/archives/eb/eb72/eb72_it_en_exec.pdf.

14. V. Capperucci, "La sinistra democristiana e la difficile integrazione tra Europa e America (1945–1958)," in *Atlantismo ed europeismo*, edited by P. Craveri and G. Quagliariello (Soveria Mannelli: Rubbettino, 2003), pp. 71–93.

15. A. Varsori, *L'Italia nelle relazioni internazionali dal 1943 al 1992* (Rome: Laterza, 1998), p. 74.

16. M. Telò, "L'Italia nel processo di costruzione europea," in *Storia dell'Italia Repubblicana*, vol. 3 (Turin: Einaudi, 1996), pp. 195–96.

17. M. Cotta, "European Integration and the Italian Political System," in *Italy and EC Membership Evaluated*, edited by F. Francioni (London: Pinter, 1992), pp. 206–07; L. V. Ferraris, "Italian-European Foreign Policy," in *Italy and EC Membership Evaluated*, edited by Francioni, p. 131.

18. Craveri and Quagliariello, eds., *Atlantismo ed europeismo*.

19. N. Conti and L. Verzichelli, "La dimensione Europea del discorso politico: un'analisi diacronica del caso Italiano (1950–2001)," in *L'Europa in Italia*, edited by M. Cotta, P. Isernia, and L. Verzichelli (Bologna: Il Mulino, 2005).

20. See Craveri and Quagliariello, eds., *Atlantismo ed europeismo*, p. 571.

21. P. Soddu, "Ugo La Malfa ed il nesso nazionale / internazionale dal Patto Atlantico alla Presidenza Carter," in *Atlantismo ed europeismo*, edited by Craveri and Quagliariello.

22. P. A. Ginsburg, *History of Contemporary Politics: 1943–1988* (London: Penguin, 1990), pp. 110–12.

23. G. Scirocco, "Il PSI dell'antiatlantismo alla riscoperta dell'Europa (1948–1957)," in *Atlantismo ed europeismo*, edited by Craveri and Quagliarello,

24. J. Monnet, *Mémoires* (Paris: Fayard, 1976).

25. A. Guiso, "L'Europa e l'Alleanza Atlantica nella politica internazionale del PCI negli anni '50 e '60," in *Atlantismo ed europeismo*, edited by Craveri and Quagliarello.

26. Ibid.

27. A. Spinelli, *Diario Europeo / III* (Bologna: Il Mulino, 1992).

28. M. Cotta, "European Integration and the Italian Political System," in *Italy and EC Membership Evaluated*, edited by Francioni, p. 211.

29. *La Repubblica*, May 5, 1992.

30. *Corriere della Sera*, August 3, 1992.

31. See the website of the European People's Party: www.eppgroup.eu.

32. See the website of the Group of the Progressive Alliance of Socialist and Democrats in the European Parliament: www.socialistgroup.eu.

33. *Il Sole 24 Ore*, May 17, 1994.

34. *Il Sole 24 Ore*, July 16, 1994.

35. E. Brighi, "Europe, the USA and the 'Policy of the Pendulum': The Importance of Foreign Policy Paradigms in the Foreign Policy of Italy (1989–2005)," *Journal of Southern Europe and the Balkans* 2 (2008): 99–115.

36. *Il Sole 24 Ore*, July 17, 1994, and August 31, 1994.

37. *Il Sole 24 Ore*, September 3, 1994.

38. G. Bonvicini, "Regional Reassertion: The Dilemmas of Italy," in *The Actors in Europe's Foreign Policy*, edited by Christopher Hill (London: Routledge, 1996).

39. F. Andreatta, "La sfida dell'Unione Europea alla teoria delle relazioni internazionali," in *L'Europa sicura: le politiche di sicurezza dell'Unione Europea*, edited by S. Giusti and A. Locatelli (Milan: Egea, 2008), p. 175.

40. Brighi, "Europe, the USA and the 'Policy of the Pendulum,'" p. 104.

41. See Partito Democratico: www.partitodemocratico.it/gw/producer/dettaglio.aspx?ID_DOC=45296.

42. All of the Northern League MPs voted in favor. The other former anti-European party, Rifondazione Comunista, did not have any elected representatives in parliament. See the website of the Italian Chamber of Deputies: www.camera.it.

43. M. Cotta, P. Isernia, and L. Verzichelli, eds., *L'Europa in Italia: elite, opinione pubblica e decisioni* (Bologna: Il Mulino, 2005).

44. Gianfranco Fini, inaugural speech as president of the Chamber of Deputies, April 29, 2008 (www.camera.it).

45. Silvio Berlusconi, speech to the parliament, April 29, 2008 (www.camera.it).

Chapter Five

1. P. Norton, "National Parliaments and the European Union," *Journal of Legislative Studies* 1, no. 3, special issue (1995).

2. G. Laprat, "Parliamentary Scrutiny of Community Legislation: An Evolving Idea," in *The Changing Role of Parliaments in the European Union*, edited by F. Laursen and S. Pappas (Maastricht: European Institute of Public Administration, 1995), p. 1.

3. T. Raunio and S. Hix, "Backbenchers Learn to Fight Back: European Integration and Parliamentary Government," in *Europeanised Politics? European Integration and National Systems*, edited by K. H. Goetz and S. Hix (London: Frank Cass, 2001), p. 152.

4. A. Maurer and W. Wessels, "National Parliaments after Amsterdam: From Slow Adapters to National Players?" in *National Parliaments on Their Ways to Europe: Losers or Latecomers?* edited by A. Maurer and W. Wessels (Baden-Baden: Nomos Verlagsgesellschaft, 2001), pp. 425–75.

5. J. Di Palma, *Surviving without Governing: The Italian Parties in Parliament* (University of California Press, 1977).

6. C. De Micheli and L. Verzichelli, *Il Parlamento* (Bologna: Il Mulino, 2004), p. 77.

7. G. Amato, "My Experience as Prime Minister," speech given at the European University Institute in Florence, October 1993.

8. L. Morlino, ed., *Costruire la democrazia* (Bologna: Il Mulino, 1991).

9. Amato, "My Experience as Prime Minister."

10. De Micheli and Verzichelli, *Il Parlamento*, p. 77.

11. M. Cotta "The Centrality of Parliament in a Protracted Democratic Consolidation: The Italian Case," in *Parliament and Democratic Consolidation in Southern Europe*, edited by U. Liebert and M. Cotta (London: Pinter, 1990), p. 76.

12. M. Cotta "Il Parlamento nella prima repubblica," in *La politica italiana*, edited by G. Pasquino (Bari: Laterza, 1996), pp. 79–91.

13. D. Rometsch and W. Wessels, eds., *The European Union and Member States: Towards Institutional Fusion?* (Manchester University Press, 1996), p. 354.

14. F. Bindi and S. Grassi, "The Italian Parliament: From Benevolent Observer to Active Player," in *National Parliaments on Their Ways to Europe*, edited by Maurer and Wessels.

15. Chamber of Deputies, Rules of Procedure, art. 127 ter c.1 (www.camera.it/files/regolamento/regolamento.pdf).

16. Senate, Rules of Procedure, art. 142 (www.senato.it/istituzione/29377/articolato.htm).

17. Chamber of Deputies, Rules of Procedure, art. 126, c. 2. r. S., art. 23, cc. 2 and 4 (www.camera.it/files/regolamento/regolamento.pdf).

18. Bindi and Grassi, "The Italian Parliament."

19. M. Giuliani, "Italy," in *The European Union and Member States*, edited by Rometsch and Wessels, pp. 115–16.

20. Bindi and Grassi, "The Italian Parliament."

21. Senate, Rules of Procedure, art. 21 (www.senato.it/istituzione/29377/articolato.htm).

22. Chamber of Deputies, Rules of Procedure, art. 127-ter; Senate, Rules of Procedure, art. 144-quarter (www.camera.it/files/regolamento/regolamento.pdf).

23. Chamber, Rules of Procedure, arts. 22 and 126 (www.camera.it/files/regolamento/regolamento.pdf); and Senate, Rules of Procedure, art. 23 (www.senato.it/istituzione/29377/articolato.htm).

24. Chamber, Rules of Procedure, art. 126 (www.camera.it/files/regolamento/regolamento.pdf); Senate, Rules of Procedure, art. 23.3 (www.senato.it/istituzione/29377/articolato.htm).

25. Chamber, Rules of Procedure, art. 127-bis (www.camera.it/files/regolamento/regolamento.pdf); Senate, Rule of Procedure, art. 144-ter (www.senato.it/istituzione/29377/articolato.htm).

26. Law 11/2005, art 3.5 and 3.6.

27. Chamber, Rules of Procedure, art. 126-ter (www.camera.it/files/regolamento/regolamento.pdf); Senate, Rules of Procedure, arts. 144-bis c.6 and 7 (www.senato.it/istituzione/29377/articolato.htm).

28. Chamber, Rules of Procedure, arts. 125–127-ter (www.camera.it/files/regolamento/regolamento.pdf); Senate, Rules of Procedure, art. 142–144-quarter (www.senato.it/istituzione/29377/articolato.htm).

29. Chamber, Rules of Procedure, art. 125–127-ter; Senate, Rules of Procedure, art. 142–144-quarter.

30. Senate, Rules of Procedure, art. 29 (www.senato.it/istituzione/29377/articolato. htm); Chamber, Rules of Procedure, art. 25.4 (www.camera.it/files/regolamento/ regolamento.pdf).

31. Article 226 of the EU Treaty gives the European Commission power to take legal action against a member state that is not respecting its obligations. If the Commission considers that there may be an infringement of EU law that warrants the opening of an infringement procedure, it addresses a "Letter of Formal Notice" (first written warning) to the member state concerned, requesting that it submit its observations by a specified date, usually within two months. In light of the reply or absence of a reply from the member state concerned, the Commission may decide to address a "Reasoned Opinion" (final written warning) to the member state. This clearly and definitively sets out the reasons why it considers there to have been an infringement of EU law and calls upon the member state to comply within a specified period, usually two months. If the member state fails to comply with the Reasoned Opinion, the Commission may decide to bring the case before the Court of Justice. Where the Court of Justice finds that the treaty has been infringed, the offending member state is required to take the measures necessary to conform. Article 228 of the Treaty gives the Commission power to act against a member state that does not comply with a previous judgment of the European Court of Justice. The article also allows the Commission to ask the Court to impose a financial penalty on the member state concerned.

32. Internal Market Scoreboard 7/2007; Internal Market Scoreboard 7/2009 (http:// ec.europa.eu/internal_market/score).

33. See the website of the EU Department: www.politichecomunitarie.it/attivita/ 15141/dati.

Chapter Six

1. H. Kassim, G. B. Peters, and V. Wright, eds., *The National Coordination of EU Policy: The Domestic Level* (Oxford University Press, 2000).

2. G. Sartori, *Ingegneria costituzionale comparata* (Bologna: Il Mulino, 1994).

3. G. Amato, "My Experience as Prime Minister," speech presented at the European University Institute in Florence, October 1993.

4. G. Amato, "Italy: The Rise and Decline of a System of Government," *Indiana International & Comparative Law Review* 4 (Winter 1994): 225.

5. P. Evans, H. Jacobson, and R. Putnam, eds., *Double-Edged Diplomacy: International Bargaining and Domestic Politics* (University of California Press, 1993).

6. J. Blondel, *The Organization of Governments: A Comparative Analysis of Governmental Structures* (London: Sage, 1982), pp. 142–46; J. Blondel and F. Mueller-Rommel, eds., *Governing Together* (London: St. Martin's, 1993), pp. 130–52.

7. G. Grottanelli de Santi, "The Impact of EC Integration on the Italian Form of Government," in *Italy and EC membership Evaluated*, edited by F. Francioni (London: Pinter, 1992), p. 186.

8. G. Cananea, "Italy," in *The National Coordination of EU Policy*, edited by Kassim and others, pp. 134–35.

9. A. Ciriolo, *Il Dipartimento per il Coordinamento delle Politiche Comunitarie* (Lecce: Milella, 1991); Grottanelli de Santi, "The Impact of EC Integration on the Italian Form of Government," p. 186.

10. Decreto Ministeriale no. 298/2006.

11. See the website of the Chamber of Deputies: www.camera.it/459? shadow_organo_parlamentare=1507&eleindag=/_dati/leg16/lavori/stencomm/14/indag/ partecipazione.

12. F. Bindi, and M. Cisci, "Italy, Spain and the EU: A Comparative Analysis," in *Member States and the European Union*, edited by S. Bulmer and C. Lequesne (Oxford University Press, 2005).

13. See the website of the Dipartimento Politiche Comunitarie (EU Department): www.politichecomunitarie.it/attivita/46/riunioni.

14. Cananea, "Italy," p. 132.

15. M. Giuliani, "Italy," in *The European Union and Member States: Towards Institutional Fusion?* edited by D. Rometsch and W. Wessels (Manchester University Press 1996), pp. 115–16.

16. B. De Giovanni, "La funzione pubblica europea: una proposta," in *Europa Europe* 7, nos. 4–5 (New Series) (1998): 15–19.

17. See the Dipartimento Politiche Comunitarie (EU Department) newsletter, June 4, 2009 (www.politichecomunitarie.it/newsletter/16695/funzionari-italiani-cittadini-europei).

18. "Direttiva del Presidente del Consiglio dei Ministri sui funzionari internazionali di cittadinanza italiana, 2 August 2010," in *Gazzetta Ufficiale* No. 210, September 8, 2010.

19. G. Freddi, ed., *Scienza dell'amministrazione e politiche pubbliche* (Rome: La Nuova Scientifica, 1989), p. 30.

Chapter Seven

1. The Structural Funds and the Cohesion Fund are financial instruments of European Union regional policy that are intended to narrow the development disparities among regions and member states. For the period 2007–2013, for instance, the EU budget allocated to regional policy amounts to around €348 billion, comprising €278 billion for the Structural Funds and €70 billion for the Cohesion Fund. This represents 35 percent of the Community budget and is its second-largest budget item. There are two Structural Funds. The European Regional Development Fund (ERDF) is currently the largest. Since 1975 it has provided support for the creation of infrastructure and productive job-creating investment, mainly for businesses. The European Social Fund (ESF), set up in 1958, contributes to the integration into working life of the unemployed and disadvantaged sections of the population, mainly by funding training measures.

2. C. Engel and W. Wessels, eds., *From Luxembourg to Maastricht: Institutional Change in the European Community after the Single European Act* (Bonn: Europa Union Verlag, 1992).

3. J. Nonon and M. Clamen, *L'Europe et ses couloirs: lobbying et lobbyistes* (Paris: Dunod, 1991), p. 67.

4. M. Clamen, *Bruxelles au jour le jour: petit guide des négociations communautaire* (Paris: La Documentation Française, 1996), pp. 16–17.

5. J. M. Onhet, "Comitè des regions où comitè Theodule," *Le Monde*, October 12, 1992.

6. R. Leonardi and R. Nanetti, *Le regioni e l'integrazione europea: il caso Emilia-Romagna* (Milan: Franco Angeli, 1991), pp. 17–21.

7. F. S. Marini, "La partecipazione regionale alle decisioni statali dirette alla formazione del diritto comunitario europeo," in *L'Europa delle autonomie: le regioni e l'Unione europea*, edited by A. D'Atena (Milan: Giuffrè, 2003), p. 161.

8. E. Letta, minister for community policies, 1st National Convention of Local Government Officers for Community Policies, Palermo, October 8, 1999.

9. See the Chamber of Deputies website: www.camera.it/459?shadow_organo_parlamentare=1507&eleindag=/_dati/leg16/lavori/stencomm/14/indag/partecipazione

10. Ibid.

11. L. Badiello, "Il ruolo delle rappresentanze regionali europee a Bruxelles in Europa," *Europe*, no. 1 (2000): 166.

12. S. Profeti, "Le Regioni italiane a Bruxelles: canali e strategie di attivazione," in *Europeizzazione e rappresentanza territoriale: il caso italiano*, edited by V. Fargion, L. Morlino, and S. Profeti (Bologna: Il Mulino, 2006); CIPI, *Le Lobby d'Italia a Bruxelles* (Brussels: Centro Italiano di Prospettiva Internazionale, 2006).

13. CIPI, *Le Lobby d'Italia a Bruxelles.*

14. Ibid., pp. 103–07.

15. A. Alfieri, *La politica estera delle regioni* (Bologna: Il Mulino, 2004).

16. Ibid.

17. Badiello, "Il ruolo delle rappresentanze regionali europee."

18. For a description of the membership terms and rules, see www.cor.europa.eu/pages/PresentationTemplate.aspx?view=folder&id=90178593-c7ed-4e16-822f-ae06c1453c22&sm=90178593-c7ed-4e16-822f-ae06c1453c22.

19. V. E. Bocci, "Il potere estero delle Regioni: il caso dell'ufficio di collegamento della Regione Toscana," *Le Istituzioni del federalismo* 21, no. 1 (2000): 63–88.

20. See the Chamber of Deputies website: www.camera.it/459?shadow_organo_parlamentare=1507&eleindag=/_dati/leg16/lavori/stencomm/14/indag/partecipazione.

21. Profeti, "Le Regioni italiane a Bruxelles: canali e strategie di attivazione."

22. S. Bolgherini, *Come le regioni diventano europee: stile di governo e sfide comunitarie nell'Europa mediterranea* (Bologna: Il Mulino, 2006).

23. Ibid.

24. See Fargion, Morlino, and Profeti, eds., *Europeizzazione e rappresentanza territoriale.*

25. CIPI, *Le Lobby d'Italia a Bruxelles*.

26. Ibid., pp. 75–76.

27. Ibid.

28. Grundgesetz für die Bundesrepublik Deutschland (Basic Law for the Federal Republic of Germany), Article 50.

29. IRI: Istituto per la Ricostruzione Industriale (Institute for Industrial Reconstruction) was created in 1933 and dismantled in 2000; ENI: Ente Nazionale Idrocarburi today is an integrated company working in the field of energy, is active in seventy-seven countries, and has 78,400 employees (www.eni.com/en_IT/home.html); EFIM: Ente Partecipazioni e Finanziamento Industrie Manifatturiere was a holding initially created after World War II to support the reconversion of industries to civil manufacturing. It was dismantled in 1992.

30. F. Bindi and L. Bardi, "Italy: The Dominance of Domestic Politics," in *National Public and Private EC Lobbying*, edited by R. Van Schendelen (Dartmouth University Press, 1993).

31. Ibid.

32. CIPI, *Le Lobby d'Italia a Bruxelles*.

33. Ibid.

34. Ibid.

35. Ibid.

36. J. Boundant and M. Gounelle, eds., *Les grandes dates de l'Europe communautaire* (Paris: Larousse, 1989), p. 170.

37. *Il Sole 24 Ore*, May 30, 1992.

38. *Terra e Vita*, August 1992.

39. J. La Palombara, *Interest Groups in Italian Politics* (Princeton University Press, 1964).

40. CIPI, *Le Lobby d'Italia a Bruxelles*.

41. Ibid.

42. Ibid.

43. Burson-Marsteller Report, *The Definitive Guide to Lobbying the European Institutions* (New York, Spring 2005).

44. CIPI, *Le Lobby d'Italia a Bruxelles*.

Chapter Eight

1. A. Sbragia, ed., *Euro-Politics: Institutions and Policymaking in the New European Community* (Brookings, 1992), p. 257.

2. R. Keohane and S. Hoffmann, "Conclusions: Community Politics and Institutional Change," in *The Dynamics of European Integration*, edited by W. Wallace (London: Pinter, 1990), pp. 279–80.

3. H. Wallace and W. Wallace, eds., *Policy-Making in the European Union* (Oxford University Press, 1996), p. 439.

4. J. Lodge, *Institution and Policies of the European Union* (London: Pinter, 1995), p. 249.

5. B. Kohler-Koch, *Europäische Integration* (Opladen: Leske Budrich, 1996), p. 360.

6. S. Hoffmann, "Obstinate or Obsolete? The Fate of the Nation-State and the Case of Western Europe," *Daedalus* 95 (1966): 862–915.

7. S. Hix, "The Study of the European Community: The Challenge to Comparative Politics," *West European Politics* 17 (January 1994): 1–30.

8. S. Bulmer, "Institutions, Governance Regimes, and the Single European Market: Analyzing the Governance of the European Union," paper presented at the ECPR Joint Working Session, Madrid, April 17–22, 1994; T. Lowi, "Four Systems of Policy, Politics, and Choice," *Public Administration Review* 32, no. 4 (1972): 298–310.

9. W. Sandholtz and J. Zysman, "1992: Recasting the European Bargain," *World Politics* 42 (1989): 95–128, esp. pp. 103–12.

10. K. Middlemas, *Orchestrating Europe: The Informal Politics of the European Union* (London: Fontana, 1995), p. 144.

11. M. Thatcher, *The Downing Street Years* (London: Harper Collins, 1993).

12. Ibid., pp. 548–50.

13. See P. M. R. Stirk, *A History of European Integration since 1914* (London: Pinter, 1996), p. 210.

14. Thatcher, *The Downing Street Years*, pp. 550–51.

15. "Resolution on the ICG in the Context of the Parliament's Strategy in the European Union," *Official Journal C*, no. 231 (September 17, 1990).

16. See "Intervention de Guido Carli," Rome, December 15, 1990 (www.ena.lu/intervention-guido-carli-rome-15-decembre-1990-020005420.html).

17. Thatcher, *The Downing Street Years*, pp. 550–51.

18. *Financial Times*, November 27, 1991.

19. Middlemas, *Orchestrating Europe*, pp. 167–68.

20. L. Pistelli and G. Fiore, *Semestre Nero: Berlusconi e la Politica Estera* (Rome: Fazi Editore, 2004), p. 113.

21. Commission of the European Communities, COM 2003, 548 final (http://eur-lex.europa.eu/LexUriServ/LexUriServ.do?uri=COM:2003:0548:FIN:EN:PDF).

22. European Parliament P5_TA(2003) 0407. See www.europarl.europa.eu/sides/getDoc.do?pubRef=-//EP//TEXT+TA+P5-TA-2003-0517+0+DOC+XML+V0//EN).

23. EU Council 12293/03. See http://euce.dal.ca/Files/Paper_-_first_confer/bindi.doc.pdf).

24. CIG 2/2003 and CIG 9/2003. See http://europa.eu/scadplus/cig2004/negociations 1_en.htm

25. CIG 42/2003. See http://europa.eu/scadplus/cig2004/negociations1_en.htm.

26. CIG 50/2003. See http://europa.eu/scadplus/cig2004/negociations1_en.htm.

27. CIG 3/2003. See http://europa.eu/scadplus/cig2004/negociations1_en.htm.

28. CIG 1/2003. See http://europa.eu/scadplus/cig2004/negociations1_en.htm. The Council is "formed of a representative at a ministerial level from each member state, qualified to engage actively in the government of the member state" (art. 206 of the TEC). Legally speaking, the Council is a single entity, but it is in practice divided into several different council configurations or *(con)formations*. Over the years, the num-

ber of these formations has steadily increased. In June 2002, the European Council meeting in Seville decided to reduce the number to nine: General Affairs and External Relations; Economic and Financial Affairs; Justice and Home Affairs; Employment, Social Policy, Health, and Consumer Affairs; Competitiveness (Internal Market, Industry, and Research); Transport, Telecommunications and Energy; Agriculture and Fisheries; Environment; Education, Youth, and Culture.

29. CIG 1/2003 and CIG 36/2003. See http://europa.eu/scadplus/cig2004/negociations 1_en.htm.

30. CIG 6/2003. See http://europa.eu/scadplus/cig2004/negociations1_en.htm.

31. Council 15188/03.

32. CIG 38/2003. See http://europa.eu/scadplus/cig2004/negociations1_en.htm.

33. CIG 39/2003. See http://europa.eu/scadplus/cig2004/negociations1_en.htm.

34. CIG 37/2003. See http://europa.eu/scadplus/cig2004/negociations1_en.htm.

35. CIG 46/2003. See http://europa.eu/scadplus/cig2004/negociations1_en.htm.

36. Ibid.

37. Pistelli and Fiore, *Semestre Nero*, p. 114.

38. Joint Declaration addressed to the European Council by parliamentary members of the European Convention. See www.ena.lu/declaration-parliamentary-members-european-convention-brussels-december-2003-030005668.html.

39. Pistelli and Fiore, *Semestre Nero*, p. 116.

40. A. Ciampi, "Stillstand ist Undenkbar," *Frankfurter Allgemeine Zeitung,* December 10, 2003.

41. CIG 60/2003 ADD 1. See http://europa.eu/scadplus/cig2004/negociations 1_en.htm.

42. CIG 60/2003 ADD 2. See http://europa.eu/scadplus/cig2004/negociations 1_en.htm.

43. CIG 50/2003. See http://europa.eu/scadplus/cig2004/negociations1_en.htm.

44. Pistelli and Fiore, *Semestre Nero*, p. 117.

45. M. Banks, "Bid to Smooth Arrest Warrant Wrangles," *European Voice*, November 22, 2001.

46. "Will Laeken Be 'Hell' for Berlusconi?" *European Voice*, December 13, 2001.

47. Ibid.

48. Camera dei Deputati, XIII Commissione [Chamber of Deputies, Committee XIII], October 6, 2005.

49. M. Banks, "Italians and Czechs Resist Arrest Warrant," *European Voice*, September 16, 2004.

50. L. V. Ferraris, *Manuale di politica estera italiana (1947–1993)* (Bari: Laterza, 1996), p. 456.

51. *Corriere della Sera*, February 12, 1997.

52. *Corriere della Sera*, July 1, 1997.

53. Hearing, Joint Committees III and IV, March 15, 1997.

54. *La Repubblica*, March 3, 1997.

55. *Corriere della Sera*, March 8, 1997.

56. Hearing, Joint Committees III and IV, March 15, 1997.

57. *Corriere della Sera*, May 12, 1998.

58. *Corriere della Sera*, March 15, 1997.

59. OSCE Annual Report, 1997, p. 16 (www.osce.org/item/14116.html).

60. *New York Times*, March 29, 1997.

61. *Corriere della Sera*, March 25, 1997.

62. Chamber of Deputies, Legislative Activities. See www.camera.it/449?tipodoc= IndiceLeggi&nuove_schede=Y&anno=1997&mese=04&tipo=ElencoMensile&tipo logia=2.

63. *New York Times*, April 14, 1997.

64. *Corriere della Sera*, April 22, 1997.

65. *La Repubblica*, July 1, 1997, and August 24, 1997.

Chapter Nine

1. P. Gerbet, "The Intergovernmental Conference on Economic and Monetary Union" (www.ena.lu/intergovernmental_conference_igc_economic_monetary_union-02010 2268.html).

2. A. Colombo and N. Ronzitti, eds., *L'Italia nella politica internazionale* (Bologna: Il Mulino, 1993).

3. Ibid.

4. Treaty on the European Union (Maastricht Treaty), article 109 J; for the original text see OJ C 191 of 29.7.1992 or http://eur-lex.europa.eu/en/treaties/dat/11992M/tif/JOC_1992_191__1_EN_0001.pdf.

5. *Corriere della Sera*, December 9, 1991.

6. M. Ferrera and E. Gualmini, *Salvati dall'Europa?* (Bologna: Il Mulino, 1999).

7. L. S. Talani, *Betting for and against EMU: Who Wins and Loses in Italy and in the UK from the Process of European Monetary Integration?* (Aldershot, UK: Ashgate, 2000).

8. Ibid.

9. *Sole 24 Ore*, January 21, 1992.

10. *La Repubblica*, July 27, 1991.

11. M. Battocchi, "Italy's Admission to the Third Stage of the European Monetary Union," concept paper, Princeton University, 2003 (wws.princeton.edu/research/cases/italy.pdf).

12. A. Monorchio and L. Tivelli, *Dove va l'Italia: Democrazia, economia e Stato sociale* (Rome: Rai-Eri, 1999).

13. *La Repubblica*, March 27, 1997.

14. L. Spaventa and V. Chiorazzo, *Astuzia o virtù? Come accadde che l'Italia fu ammessa all'unione monetaria* (Rome: Donzelli, 2000).

15. Joint hearing by Committee V (budget) of the Chamber of Deputies and the Senate with the governor of the Bank of Italy, July 9, 1996.

16. *Corriere della Sera*, September 19, 1996.

17. *Corriere della Sera*, May 1, 1996.

18. *Corriere della Sera*, September 25, 1996.

19. Ibid.

20. Battocchi, "Italy's Admission to the Third Stage of the European Monetary Union."

21. *Financial Times*, September 30, 1996.

22. Battocchi, "Italy's Admission to the Third Stage of the European Monetary Union."

23. *La Repubblica*, October 9, 1998.

24. *Corriere della Sera*, November 17, 1996.

25. *La Repubblica*, November 21, 1996.

26. Ibid.

27. *Corriere della Sera*, November 24, 1996.

28. *Corriere della Sera*, November 25, 1996.

29. See European Parliament, Task Force on Economic and Monetary Union (www.europarl.europa.eu/euro/country/general/i_it.pdf) (in Italian).

30. Ibid.

31. "Quando Ciampi alzo' la voce per portare l'Italia nell'Euro," *Sole 24 Ore*, June 11, 2008.

32. Council of the European Union, press release; for the original text see OJ C 191 of 29.7.1992 or http://eur-lex.europa.eu/en/treaties/dat/11992M/tif/JOC_1992_191__1_EN_0001.pdf.

33. Ibid.

34. Dipartimento Politiche Comunitarie [EU Department], Annual Report for 2009 (www.politichecomunitarie.it/attivita/17389/relazione-annuale-2009).

35. "Ue 2020: Sfida immane, Italia a rischio," *Quotidiano Energia*, January 25, 2008.

36. "Ue 2020, ora parte la trattativa," *Quotidiano Energia*, January 24, 2008.

37. "Una politica dell'energia per conciliare mercato e sicurezza," *Newsletter Gestore del Mercato Elettrico*, February 2008 (www.mercatoelettrico.org/).

38. "Pacchetto clima, tra delusi ed entusiasti," *Rinnovabili*, January 24, 2008 (www.rinnovabili.it).

39. Dipartimento Politiche Comunitarie, Annual Report for 2009.

40. "Ue 2020, l'Italia riapre i giochi," *Quotidiano Energia*, July 4, 2008.

41. "Ue 2020, Governo in pressing," *Quotidiano Energia*, August 5, 2008.

42. "I Don Chisciotte dei numeri: la disputa in atto," *La Voce*, October 21, 2008 (www.lavoce.info).

43. "Ue 2020: Si cercano alleati," *Quotidiano Energia*, September 18, 2008.

44. "UE 2020, Governo in pressing sulla Francia," *Quotidiano Energia*, September 19, 2008.

45. "Ue 2020, Bruxelles ha rifatto i conti," *Quotidiano Energia*, October 6, 2008.

46. "Stop a Kyoto, nove stati con l'Italia," *La Repubblica*, October 20, 2008.

47. "Scontro sul clima, Italia pronta al veto," *La Repubblica*, October 16, 2008.

48. "Stop a Kyoto, nove stati con l'Italia."

49. "Ambiente: Marcegaglia, giusto rivedere il pacchetto clima," *Sole 24 Ore*, October 20, 2008.

50. "Clima Altolà dell'Italia a Bruxelles," *Corriere della Sera*, December 5, 2008.

51. Dipartimento Politiche Comunitarie, Annual Report for 2009.

52. "Ambiente, Compromesso Ue Auto meno inquinanti dal 2012," *Corriere della Sera*, December 2, 2008.

53. "Clima, l'Italia Contro l'UE passi avanti ma non bastano cosi boccieremo l'intesa," *La Repubblica*, December 9, 2008.

54. "Frattini, Clima, Italia Insoddisfatta," *La Stampa*, December 8, 2008.

55. Dipartimento Politiche Comunitarie, Annual Report for 2009.

56. "Ue, raggiunto l'accordo sul clima Sarkozy: Voto all'unanimità," *Corriere della Sera*, December 12, 2008.

Chapter Ten

1. F. Bindi and M. Cisci, "Italy, Spain and the EU: A Comparative Analysis," in *Member States and the European Union*, edited by S. Bulmer and C. Lequesne (Oxford University Press, 2005).

2. D. Spence, "The Co-ordination of European Policy by Member States," in *The Council of the European Union*, edited by M. Westlake (London: Cartemill, 1995), pp. 353–72.

3. J. La Palombara, *Interest Groups in Italian Politics* (Princeton University Press, 1964).

4. A. Moravcsik, "Negotiating the Single European Act," in *The New European Community: Decisionmaking and Institutional Change*, edited by R. Keohane and S. Hoffmann (Oxford, UK: Westview Press, 1991), pp. 41–84.

5. The EU governments began an Intergovernmental Conference (IGC) on October 4, 2003, to revise the draft Constitutional Treaty that had been adopted by the European Convention on July 10. During the IGC session of December 12–13, 2003, however, the EU heads of state and government failed to agree on the Council voting system. On June 17–18, 2004, the European Council finally brought the IGC to a conclusion.

6. An agreement on European monetary union was reached at Maastricht, the Netherlands, in December 1991. The EU heads of state and government set a fixed timetable for the implementation of a single currency and agreed on five criteria for EMU qualification: a country should have an inflation rate within 1.5 percent of the inflation rate of the three EU countries with the lowest rate; a country's long-term interest rate must be within 3 percent of the three lowest interest rates in the EU; a country's currency exchange rate must be kept within a "normal" range of fluctuation within Europe's exchange rate mechanism; a country's budget deficit must be below 3 percent of GDP, although in "exceptional circumstances" a country with a higher rate might still qualify; the country's public debt must be less than 60 percent of GDP or "tending toward it."

7. J. Blondel and F. Mueller-Rommel, eds., *Governing Together* (London: St. Martin's, 1993).

8. J. Blondel and J. L. Thiebault, *The Profession of Government Minister in Western Europe* (Basingstoke, UK: Palgrave Macmillan, 1991).

9. M. Westlake, ed., *The Council of the European Union* (London: Cartemill, 1995), pp. 353–72.

10. J. Beyers and G. Dierick, "The Working Groups of the Council of the European Union: Supranational or Intergovernmental Negotiations?" *Journal of Common Market Studies* 36, no. 6 (1998): 289–317.

11. A. Moravcsik, *The Choice for Europe: Social Purpose and State Power from Messina to Maastricht* (Cornell University Press, 1998).

12. E. Letta, *Euro sì: morire per Maastricht* (Rome: Laterza, 1997), pp. 70–75.

13. L. Caracciolo, *Euro no: non morire per Maastricht* (Rome: Laterza, 1997), pp. 5, 63.

14. C. M. Santoro, *La politica estera di una media potenza: l'Italia dall'Unità ad oggi* (Bologna: Il Mulino, 1991).

15. Italian Foreign Ministry, "Italy 2020," 2006 (www.esteri.it/mae/doc/MD_COMPLETO.doc).

16. *Sole 24 Ore*, May 31, 1997; *Il Mundo*, May 26, 1997.

17. Lloyd's List International, May 12, 2008.

18. Bindi and Cisci, "Italy, Spain and the EU."

19. S. Fabbrini and S. Vassallo, *Il governo: gli esecutivi nelle democrazie contemporanee* (Rome: Laterza, 2002).

20. G. Freddi, ed., *Scienza dell'amministrazione e politiche pubbliche* (Rome: La Nuova Scientifica, 1989).

21. H. A. Simon, *Models of Man* (New York: Wiley, 1957), pp. 133–34.

22. G. Almond and S. Verba, *The Civic Culture: Political Attitudes and Democracy in Five Nations* (Princeton University Press, 1963).

Index